RELIGIONS
of the
WORLD

Religions of the World: The Illustrated Guide to Origins, Beliefs, Traditions & Festivals was produced for Transedition Limited and Fernleigh Books Limited by Bender Richardson White.

Project Manager: Lionel Bender
Designer and Art Editor: Ben White
Text Editor and Make-up: Peter MacDonald
Editorial Assistant: Kim Richardson
Picture Research: Jennie Karrach & Lionel Bender

Production: Richard Johnson
Origination: Emirates Printing Press
Cover Design and Make-up: Mike Pilley, Radius

Library of Congress Cataloguing-in-Publication Data
Religions of the world: the illustrated guide to origins, beliefs, traditions and festivals / by Elizabeth Breuilly, Joanne O'Brien, and Martin Palmer; consultant editor Martin E. Marty.
        p.   cm.
Includes bibliographical references and index.
ISBN 0-8160-6258-7
I. Religions. I. Breuilly, Elizabeth II. O'Brien, Joanne. III. Title.
BL20.2.R443 2005 and 1997   97-22829
291-dc.21

The authors' acknowledgements
Our gratitude is due to the many people who have helped in the research and planning of this book. We would particularly like to thank Alex Gooch for his contributions to the Buddhist and Hindu chapters, Ranchor Prime for his work on the Hindu chapter, and James Palmer for his contribution to the Jain chapter. We are grateful to Amrit Kaur Singh, Rabindra Kaur Singh, Dr. Mawil Izzidien and Rabbi Mark Goldsmith for their help with the text of the revised edition. We would also like to thank Fazlun Khalid, Dr W. Owen Cole, Kevin Fossey and Bradley Rowe for their guidance and advice, the Manchester Metropolitan University and the Resources Centre at Westhill College, Birmingham, England, for making facilities available, and finally our colleagues at ICOREC for their support throughout the project.

Photo Credits
COP = Christine Osborne Pictures, CPL = Circa Photo Library,
EU = Eye Ubiquitous Photos, Hutch = The Hutchison Library,
JD = James Davis Travel Photography, RHPL = Robert Harding Picture Library, Z = Zefa.
From left to right on double-page spreads, pages 3: CPL/Zbigniew Kösc. 6-7: Z/Damm. 12-13: CPL/William Holtby, CPL/William Holtby, CPC/Barrie Searle. 14-15: CPC/John Smith, CPL/Zbigniew Kosc 16-17: Z, CPC/Maxim Shaposhnikov, CPC/William Holtby. 18-19: e.t. archive, Z. 20-21: Z, CPL/John Smith, CPL/William Holtby. 22-23: Z. 24-25: Cephas/Hervé Champollion, Z/R. Bond. 26-27: CPL/Barrie Searle. 28-29: Z, CPL/Zbigniew Kösc, Z. 30-31: CPL/Barrie Searle, Hutch/Libby Taylor. 32-33: Z, CPL/Zbigniew Kösc, CPL/John Smith. 34-34: Z, Z, CPL/Barrie Searle. 36-37: COP, CPL/Zbigniew Kösc, Panos Pictures/Nancy Durrell McKenna. 38-39: EU/Tim Hawkins, Panos Pictures/Penny Tweedie. 40-41: Z, Hutch/Simon McBride. 42-43: Z/CLI, EU/C.J. Hall. 44-45: e. t. archive, CPL/Martin Palmer. 46-47: CPL/Martin Palmer, CPL./Martin Palmer, Manchester Museum/The University of Manchester. 48-49: CPL/John Smith, CPL/John Smith. 50-51: EU/Felix Kerr. 52-53: CPL/Tjalling Halbertsma, EU/Dave Cumming. 54-55: CPL/William Holtby, CPL/John Smith. 56-57: Hutch/J. Wright, Hutch/Eric Lawrie, Hutch/B. Régent. 58-59: Z/Trenkwalder, CPL/John Smith. 60-61: Hutch/Lesley McIntyre, Cephas/Hervé Champollion, Hutch/B. Régent. 62-63: CPL/Martin Palmer, Topham Photo Library/The Image Works. Wiseman, Hutch/Michael MacIntyre. 64-65: Impact Photos/Colin Jones, EU/Andy Hibbert, Panos Pictures/Lucy Anderson. 66-67: COP, CPL/Martin Palmer. 68-69: COP. 70-71: COP, COP, EU. 72-73: Zefa, CPL/John Smith. 74-75: EU/Thelma Sanders, Hutch/Robin Constable. 76-77: Hutch/Silvertop, COP. 78-79: COP, CPL/William Holtby, COP. 80-81: Hutch/Errington, CPL/John Smith, CPL/John Smith. 82-83: Hutch/J. C. Tordai, CPL/Zbigniew Kösc. 84-85: CPL/Robyn Beeche, CPL/William Holtby. 86-87: CPL/John Smith, CPL/William Holtby. 88-89: JD, CPL/Bipinchandra J. Mistry. 90-91: CPL/Bipinchandra J. Mistry, CPL/John Smith, CPL/John Smith. 92-93: CPL/Bipinchandra J. Mistry, CPL/Ranchor Prime. 94-95: RHPL/Gina Corringan, Hutch/Edward Parker. 96-97: CPL/John Smith, CPL/John Smith. 98-99: CPL/Bipinchandra J. Mistry, Hutch/Joan Klatchko. 100-101: CPL/Robyn Beeche, CPL/John Smith. 102-103: CPL/William Holtby, Hutch/Isabella Tree, CPL/John Smith. 104-105: COP, CPL/John Smith, CPL/Bipinchandra J. Mistry. 106-107: Hutch, Stone Routes/Bradley Rowe. 108-109: Hutch/Michael MacIntyre, Hutch/Vanessa Boeye. 110-111: Hutch/Jenny Pate, COP. 112-113: EU/P. M. Field. 114-115: CPL/John Smith, Stone Routes/Bradley Rowe, Stone Routes/Bradley Rowe. 116-117: Hutch/Jon Burbank, Stone Routes/Bradley Rowe. 118-119: CPL/William Holtby, COP, Impact Photos. 120-121: Hutch/Michael MacIntyre, CPL/William Holtby, Hutch/Stephen Pern. 122-123: Hutch/Christine Pemberton, Hutch/John Hatt. 124-125: RHPL, RHPL/J.H.C. Wilson. 126-127: CPL/John Smith, CPL/Tjalling Halbertsma. 128-129: Z/Orion Press, JD. 130-131: Hutch/Michael MacIntyre, Hutch/Jon Burbank, Panos Pictures/J. Holmes. 132-133: CPL/John Smith, CPL/Martin Palmer. 134-135: CPL/Tjalling Halbertsma, CPL/Tjalling Halbertsma. 136-137: CPL/William Holtby, CPL/Tjalling Halbertsma. 138-139: JD, CPL/John Smith. 140-141: CPL/John Smith, COP, Impact Photos/Javed A. Jafferji. 142-143: CPL/John Smith, CPL/Twin Studio. 144-145: COP, CPL/John Smith. 146/147: Hutch, Hutch/Libby Taylor. 148/149: COP, CPL/William Holtby, CPL/ John Smith. 150/151: Hutch/John Hatt, CPL/Martin Palmer. 152/153: CPL/Bahai Community UK, JD. 154: CPL/Michael Shackleton.

Cover photos Front: (clockwise from top left) CPL/Ged Murray, Robert Harding Photo Library, CPL/Ged Murray, CPL/Ged Murray, CPL/Mike Edwards, CPL/Ged Murray, Fernleigh Books/Transedition. Back: (bottom left) CPL/John Smith, (top right) CPL/William Holtby. Back flap: CPL/Martin Palmer.

Artwork (book and cover) Cutaway illustrations by Jonathan Adams. Diagrams and calendars by Bill Donohoe. Maps by Stefan Chabluk.

RELIGIONS
of the
WORLD

The Illustrated Guide to Origins, Beliefs,
Traditions & Festivals
Revised Edition

Elizabeth Breuilly • Joanne O'Brien • Martin Palmer
Consultant Editor • Professor Martin E. Marty

Facts On File, Inc.

FOREWORD

Asked to evaluate *Religions of the World* for potential readers, I am pleased now to recommend it. Designed to guide lay readers through the maze of religions around the world, it is a first-rate introduction, one that will also be of use to experts of one religion who also will welcome a perspective on others.

Two centuries ago during the event called the Enlightenment in the Western World, many prophets foresaw the dwindling if not the disappearance of religions from the global scene. Now at the end of the second millenium CE, most of the world religions are prospering. The Enlightened prophets also predicted that any left-over religious movements by now would be cosmopolitan, passive, tolerant and "soft". Instead many of these movements are "tribal", highly activist, intolerant, and hardline.

Several years ago an American political scientist, Benjamin Barber, published a book called *Jihad versus McWorld*. In his view, in the future there would be conflict between two sets of people or two tendencies: *jihad* represented the holy cause, including holy war; *McWorld* he coined, thinking of McDonald hamburgers, Macintosh computers, and the other "Macs" that symbolize international standardization and the potential for communicating and transacting on levels of least common denominators.

The editors and sponsors of *Religions of the World* consider that those are not the only two alternatives. They believe that it is urgent for people of the world and peoples of the world to deal with each other in positive ways. "Positive ways" means: we must do justice to the particular and separate features of each religion and we must better understand the special character of other people's lives, including their beliefs and religious behaviors.

The book is an excellent, accessible and, I find, clear introduction to the particular elements of the religions of the world. The authors took great pains to be empathic and understanding about the various faiths; they succeeded in presenting fair-minded, balanced treatments. Whoever uses the book will be able not only to gain a general comprehension of these world religions but can satisfy curiosity about the elements that make them attractive, healing forces in the lives of billions.

Someone once said that it was easy for Christians to send missionaries to the world of Buddhists so long as they only heard other missionaries tell them how bad the Buddhists were. (You can translate that sentence to other religions, too.) But, he asked, what do you do to explain the *good* Buddhist next door? In an ever-shrinking globe, full of refugees and immigrants from land to land, and as travel and communications become ever more efficient and rapid, it is as important to learn why religions produce "good" people and reconciliation as it is to understand why they evoke militancy. *Religions of the World* is a fresh, attractive guide to such understanding.

Martin E. Marty
Professor of Religion, University of Chicago, Chicago, Illinois

PREFACE

It is no longer possible to publish a book on world religions that will remain useful and topical through several reprints. The worlds of religions are interwoven with the increasingly complex and fluid worlds of politics, social affairs and economic development. Developments and disagreements within faiths challenge both the community of faith and the world at large. The role, status and place of religion is changing more rapidly today than it has done for decades and makes it necessary to revise parts of this book.

It is eight years since we wrote the texts and researched the issues. The attack on the World Trade Center in 2001, conflicts in Afghanistan, Iraq, the continued decline of communism world-wide, and the increasingly influential voice of religions in scientific debates have meant that we needed to visit again some of the core concerns of the faiths and the way these manifest themselves today.

Obviously, the core teachings, the details about festivals and rites of passage remain the same. But how and why people express their beliefs in a world context are changing with a rapidly changing world. This is why we have revised the Modern Developments section of the major faiths.

One of the remarkable characteristics of faiths is that while they give an impression of being unchanging, eternal and true, they are in fact continually changing, sometimes almost imperceptibly, sometimes cataclysmically. Faith works because it makes the world we live in workable. For some today, that means trying to make the world more socially just, economically equitable or environmentally protected. For others, it is about trying to align vision and beliefs into an overarching world-view, often through forms of what is commonly called "fundamentalism".

In revising the book, we have mentioned the new challenges the faiths are facing and what new challenges they are also creating. Whatever else we can say about the future, it is clear that religions will need deeper understanding about themselves, between themselves and by others as the faiths become more and more heavily involved with each other and with secular cultures in the wider world that we all inhabit.

Elizabeth Breuilly, Joanne O'Brien, Martin Palmer

Contents

World Religions— Making Sense of Diversity

T his book aims to describe the most important aspects of the world's major faiths—their roots, beliefs, and practice. This is an enormous and complex task, since some religions have evolved over millennia and continue to be practiced, while others have faded away. The section in this introduction on early religions (pages 16-19) covers those faiths that are now no longer practiced, or whose influence has waned so that they are but vestiges of their former selves.

However, our main concern is with living religion. Attempts to categorize religions are always inadequate, for a study of any group of religions will show that there are more differences than similarities between them. But in order to provide an accessible framework, we have divided the book into three broad categories of contemporary faiths: the Abrahamic faiths, the Vedic faiths, and other major traditions.

The Abrahamic faiths are Judaism, Christianity, and Islam. These have sometimes been called the prophetic traditions, for one of their distinctive aspects is the role of prophets, sent to recall the people to their proper role in God's plan, God's creation. The Vedic traditions include Hinduism, Buddhism, and Jainism, linked by a common root in the Vedic culture of ancient India and by a belief that all existence is cyclical: Universes arise, exist, decline, and fade to be replaced by other universes, just as every being in these universes passes through many existences or reincarnations. The characteristics of these two groups of faiths are discussed at greater length in the introductions to their respective sections of the book.

Apart from these two major strands of religious tradition there are several major faiths that have developed in individual ways. Some are indigenous religions such as Taoism in China and Shinto in Japan, which have evolved complex rituals and written texts. Others, such as Sikhism and to a certain extent the Baha'is, have been influenced by elements of Abrahamic and Vedic faiths. These are discussed in the section on other major traditions (pages 126-153).

This book is designed as an introduction and reference to the main beliefs and practices of the world's major religious traditions. The chapters on the major faiths look at history, basic beliefs, scriptures, places of worship, lifestyles, festivals, and modern developments. Because of the diversity of these faiths they cannot all be described under the same headings— each has its own story, its own rituals and beliefs, its own idea of spirituality. We have tried to indicate in each chapter the main varieties and divisions within the faiths, but it is impossible to describe or summarize all the variations that may be found. In general, we have tried to give an objective account of each faith from the point of view of its adherents, without making claims about the truth of their teachings. We have told some of the central stories from each faith, without entering into debates regarding their historical accuracy.

The religions of today are alive because they adapt, grow, and develop. In *Religions of the World* we have therefore sought to bring together classic teachings and new developments, to balance history with contemporary events and to combine the formal teachings with the reality of being a follower today. We range from the vast cosmic view to the everyday rituals of the believer, for it is between and within these that the true life and power of religion resides.

Calendars and dating

Different cultures and different faiths have always used their own calendars to document the cycle of the year and to name each year within recorded or remembered history. It is only quite recently that the system used by Western Christians has become the standard in most parts of the world. This calendar itself is curious, combining as it does the month names based on Roman gods and deified emperors with year numbers derived from the supposed year of the birth of Jesus (*AD* stands for *Anno Domini*, "the year of the Lord"; *BC* stands for *Before Christ*).

However, the use of such specifically Christian references in relation to other faiths is sometimes inappropriate, and the convention has developed of using the same year numbers—as they are now almost universally understood—but referring to them as CE (Common Era) and BCE (Before the Common Era). This is the system we have adopted in this book..

For most of the faiths covered in this book we have also given a calendar of festivals based on their religious year rather than on the Western calendar. Where possible we have shown an approximate correspondence between the two, but this should not be regarded as providing an accurate date for a festival according to the Western calendar, since the correspondence is never exact, and may vary from year to year. This is particularly so for the Muslim calendar (see page 79).

Buddhist prayer flags left by travelers through the Khambala Pass in Tibet. Each flutter of the flag is regarded as a repetition of the prayer printed upon it.

Explanation of terms

Unfamiliar or specialist words or use of words are explained where they first appear in the text. For convenience, many of these terms are also explained briefly in the glossary on pages 155-157. Glossary entries are intended more as reminders than as complete explanations of words; for detailed explanations we suggest the reader uses the index to find the relevant pages in the book. The glossary does not include general religious vocabulary, which can be found in a modest-sized dictionary.

Quotations from scripture

Many chapters contain quotations from scripture. Often there are agreed ways of dividing and numbering the scriptures; for example, the Bible consists of books conventionally divided into chapters and verses, the Qur'an is arranged in chapters called surahs, and the Bhagavad Gita is divided into chapters and verses. We have given brief references to enable the reader to follow up the sources of the passages quoted, but these are not a complete reference to a given English translation.

In some cases the translation may use a different term from the one we use in the book: For example, in the chapter on Islam we have used the English word *God* rather than the Arabic *Allah*, which means exactly the same. In some quotations, however, *Allah* is used and we have not altered this.

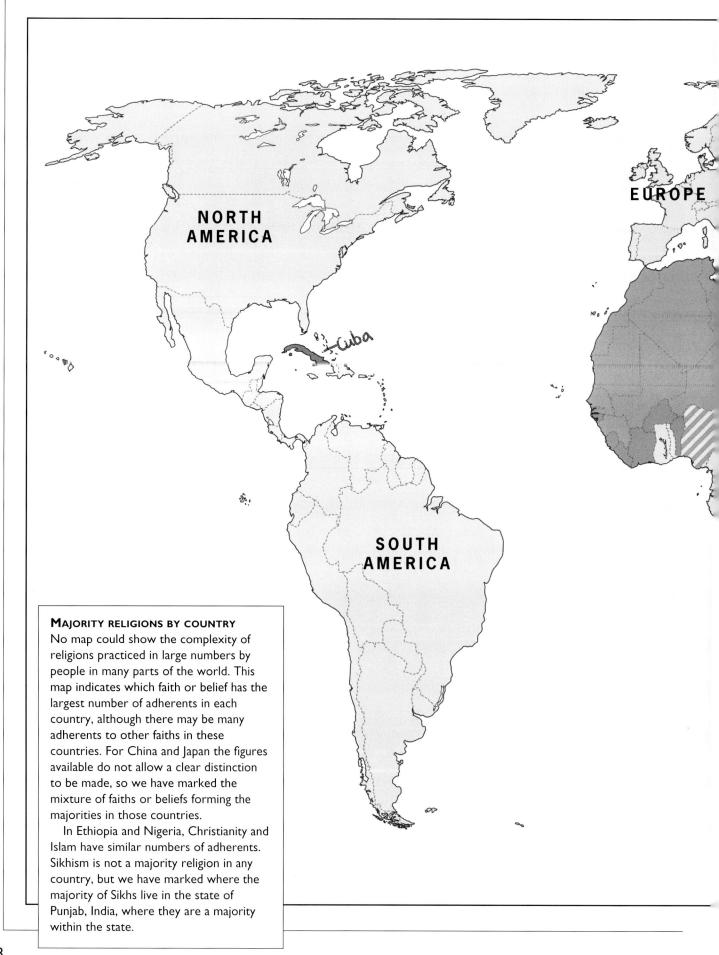

NORTH AMERICA

EUROPE

Cuba

SOUTH AMERICA

MAJORITY RELIGIONS BY COUNTRY
No map could show the complexity of religions practiced in large numbers by people in many parts of the world. This map indicates which faith or belief has the largest number of adherents in each country, although there may be many adherents to other faiths in these countries. For China and Japan the figures available do not allow a clear distinction to be made, so we have marked the mixture of faiths or beliefs forming the majorities in those countries.

In Ethiopia and Nigeria, Christianity and Islam have similar numbers of adherents. Sikhism is not a majority religion in any country, but we have marked where the majority of Sikhs live in the state of Punjab, India, where they are a majority within the state.

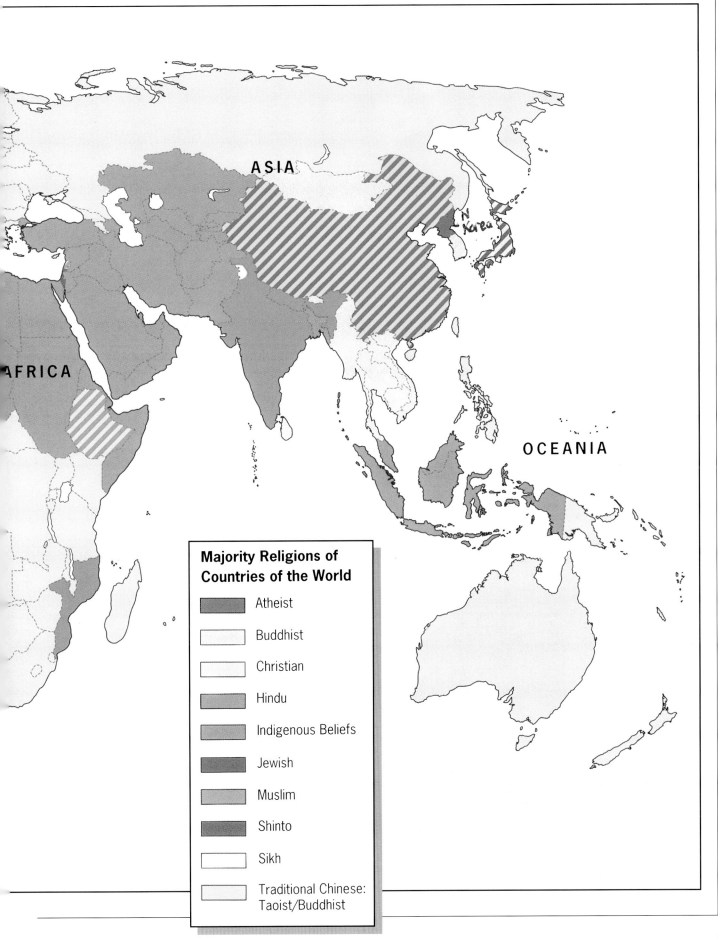

ASIA

N Korea

AFRICA

OCEANIA

Majority Religions of Countries of the World

- Atheist
- Buddhist
- Christian
- Hindu
- Indigenous Beliefs
- Jewish
- Muslim
- Shinto
- Sikh
- Traditional Chinese: Taoist/Buddhist

JUDAISM	CHRISTIANITY	ISLAM	HINDUISM	BUDDHISM
Jews believe in one God who is the Creator and Lord of the universe. They believe that God has a special relationship—the Covenant—with the Jewish people. This relationship has been guiding and will continue to guide Jewish people: "Obey my voice, and I will be your God, and you shall be my people; and walk in all the way that I command you, that it may be well with you." (Jeremiah 7:23) The Law, written in the Jewish holy book, the Torah, was given to Moses on Mount Sinai and is the Jewish people's guide to how to live in accordance with the Covenant. Jews look forward to the coming of the Messiah, a leader from God, who will bring a time of peace, fruitfulness and security to the whole world, but also a time when the dead will be brought back to life and judged by God.	"The saying is sure and worthy of full acceptance, that Christ Jesus came into the world to save sinners." (1 Timothy 1:15) Christians believe in one God, who created the universe and created human beings to have a special relationship with him. Through human wilfulness, exemplified in the story of Adam and Eve, this relationship was broken. God showed his love for all humanity by sending his son Jesus to bring humanity back to a personal relationship with God. Christians take their name from the title given to Jesus: the Christ, meaning the "anointed one of God." After three years of teaching, Jesus was executed by crucifixion but brought to life again, showing God's power over death and suffering and that death is not the end. Christians believe that they are called to be like Christ in the world.	"There is no god but God, and Muhammad is the Prophet of God." Islam means "peace" or "submission" and a Muslim is "one who submits to God." Muslims believe that by submitting to the will of God they can find peace within themselves and between all people. Muslims believe in one God, Allah in Arabic, who is known by titles such as the Creator, the Merciful or the Compassionate. At different times God has sent prophets to give his message to humanity. The final, complete message was given by the Prophet Muhammad, who lived in Arabia in the sixth century CE. Muslims believe that their holy book, the Qur'an, was written by God before time began and dictated to the Prophet Muhammad by the angel Jibra'il, a messenger from God.	Hinduism encompasses a wide variety of beliefs originating in India. Most Hindus believe that God takes many forms and is worshipped by many different names. Each person and every creature embodies a spark (*atman*) of the universal soul, equated with God. After death the atman is reborn in a new body. Thus God is in every object in the universe, and everything that exists—humans, animals, earth, air, water, fire—is part of God: "I am pervading the universe. All objects rest on me as pearls upon a thread." (*Bhagavad Gita*) Hindus believe that every action, good or bad, hurtful or compassionate, has an effect on this life and on future lives. This is called *karma*. By letting go of karma Hindus can eventually break free from the cycles of birth and death to achieve liberation or *moksha*, which is complete union with God.	Buddhists follow the teachings of Siddhartha Gautama, given the title the Buddha—"the enlightened, or awakened, one." The Buddha lived in northern India in the fifth and sixth centuries BCE. He spent many years trying to understand the cause of suffering and find the way to end it, before he reached enlightenment. Buddhists believe that we are tied to the cycles of death and birth through desire and can be born again in many different forms. But they believe they can find a way to escape this cycle, to be finally released from reincarnation to reach *nirvana*. As the Buddha taught: "If you walk towards knowledge you leave these rebirths behind. You do not go on becoming." The Buddha's teachings are a guide for all Buddhists, who try to perfect the qualities of wisdom, compassion and harmlessness. Eventually they can be "awakened" to obtain the highest peace and freedom, which is nirvana.

The menorah, a seven-branched candlestick, stood in the Temple in Jerusalem in ancient times, and its design is described in the Torah. The central branch is said to represent the sabbath, the day when God rested after creating the world.	Jesus died on the cross, the normal method of execution in the Roman Empire at that time. It was a shameful and painful death, but Christians believe that through it God showed his power over shame, pain and death.	Muslims say that Islam guides a person's life just as the moon and stars guide a traveler in the desert. This symbol on a country's flag often indicates a Muslim state.	This is the written form of the sacred sound "Aum," (sometimes spelt "Om"). According to the Hindu scriptures, Aum was the first sound, out of which the rest of the universe was created.	The Buddha spoke of an Eightfold Path to enlightenment. This is traditionally represented as an eight-spoked wheel. The path is a guide to living life compassionately and non-violently.

WORLDWIDE NUMBERS

There are 13 million Jews living worldwide. Over 44% live in North America, 37% in Israel and above 12% in Europe. The 20th century saw a dramatic shift in numbers away from Europe following the Holocaust.	Christians number over 2 billion worldwide. The largest branch (denomination) of Christianity is Catholicism, with almost 1 billion followers. Other major branches are Orthodox and Protestant.	There are 1.25 billion Muslims worldwide, principally in the Middle East, North and West Africa, southeastern Europe and Southeast Asia. In nineteen countries of the Middle East and North Africa more than 90% of the population is Muslim.	There are 850 million Hindus worldwide, almost all living in southern Asia. In India, where the Hindu religion began, there are up to 800 million Hindus. Their traditions and beliefs have shaped the unique culture of the country.	There are over 250 million Buddhists worldwide. Most Buddhists live in Asia. More than 85% of the population of Myanmar (Burma) and Thailand and Cambodia are Buddhist, as are more than 70% in Laos and Japan. Buddhism is the state religion in Thailand and Bhutan.

HOLY PLACES

Israel is regarded as the historic "Promised Land." The Western Wall in Jerusalem, an important place of prayer, is all that is left of the last Jewish Temple, destroyed in CE 70.	There are hundreds of Christian pilgrimage sites around the world. Israel is important because of its links with Jesus. Rome is the seat of the pope, spiritual leader of the Catholics.	All Muslims try at least once in their lives to make the pilgrimage to Makkah in Saudi Arabia, site of the first House of God on earth and the birthplace of the Prophet Muhammad.	There are Hindu pilgrimage sites all over India. Among the most important are the Himalayas and the river Ganges, especially where it flows through the city of Varanasi (Benares).	Each Buddhist country has its own pilgrimage sites. However, the sites in northern India associated with Siddhartha Gotama's life are significant for almost all Buddhists

HOLY WRITINGS

The Hebrew Bible consists of the Torah (Five Books of Moses), the Prophets and other writings including the Psalms. The Torah contains laws and guidance and tells the early history of the Jewish people. It is written in Hebrew.	The Bible consists of the Old Testament, written in Hebrew, and the New Testament, written in Greek. It contains accounts of the life and teachings of Jesus, and letters from early Christians. The Bible has been translated into many languages.	The revelations written in the Qur'an are central to Muslim life, whether used as a system of law or a guide for everyday life. The Qur'an is written in Arabic and, although Muslims speak many native languages, it is always recited in Arabic.	There are many sacred books, mostly written in the ancient Indian language Sanskrit. The major texts are the Vedas, the Upanishads, the Puranas, the *Mahabharata* and the *Ramayana*.	The teachings of the Buddha have been handed down in a collection of writings called the Tripitaka in the Theravada tradition. These and the writings of sages and scholars are included in the scriptures of the Mahayana tradition.

JAINISM

The word *Jain* refers to a follower of the *Jinas*—"those who overcome." Altogether there are 24 Jinas, who are also called Tirthankaras (bridge-makers). They are regarded by the Jains as great teachers. The last of them was Mahavira, who lived in India in the fifth century BCE. The Jinas continue to be regarded as teachers whose example helps others to escape the cycles of birth and death and to achieve freedom from reincarnation. The belief in non-violence, *ahimsa*, is central to the Jain tradition, and Jains try to avoid violence toward humans and toward life in any other form, including animals and plants.

Jains believe that all life is closely bound up in a web of interdependence and that all aspects of life belong together and support each other.

The upright hand represents non-violence and reassurance and is a reminder of the responsibility of every individual to act with wisdom and peace. The word *ahimsa* appears on the palm of the hand.

More than 98% of the 6.5 million Jains in the world today live in India. The two largest Jain communities outside India are in the United Kingdom and the United States.

There are many Jain holy sites in India connected with the lives of the Tirthankaras. The most important sites are often places where different Tirthankaras achieved enlightenment.

Sources of Jain teaching include early scriptures called the Siddhanta and Anuyoga. The core Jain teaching of non-violence has had a powerful effect on Indian culture and was highlighted by the teaching of Mahatma Gandhi.

SIKHISM

Sikhs believe in one God who is timeless and without form. The world and the universe are a reflection of God, who created them and directs them. The Sikh scriptures say:

"God is the sole creator and judge.
Keep him ever in mind.
Nothing but God has any power."

God cannot be found by human effort, but reveals himself to those who seek him through prayer and an unselfish lifestyle. Sikh teachings emphasize equality, service, and protection of the weak against injustice. Sikhs follow the teachings of ten human Gurus (teachers), who lived in India during the fifteenth to seventeenth centuries CE, and now regard the book of their hymns and poems as the Guru for all time to come.

In the center of this symbol is the two-edged sword used to prepare a sweet food during Sikh services. The circle symbolizes one God with no beginning or end. The two swords on the outside show Sikh readiness to defend truth and justice.

There are 23 million Sikhs worldwide. Over 85% of them live in India, mainly in the Punjab in northwestern India. There are sizable communities in the UK, United States and Canada and smaller ones in East Africa, Europe, Malaysia, Indonesia, Australia and New Zealand.

The city of Amritsar in the Punjab was founded by the fourth Guru of Sikhism, and the Golden Temple there was built by his successor. Amritsar has become the center of Sikh pilgrimage.

The Guru Granth Sahib contains hymns written by some of the Sikh Gurus and other writers. It is written in Gurmukhi, a form of written Punjabi, and is regarded by Sikhs as a living Guru.

SHINTOISM

Shinto is the traditional religion of Japan. The name means "the way of the gods." Shinto religion is closely involved with the landscape of Japan, and with the ancestors of believers. Shinto ceremonies appeal to *kami*, the mysterious powers of nature, for protection and benevolent treatment. Kami are associated with natural features such as caves, rocks, streams, trees, and particularly mountains.

At fixed times during the year believers gather to celebrate community ceremonies in Shinto shrines, but individuals often visit shrines to mark important stages or events in their lives. Some shrines are linked to particular kami, for example there are fox shrines, horse shrines, and wolf shrines. There are also certain kami which are associated with areas, groups of people, or with different aspects of life such as youth or old age.

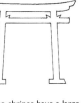

All Shinto shrines have a large gate called a *torii*, consisting of two upright bars and two crossbars. The torii can be seen standing alone in lakes, mountains or trees and other places associated with these mysterious powers in nature.

Shinto worship is found only among the Japanese. Many Japanese follow both Buddhist and Shinto beliefs and hold ceremonies in the different traditions, depending on the occasion, so numbers are hard to estimate.

The whole Japanese landscape is central to Shintoism, but Mount Fuji is regarded as the supreme home of the gods. Pilgrims usually ascend this snow-capped mountain on foot.

Shinto literature explains Shinto mythology and describes the laws governing the religion, the administration of the shrines and the order and detail of the ceremonies.

TAOISM

Taoism takes its name from the Chinese word *Tao*, which means the "way" or "path" and refers to the Way of the Universe. The Tao is a natural force that guides all life throughout the universe. "It is the deep source of everything. It is nothing and yet in everything." (*Tao Te Ching* 4)

Taoists believe that distress and suffering arise when people struggle against the Way of Nature, but that if they travel with the Tao their lives will be in harmony with the order of the universe.

This order is kept in balance by the opposing forces of *yin* and *yang*—forces that are continually changing and interacting with each other, giving order to all life. Many Taoists believe that if they withdraw from the world to remote mountains or other secluded places they are much closer to nature and can discover the true meaning of the Tao.

This symbol represents the interaction and balance of yin and yang. Yin is a cool dark force that is seen in rain, clouds, winter and snow; yang is a hot bright force that is seen in thunder, the Earth, summer, and the Sun.

There are almost 20,000 Taoist priests, both male and female, in China. Taoist traditions are followed by Chinese communities all over the world and Taoist thought, literature, and philosophy is becoming increasingly popular with non-Chinese followers.

There are many temples and shrines in China that are centers of local pilgrimage. The major pilgrimage sites, however, are the five Taoist mountains.

There are hundreds of sacred Taoist texts. One of the most influential writers is the great sage Lao Tzu, author of the *Tao Te Ching*. This book of poetry and philosophy explains the Way of the Tao and is also widely read by non-Taoists.

BAHA'I

Baha'is follow the teachings of Baha'u'llah, who lived in Iran in the nineteenth century. He taught his followers that God has provided successive revelations to mankind through a series of Divine Messengers to bring humankind to spiritual maturity. Each of these messengers has been the founder of one of the world's greatest religions, and Baha'u'llah taught that he was the last of these. The central message of his teachings was the unity of all people. The Baha'i faith is summed up in the words of Baha'u'llah, "The Earth is but one country and mankind its citizens."

The Baha'i teachings are based on the principles of economic justice, equal rights for women and men, education for all people, and the breaking down of traditional barriers of race, class and creed.

The interlocking triangles represent the interdependence of all people in one essential unity.

WORLDWIDE NUMBERS

There are 5 million Baha'is worldwide in more than 200 countries, with the largest concentrations in Africa (about 1 million) and the United States (about 300,000).

HOLY PLACES

Baha'is meet in local assemblies but their administrative and spiritual center is in Haifa, Israel. The two most holy places are the tomb of Baha'u'llah and the shrine of the Bab, both in Israel.

HOLY WRITINGS

All the writings of Baha'u'llah are revered and studied, especially the Kitab-i-Aqdas—"The Most Holy Book." He wrote in both Arabic and Persian, and his works have been translated into many languages.

11

Living Religion:
Beyond the Here and Now

Tibetan monks gathered to listen to Buddhist teachings in Dharamsala, India. Many of the Buddhists here followed the Dalai Lama into exile from Tibet and the community in Dharamsala is now flourishing.

hroughout the world people make sense of life, and give purpose and meaning to it, through living their faith. High in the icy mountains of the Himalayas, pilgrims who have saved for years journey to wash in the freezing waters above the snow line, joyful that they are at the birthplace of the sacred river Ganges. In the midst of troubled Afghanistan, the hope and strength of a family lies in the teachings of the Qur'an, the Muslim holy book. In South Africa, Christian churches provide refuge and support networks for children suffering the loss of their parents through AIDS. In North America, native peoples, members of the First Nations, use traditional healing and spiritual traditions to help others overcome drug addiction.

It is estimated that well over half the world's population practice, to a greater or lesser degree, one or other of the world's religions or indigenous spiritual traditions. They might be members of the largest religious community in the world, the Roman Catholic church: a community of nearly 1 billion, from every nation on Earth, united by a shared faith and tradition. Or they might be members of a community whose numbers are small but whose faith is central to their lives, such as the Druze of Lebanon, whose form of Islam is so secret that the inner teachings are known only to those born into the community.

Followers of the religions also range from those who have devoted their entire lives to religious practice, such as monks and nuns, to those for whom it is something that happens only at set times of the year—perhaps a weekly

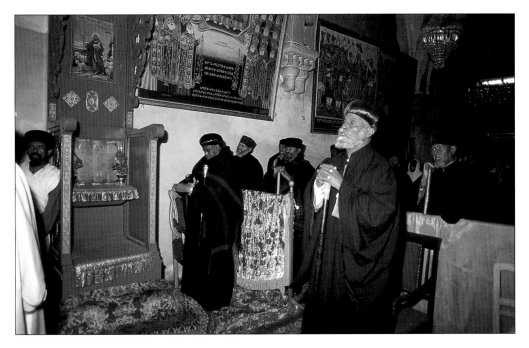

visit to a place of religious worship such as a synagogue, temple, or church, or participation only at major festivals such as New Year or rites of passage.

Members of the Ethiopian Orthodox church gathered to celebrate a liturgy in their chapel within the Church of the Holy Sepulcher in Jerusalem

The world of living religion is very diverse, embracing the kaleidoscope of human experience, action and emotion. It also encompasses the divine, the encounter with God or gods. Religion teaches that this physical, material world is not the only reality, that there is something greater than the here and now, a purpose more profound than simple survival. Here in this material world it is possible to touch and be touched by this sense of the Divine.

For some, this leads to renunciation of the temporal pleasures of this world in the search for something greater. For example, some Jain monks do not wear any clothes at all, seeing themselves as "sky clad"—clothed by the sky. For others, it leads to a desire to make this world a better place by tackling social issues such as poverty. Muslims, for example, campaign for fairer trading between nations; Christians work to improve health or education facilities or develop environmental programs.

Hindu pilgrims bathing at Varanasi in the sacred waters of the river Ganges. It is a major site of pilgrimage, and the hope of many Hindus is to have their ashes scattered over the waters of the Ganges.

Religion in the Modern World

Almost all the world's major faiths have moved out from their historic centers and old homelands and are now present worldwide. For example, the majority of Christians today live in developing countries far from the Middle Eastern and Mediterranean beginnings of Christianity, and in many European countries Islam is now the second largest religious group. Within most faiths there is a bewildering variety of cultures, languages and traditions. It is important to realize what a vast array of different expressions of faith and experience lie beneath a broad term such as *Christianity* or *Buddhism*.

Religion and science

For many people, just as there is no distinction between religion and life, so there is no distinction between religion and science. Taoism, for example, is dedicated to discovering "the way of the universe" and working with it, rather than against it. Islam lays great stress on the value of knowledge and discovery about the natural world, but always in the context of submission to God and his laws.

Scientific discoveries such as genetic engineering can cause great soul-searching and heated debate in religions. For some, scientific theories, such as evolution or the "selfish gene" raise moral and theological issues. Medical advances in DNA research and its consequences arouse debate in religious and secular leaders about what it really means to be human and the moral and medical responsibilities that need to be addressed in relation to issues such as human cloning.

Islam has always encouraged scientific exploration, and many scientific discoveries owe their origin to Islam. Christianity has been credited with laying the foundations of modern empirical research by creating a world view in which everything was seen to be made by God, and thus open to investigation as a way of knowing God better.

Modern science has sometimes seemed to answer certain questions about the nature of life traditionally answered by religion, and there are many who believe that religions will decline as scientific knowledge continues to grow. But in recent years there has been a resurgence of interest both in religion and in mediums and divination. For many people, the answers given by science fail to address deeper questions of meaning.

Religion and politics

For many people there is also no distinction between religion and politics. Indeed, the whole idea that religion should have nothing to do with politics arises mainly from the European historical experience of religious warfare in the sixteenth and seventeenth centuries. In the ancient past, no ruler would go to war or sign peace treaties without first consulting the gods or God. In Rome, when the state was at war, the temple gates of Mars, the god of war, stood open, and were only closed when peace was restored. For many communities, religion, life, and politics are the same.

However, when religions clash or cultures are overwhelmed by invasion, then religious differences become political differences and vice versa. The early Christians were seen to be

A wall hanging depicting the risen Christ, made by members of a Catholic community in South Africa. Many Christian churches play an active role in campaigning for peace and justice. In South Africa, churches were instrumental in bringing about the end of apartheid.

dangerous to the Roman Empire because they would not worship the emperor and thereby threatened the whole balance between state and religion. In the 20th century, Japan under State Shinto practiced persecution, not just of newer religions such as Christianity, but also of the ancient religion of Buddhism. Again, it was the desire for the state to embody a unified vision of life that led to these persecutions. It is no wonder, therefore, that the often bitter experiences of being a minority faith within a political entity have led to calls for political separatism on religious grounds. All too many communities around the world know the fears involved in belonging to a religious minority.

Even without overt persecution, the institutions and expectations of a society may be based on a particular religion or outlook, making life difficult for those of another belief. In Saudi Arabia, non-Muslims can worship only privately, and must never attempt to convert a Muslim. In France, no religious clothing may be worn in schools, yet for many Muslims, a certain kind of headwear is necessary for modesty. The conflict of values and of understandings has created deep divisions in France.

The growth of terrorism in the name of religion such as the September 11th, 2001 attacks by Islamic extremists on New York and Washington, D.C. has arisen from feelings of powerlessness and anger by some Muslims who feel that Western secular values and politics are undermining traditional Muslim cultures. Denounced by mainstream Muslims, the terrorists must not be seen as being representative of Islam itself.

Rejection and response

The world contains many people for whom religion in any form is a curse, an irrelevance or a hindrance. Religions are notoriously slow at changing, and at times can be a major obstacle to social progress. In many religions today, the issue of the role of women is setting radicals against traditionalists. Racism and warfare in certain parts of the world are often linked to religious differences. The rejection of religion arises from such harsh realities. Atheism and

humanism have few formal structures, but perhaps as many as one quarter of the world's population reject the faith choices around them or are simply indifferent to religious questions. The attacks of communism and Marxism in the twentieth century have done untold damage to religions and have also helped to create a climate in which many people have chosen not to have a faith. Terrorism in the name of religion only adds to this trend.

Until recently, many thought that secularism would soon sweep all religion into a small corner, away from the main events of the real world. This idea has now receded as religions have reasserted themselves across the globe and shown their ability to adapt and develop. Today no one can understand the social, political or cultural life of the world without understanding something of religion. As the older faiths regain lost ground in many places and newer forms of religion emerge from the changing circumstances of modern life, the place of religion in the affairs of the world is without question. The question is, perhaps, what exactly will be its role.

Jerusalem is a holy city for Judaism, Christianity, and Islam, but it has also often been a place of tensions.

RELIGION, CULTURE AND LIFE
In many cultures there is no distinction between religion and everyday life. People simply see themselves as living according to the ways and wisdom of their people and traditions. Muslims, for example, say that Islam is not a religion—it is a way of life. Most Hindus do not realize they "belong" to that religion, for it is a name given by outsiders.

What people in the West mean by "religion" is often seen by other cultures as a narrow perception of the role of God and of humanity. The distinction between secular society and religion in the West, expressed in the separation of church and state in the American and other constitutions, is impossible for many of the peoples of the world to understand: Life is faith and faith is life.

Prehistoric Religion

A prehistoric painting of a bird, man, and deer from Lascaux Cave in France. Many of the scenes found painted in caves by prehistoric people are thought to represent ancient rituals and may indicate early forms of religious activity

O n December 18, 1994, three friends out climbing in southeastern France stumbled upon a small opening into the hillside. They found themselves in a long cave, or series of caves, and by the light of their torches they could see that the walls were covered with the most exquisite prehistoric cave paintings. Long-extinct creatures rose up before them, depicted in dramatic, lifelike poses. Cave paintings have been found before in France and elsewhere in the world, but these, in the Chauvet Cave, have turned out to be the oldest known paintings in the world over 30,000 years old.

At various places through the complex of linked caves were signs that some form of religious activity had taken place here. Patterns in the dirt of the floor, which had lain there undisturbed for perhaps 25,000 years, indicate dancing. A stone block with a bear skull on it seems to indicate a possible shrine. At the very back of one of the last caves is a strange figure, half human and half bison. This figure, which is unlike any other in the caves, is thought to be a religious figure, similar to the antler-headed humans found in other prehistoric cave paintings in France.

It could be that this is the earliest evidence of religious activity. If it is, there is a strong possibility that this cave was a religious center for shamanic activities—activities of a type which can still be observed today.

Where no written records exist (the earliest written religious texts date from only around 2500 BCE), it is impossible to be certain what people believed in or what their religious practices were. However, it is reasonable to suggest that the Chauvet Cave shows signs of shamanic practices. If this is so, our knowledge of contemporary and historical shamanism makes it possible to speculate on what was being done here in the name of religion.

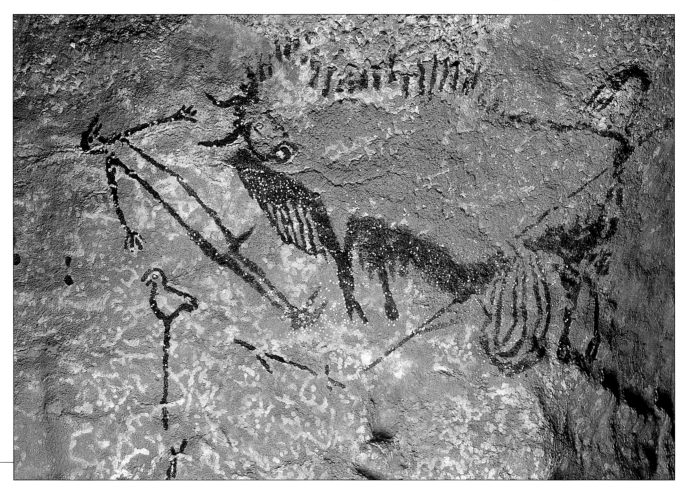

Shamanic offerings being made to the spirits of a tree during a festival in the Altai region of southern Siberia. Offerings include water and strips of cloth tied to the branches.

Shamanism

Shamanism is often described as the first world religion. This is an exaggerated title, for it is highly unlikely that shamanism ever saw itself or organized itself as a coherent faith, or indeed that any of its diverse expressions around the world were aware of the existence of other shamans beyond their own group. But the evidence is that shamanic practices spread from Siberia south to China and beyond, east across the land bridge between Siberia and Alaska well before this was breached by the rising oceans 10,000 years ago, west to Russia and Finland, and into Mongolia and the Central steppes of Asia.

The shaman is one who can enter into a trance and, in this trance, act as a communication bridge between the two worlds of shamanic belief. These two worlds are the physical, material world and the more powerful but highly unpredictable spirit world.

In the shamanic tradition problems in the physical world such as illness and bad luck, or hopes such as for good hunting, power and wealth, can all be affected by the spirit world and the intervention of the spirits. The shaman is the man or woman (as far as is known, the gender balance has always been roughly equal) who is able to speak to the spirits and to receive their messages.

Shamanism lies behind much of the folk religion and religious philosophy of China, Japan, Siberia, much of Mongolia, and to some extent the pre-Buddhist religion of Bon in Tibet. Shamanism spread from Alaska down to South America as tribes from Siberia and the Mongolian steppes spread down, crossing over the land bridge that once existed across the Bering Sea.

It is too early yet, and may indeed never be possible, to be sure whether the Chauvet Cave shows shamanism in France 30,000 years ago, or whether it shows a similar development of religious attitudes unconnected with Siberia.

Other prehistoric religions

Shamanism was not the only prehistoric faith. Across the globe traces can be found of sacred sites and burial places of devotion. Cults of ancestors and veneration of the immediate and major natural features seem to have been common. In Europe, female figurines from around 30,000 years ago seem to indicate a veneration of the feminine. But what that consisted of, or meant, we have no idea. Simple markings, circles in particular, have been found carved on rocks in Australia. Dating suggests they are around 100,000 years old. Are these religious? Humanity's earliest attempt to leave a mark on the environment? The great problem with prehistoric sites is that on the whole we simply do not know. We do not know what was happening at Stonehenge, nor much about the burial mounds that lie scattered across Europe dating from over 5,000 years ago. All that is clear is that in some fashion or another, people have worshiped, venerated and related ritually to their ancestors, to nature and to their own land for millennia.

A wooden pole with shamanic carvings from Khakassia in southern Siberia. These are erected at special worshiping-places in the mountains. During a ceremony, ribbons are tied directly to the pole and offering made throughout the night, but invitations to the spirits do not begin until the dawn.

THE BEAR CULT

A key aspect of shamanism is the bear cult. The shaman has an animal spirit through whom he or she can most easily enter into the spirit world. Ancient legends abound with such spirit animals—for example, in ancient China the legendary shamanic bringers of civilization, Fu Tzu and Nu Kua, were half snake, half human. In Druidic culture, deer were a common form. But most powerful of all is the bear. A young bear cub is taken from the wild in the autumn. Throughout the winter and early spring the cub is reared and cared for by the shaman. Then the cub is killed in order to unite bear and shaman, and the bear's skull becomes an object of veneration.

Early Historic Religions

Many great religions arose in the ancient world, blazed brightly, then faded. However, their insights, even their specific beliefs and deities, can often still be found within current religions.

Egypt

Texts dating from around 2500 BCE onward give an idea of the beliefs of the ancient Egyptians. Central aspects in Egyptian religion were the renewal and fertility that the annual inundation of the Nile brought to the land of Egypt. With the regular flooding of the Nile, stability and order were maintained and Egypt flourished through the divine authority of the pharaoh and the temple rituals. The rituals surrounding death reflect the hope of the ancient Egyptians that life continued after death in the way that it had in the land of Egypt.

The Egyptian pantheon ranges from powerful national gods such as the Sun god, Re, or the god of Thebes, Amun, to gods who governed specific areas of life. Examples are Thoueris, the hippopotamus goddess of childbirth, and Ma'at, the goddess of truth and order, whose symbol was a feather.

The Egyptians believed that the soul of the dead was judged after death against the feather of truth and justice. The ibis-headed god of learning, Thoth, and the jackal-headed god of embalmers, Anubis, watched over the ceremony while Osiris waited to welcome those who were judged favorably.

OSIRIS, ISIS, AND HORUS

The great god and ruler Osiris married his sister Isis, but his wisdom and power were resented by his brother Seth. In a fit of jealousy Seth killed Osiris, chopped his body into pieces and scattered them across the marshy land of the Delta. Isis went in search of her beloved husband and finally, when she had gathered the pieces of Osiris's body together, she leant over him and conceived a child.

The child, called Horus, was born in the marshy waters of the Nile and raised secretly, grew to manhood and avenged his father's death by killing Seth to take the throne of Egypt.

The pharaohs who ruled Egypt became associated with the god Horus. They embodied the qualities of order, strength, duty, and divine authority. Osiris, the father of Horus, once the god of the living, became the god of the dead and the symbol of renewal. In his mummified form he welcomed those who had died to their next life in the land of the West.

The ancient Middle East

In Sumeria (present-day Iraq), texts from 2500 BCE onward contain stories of cosmic battles between the firm and dependable elements of creation (the land, the agricultural crops and in particular the cosmic tree) and the unstable

elements, such as the waters and floods, and in particular the primeval monsters that live in the oceans. Humanity was a pawn in these struggles. The *Epic of Gilgamesh*, from around 1700 BCE, is a classic account of the struggle between order and chaos. It tells the story of Gilgamesh and his search for eternal life. But it also contains many themes also found in the Bible, such as creation in six days, the idea of an original Paradise and the story of a survivor of the great Flood.

Zoroastrian religion

In Zoroastrianism (named after its founder or reformer, Zarathustra—Zoroaster in Greek) the struggle between good and evil was personified in two mighty gods who fought each other and caught up the world in their struggle. The Zoroastrian religion dominated the area of Persia from around 600 BCE, when it became the state religion, until the area fell to Islam in the seventh century CE. Today small communities still exist in Iran, and the Parsees of India are Zoroastrians who migrated to India in the early Middle Ages. Many of the ideas in Jewish and Christian mythology are first seen in Zoroastrianism—angels, heaven and hell, and the idea of a struggle between good and evil.

Indo-European religions

The Indo-European traditions share many names and attributes of gods, passed on as tribes migrated from India and central Asia into Europe. Many tribes of Europe originated from the cultural melting-pot of the central Asian steppes, where tribes from Mongolia met Turkic peoples and Indian and Persian culture. For example, the ancient Celts were originally a people of the steppes of central Asia, and many tribes who descended upon ancient India came from the same area.

One example of a theme common to Indo-European religions is the mother goddess Danu. In the *Rig Veda*, an ancient Indian text, she is the mother of various demons, and fights against Indra, the king of the gods. In the myths of the Celts she emerges as a more benign mother goddess figure. Her name lies

behind the name of the river Don in Russia, the Danube in central Europe, and the mountains known as the Paps of Danu in Ireland. Her link with waters emerges again in the name Ana as a common saint's or deity's name for holy wells in Britain.

GREEK AND ROMAN RELIGION

Mount Olympus in northern Greece was believed to be the home of an array of gods and goddesses whose behavior mirrored, or according to the Greeks, shaped, the behavior of the humans on the plains below.

For example, the *Iliad* (c. 900 BCE), which recounts episodes in the Greek siege of the city of Troy, depicts the gods fighting between themselves and using the Greeks and Trojans as surrogates in the struggle.

Greek mythology borrowed from the traditions of Egyptian and Indo-European religions. While there were solely Roman gods, such as Vesta, goddess of the hearth and of Rome, the Romans picked and chose their deities from the peoples they conquered. They borrowed almost wholesale the mythology of Greece; thus Zeus, king of the Greek gods, becomes Jupiter. Aphrodite, the Greek goddess of love becomes Venus. Isis, the divine wife of Osiris in ancient Egypt, continued to be worshiped as Isis.

The Romans were also fascinated by the mystery religions that arose from the ancient Middle Eastern cultures of Babylon and Persia. Induction into a mystery cult was common among Roman soldiers. The most popular cult from the first century CE onward was that of Mithra. Mithra is a god named in the Zoroastrian texts of ancient Persia.

Why Mithra became so popular in Roman culture is unclear. The main secret ritual for those being initiated was to stand in a darkened pit while a bull was sacrificed above them. Mithra is usually shown slaying such a bull—a symbol of dark elements and brute force.

Artemis, the Greek goddess of hunting and of the forests, was worshiped as a fertility goddess in the ancient city of Ephesus on the coast of Turkey. Artemis was assimilated into Roman mythology as the goddess Diana.

Indigenous Traditions Today

A Hindu temple ceremony in Bali. Hinduism is the religion of the majority of people who live on the island of Bali in Indonesia. Balinese Hindu ritual is influenced by the indigenous traditions of this area.

In many parts of the world, the older, indigenous religions continue today. In Siberia, for example, shamanism has emerged from many decades of Communist persecution and is once more being practiced openly. In China, shamans are still strongly disapproved of by the government but can be found all over the country. In Japan, shamans operate on the fringe of the more formal religious worlds of Buddhism and Shinto.

Indigenous traditions are also reviving in North, Central, and parts of South America, as part of the recovery of self-identity among native peoples (often now called First Nations). However, here as in other parts of the world where traditional religions persist, notably sub-Saharan Africa, the traditional religions are almost all now affected by their contact with world religions such as Christianity and Islam. New expressions of both traditional religion and of the major world religions often arise from this interaction.

In North America, ritual practices that have been passed down through generations of traditional healers are now being used to help people recover from psychological as well as physical breakdown. The notion of healing not just the physical body but the mind and spirit as well is one many traditional religions have retained, and their insights are proving important as the world seeks a balance between the advances of medical science and the needs of the spirit.

But the encounter does not always favor the indigenous peoples and their traditions. Many have been pushed to the edge of extinction in the last hundred years. The loss of traditional wisdom about how to live in a given area, expressed in the myths, rituals, legends, and cultures of these peoples, is incalculable. It is unrealistic to think that any culture, religion, or tradition today is untouched by the wider world. All traditions are changing or dying. But the relationship between the older indigenous traditions and contemporary societies is often far from being an equal one. This dilemma was expressed by the leader of the small and threatened Yanomamo people of the Amazon:

Everyone likes to give as well as to receive.
No one wishes only to receive all the time.
We have taken much from your culture...
I wish you had taken something from our
culture...for there were some good and
beautiful things in it.

Major religions and old traditions

Even within the great world religions, elements of earlier religious beliefs have a tendency to re-emerge. In some Buddhist countries, pre-Buddhist indigenous deities have their own shrines within the grounds of Buddhist temples, and people turn to them for everyday problems such as illness or marital troubles. In

An Australian Aboriginal wooden carving of a bird representing one of the Dreamtime Ancestors. According to tradition, these Ancestors moved across the land, creating life and shaping the natural features. They taught the people secret ceremonies before they sank back into the land, which is still alive with their spirits.

central Asia, in spite of its long Muslim tradition, the tombs of warriors such as the Mongol conquerors Genghis Khan and Tamerlane are among the most popular centers of religious revival following the collapse of the Soviet Union. In China, ancestor worship has arisen again following the suppression of religion in the Cultural Revolution (1966-76). The picture in Christianity is even more varied. For example, many of the traditional customs of Christmas pre-date Christianity. Christmas Day was chosen because it was the ancient feast-day of the Sun, in the depths of winter.

New forms of religious practice are also emerging that combine old and new faiths and traditions. But what persists throughout recorded time is humanity's search for meaning and the belief that in some way the divine reaches out to offer such meaning.

Followers of Cao Dai gathered in a temple in Vietnam. This new movement, founded in 1926, aims to draw together Taoism, Confucianism, Buddhism, and Christianity into a single religion. Cao Dai is an example of one of the emerging forms of religion that combine beliefs and traditions of older faiths

The city of Jerusalem: on the right is the Dome of the Rock mosque; on the left is the Church of Maria Magdalena; in the center is the ancient Judeo-Roman town wall. Jerusalem is an important religious site for Jews, Christians and Muslims. For Jews it is the city of King David and is Holy Zion, where the Messiah will come. For Christians it is the place where Jesus was crucified and rose from the dead. In Islam it is associated with several of the early prophets, and from here Muhammad rose to Heaven on the night journey he made to see God. Sadly this shared holy site has led to much bloodshed and war over the centuries, and tension continues to this day.

The Abrahamic Faiths

The term *Abrahamic* describes the faiths of Judaism, Christianity, and Islam, which all trace their tradition back to Abraham. Abraham's life is described most fully in the Hebrew Bible, used by both Christians and Jews, and there are somewhat different accounts of him in the Qur'an, the sacred text of Islam. Some scholars question whether he was a historical figure, but he may have lived in the nineteenth century BCE.

The three faiths are closely connected historically. Christianity arose out of Judaism, although it rapidly became a separate religion. Islam also sees itself as building on, completing, and correcting the Jewish and Christian scriptures, which are regarded as being incomplete and flawed accounts of God's revelation.

One all-powerful God

The belief in God as creator and sustainer of the universe is central to the Abrahamic faiths. Early Jewish texts indicate that "the God of Abraham, Isaac and Jacob" was seen as the most powerful among the many gods and goddesses of the ancient Middle East. But by about 700 BCE, belief in the existence of only one God (monotheism) had become common in Judaism. Christianity strongly upholds monotheism, but has developed the idea of three aspects of God, known as the Trinity. The basic statement of faith of Islam—"There is no god but God and Muhammad is his prophet"—underlines the belief in one God. Islam explicitly opposes the Christian doctrine of the Trinity, seeing it as denying God's unity and treating a human being (Jesus) as his equal.

In all three faiths, God is the absolute power, and humanity's first duty is to follow God's way in daily life. This aspect is especially expressed in Islam. Christianity and Judaism, however, also have a scriptural tradition of arguing and debating with God.

Creation and the first humans

The book of Genesis in the Bible relates that God created the universe in six "days," and rested on the seventh. There is much discussion in Judaism and Christianity as to the nature and truth of this account in relation to scientific evidence. Some maintain that the biblical account is literally true, and that the scientific account of the origin of the universe is wrong. Others argue that scientific accounts of the "big bang" and evolution may well be more or less accurate descriptions of the mechanisms that God used to create the universe.

The Qur'an gives a similar account, specifying that a "day" in this context is equivalent to 50,000 years. The important difference is that Muslims do not believe in a seventh day when God "rested," for how can the all-powerful and infinite God need rest?

The Abrahamic faiths each tell in their own way the story of the first humans, Adam and Eve. God created them and put them to live in a garden, where they could eat the fruit of any of the trees except one, which the Bible describes as "the tree of the knowledge of good and evil." Adam and Eve ate the fruit of this tree, apparently in the belief that it would give them greater knowledge and power. The immediate consequence was that they became aware of their own nakedness and were shamed. Popular tradition has interpreted this as the discovery and temptation of sex, but this is not part of the mainstream teaching of any of the three faiths. Because of their disobedience, breaking a primordial relationship with God, Adam and Eve were expelled from the garden to live in the world as we know it now—a place of difficulty, strife, and hard work.

All three faiths teach that each person has only one earthly life and that there is life after death. In Judaism, according to some texts, when the Messiah comes all the just will be raised and all the damned will be cast into hell. Although the specific beliefs differ, both Christianity and Islam teach that there will be a Day of Judgment when God will judge the dead, bringing the good to Heaven and casting away the evil.

CHAPTER ONE

JUDAISM

Historic Judaism teaches that Jews are the "chosen people" through whom God has spoken to the world and revealed how to live in accordance with his laws. They are a nation in the sense that a Jew is the child of a Jewish mother, and they therefore form a distinct ethnic group. But in addition to this ethnic identity, an observant Jew chooses to follow the laws given by God to Moses, and thus to be a religious Jew.

The war memorial opposite the Knesset (Israeli parliament building) in Jerusalem is based on the menorah, the seven-branched candlestick that stood in the Temple in Jerusalem in ancient times. It has become a symbol of the Jewish faith.

The main picture shows the scrolls of the Torah, the Jewish scriptures, being held aloft during bar mitzvah celebrations next to the Western Wall in Jerusalem, the last remnant of the Temple.

Abraham, said to have lived around 1900 BCE, is regarded as the father of the Jewish people. The Jewish scriptures tell how God made a covenant, or agreement, with him that his descendants would be God's chosen people. The people's part in this covenant is to keep God's laws. The laws were given to the Jewish leader and prophet Moses as he led the people out of captivity in Egypt. At Mount Sinai God called Moses to the top of the mountain and gave him the laws on tablets of stone. The best known of these are the Ten Commandments, but there are many more that Jews follow in daily life.

Although there are Jews living all over the world, the history of Judaism is rooted in the land of Israel, the land promised to Abraham in the Bible. This was the land to which God led the people on their journey out of Egypt. The city of Jerusalem, capital city of David, Israel's greatest king, is especially important to Jews. David's son Solomon built a temple in Jerusalem. It was destroyed and rebuilt many times, but was finally destroyed in CE 70. The site of the Temple is an important place of pilgrimage, celebration and prayer for Jews, as is the single remaining wall of the last Temple, widely referred to as the Wailing Wall, but more correctly named the Western Wall.

Origins of the Jews as God's Chosen People

T he Covenant, described in the Jewish scriptures, is the promise that God gave to Abraham that his descendants would become a great nation. These are the words of the Covenant:

Now the Lord said to Abram, "Go from your country and your kindred and your father's house to the land that I will show you. And I will make of you a great nation, and I will bless you, and make your name great, so that you will be a blessing. I will bless those who bless you, and him who curses you I will

curse; and by you all the families of the earth shall bless themselves."
(Genesis 12:1-3)

Abraham obeyed God's words, and after many years of wandering arrived in Canaan. On the journey God tested his faith by asking him to sacrifice his son Isaac. Abraham was willing to obey, but at the last moment God intervened to prevent this sacrifice, and repeated his promise that Abraham would be the father of a great nation. Abraham's descendants settled in Canaan, but when the land was threatened by famine, Abraham's grandson Jacob left with his family for the land of Egypt.

The Exodus

The descendants of Jacob's sons, who had become the twelve tribes of Israel, lived and prospered in Egypt for several generations. But when a new pharaoh arose in Egypt he treated the Israelites as slaves. In order to control their numbers he gave an order that all Israelite boys should be killed at birth, but one child was hidden in a reed basket on a river. He was found by the pharaoh's daughter and named Moses.

When Moses reached manhood he fled Egypt after killing an Egyptian slave master for mistreating an Israelite. God commanded Moses to return and say to the Egyptian

The desert near Sinai. After leaving Egypt, the Jews traveled through this landscape before reaching the Promised Land.

The Jews are descended from the twelve sons of Jacob, whom God renamed Israel, "to struggle with God." Those shown in bold print in this family tree are honored as Patriarchs and Matriarchs because of the central part they play in the transmission of the Covenant.

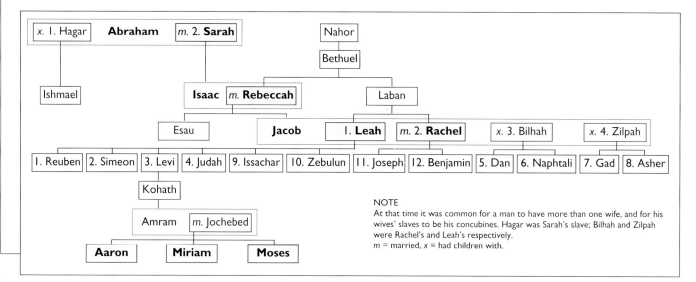

NOTE
At that time it was common for a man to have more than one wife, and for his wives' slaves to be his concubines. Hagar was Sarah's slave; Bilhah and Zilpah were Rachel's and Leah's respectively.
m = married, *x* = had children with.

pharaoh, "Let my people go." The pharaoh refused his demand, and in punishment God sent ten plagues to the Egyptians. The final plague brought death in one night to the first-born son of every Egyptian family. God told Moses that all Israelite families should smear lamb's blood on their doorposts; then their sons would not be killed on that night.

Overwhelmed by the catastrophe, the pharaoh let the Israelites go, but once they had gone he changed his mind and sent an army in pursuit. The Egyptians caught up with the Israelites at the shores of the Red Sea. God then parted the waters of the Red Sea so that the Israelites could pass safely across, but the Egyptian soldiers who tried to follow were drowned in its waters.

Moses the Lawgiver

As the leader of a people on the move, Moses had many problems to contend with, such as pursuit, hunger and thirst, and rebellion. At every point God told Moses what to do. Three months after leaving Egypt the people came to the foot of Mount Sinai at the head of the Red Sea. Here God revealed to Moses the Commandments, written on tablets of stone: ten main commands dealing with the people's relationship with God and with each other (see page 29) and hundreds of more detailed commandments enlarging on those principles.

After many years of wandering, the Israelites crossed the river Jordan and made their home in the land of Canaan—the Promised Land.

The Promised Land

At first the Israelites were ruled by prophets known as judges. Later they were ruled by kings, beginning with Saul, followed by David, to whom many of the psalms in the Bible have been attributed. David's son Solomon then ruled, but after his death the kingdom of Israel split into Judah and Israel. Both were eventually conquered by foreign powers.

In the centuries that followed, the Israelites endured exile to Babylon and although many returned they experienced further periods of invasion. In 63 BCE the Romans conquered the land and named it Palestine. The Jews rose in revolt against Roman rule in CE 66, but were defeated. The Temple in Jerusalem, rebuilt after the Israelites returned from exile in Babylon, was finally destroyed in CE 70.

Jerusalem fell to the Babylonians in 587 BCE and the last remnant of ancient Israel was swept away. The people were carried off into exile in Babylon. The exile lasted until around 550 BCE, when the Jews were allowed back to rebuild Jerusalem and the Temple. The exile is one of the most dramatic points of transition in Jewish thinking—comparable to the experience of the Holocaust in the 20th century.

THE COVENANT

Abraham is the only person in the Bible to be described as God's friend. Their relationship was one of debate, even argument. The Covenant marked the beginning of a special relationship that, according to Jewish belief, will continue until the coming of the Messiah. The relationship entailed privilege, but also responsibility: the Bible describes how the people suffered the consequences for breaking the Covenant.

At first the Jews believed, like other nations, that each people had its own god. But gradually the understanding developed that their god was God of all the world—"King of the Universe" to quote Jewish blessings:

Blessed are you, O Lord our God, King of the Universe, who has chosen us from all the nations and given us the Torah.

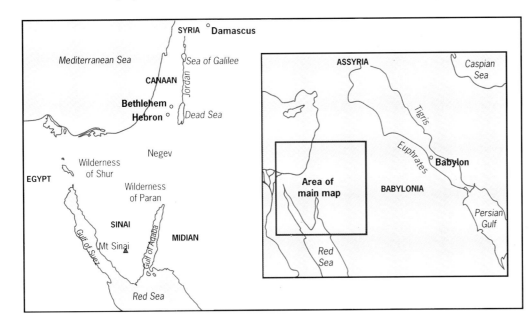

The Torah, the Prophets and the Writings

 Study of the Hebrew Bible is one of the most important religious duties for Jews. It is a collection of texts, written at different periods of Jewish history, which fall into three different types of book: the Torah, the Prophets and the Writings.

The Torah
The most important section consists of the first five books of the Bible, regarded as having been revealed by God directly to Moses. These five books are known collectively as the Torah, or by the Greek term, the Pentateuch. They contain stories of Creation, the Patriarchs, the Exodus from Egypt and details of the Jewish law. The word "Torah" is also sometimes used to mean the whole Hebrew Bible.

The Prophets
A prophet is a person who speaks or acts on behalf of God. The early books of the Prophets record the history of Israel and Judah, forever bound up with the words and deeds of such great prophets as Deborah, Samuel, Elijah and Elisha. Later books are often a detailed record of particular prophecies. For example, Isaiah speaks of a new form of covenant to replace the broken Covenant.

Writings
Much of the Hebrew Bible is poetry. The best known poems are the psalms, many of which are credited to King David. They are songs that express every shade of emotion: love, anger, despair, triumph, repentance. The Song of Songs, sometimes known as the Song of Solomon, is a love poem, while the Book of Job explores the question of suffering. The Book of Esther tells how the Jewish wife of a foreign king took great risks to protect the Jews whose lives were threatened while they were in exile in Babylon.

Mishnah and Talmud
Religious life and practice is based on the Torah and its commandments, but since these were given thousands of years ago for a very different world, learned teachers have discussed and passed down orally a series of interpretations and judgments based on the Torah.

Study of the Torah is one of the most important religious activities. There may be daily or weekly classes and study groups for different ages.

When the Temple in Jerusalem was destroyed in CE 70 following a revolt against the Romans, Judaism had to develop new ways of handling its religious life, focusing upon the synagogue and the rabbi. The Mishnah was compiled in the second century CE to assist this process, and the Talmud was finalized by the sixth century CE. These are used to help rabbis make decisions on new cases.

THE TEN COMMANDMENTS

1 *You shall have no other gods before me.*

2 *You shall not make for yourself graven images, you shall not bow down to them or serve them.*

3 *You shall not take the name of the Lord your God in vain.*

4 *Observe the sabbath day, to keep it holy. Six days you shall labor, and do all your work; but the seventh day is a sabbath to the Lord your God; in it you shall not do any work.*

5 *Honor your father and your mother.*

6 *You shall not kill.*

7 *Neither shall you commit adultery.*

8 *Neither shall you steal.*

9 *Neither shall you bear false witness against your neighbor.*

10 *Neither shall you covet your neighbor's wife, or anything that is your neighbor's.*

(Extracts from Deuteronomy 5:6-22).

The Messiah

The Jewish scriptures promise that God will send a Messiah. He will be chosen by God and will herald a new age. At a time determined by God, the Messiah will be born and will be the wisest of all the prophets whose line began with Moses. As God's representative on earth, the Messiah will bring a time of peace, justice and unity that will create the Kingdom of God on earth, and war and violence will cease. In the words of Isaiah:

> *The wolf lives with the lamb,*
> *the panther lies down with the kid,*
> *calf and lion cub feed together,*
> *with a little boy to lead them.*
> (Isaiah 11:6)

BASIC BELIEFS AND TRADITIONS

At the heart of Jewish belief is the Shema, the first commandment: *Hear, O Israel: The Lord our God is one Lord; and you shall love the Lord your God with all your heart, and with all your soul, and with all your might. And these words which I command you this day shall be upon your heart; and you shall teach them diligently to your children, and shall talk of them when you sit in your house, and when you walk by the way, and when you lie down, and when you rise.*
(Deuteronomy 6:4-7)

THE LAW

The Law was given to Moses at Mount Sinai. Its main principles are the Ten Commandments, but more detailed laws are given elsewhere in the five books of Moses, and these are worked out in further detail for changing circumstances in the Talmud. Jews of different traditions differ as to how literally the Law is to be interpreted, but they agree that a Jew's first duty is to live according to God's law.

For Jews, the Law is God's merciful provision of guidelines, without which it would not be possible to remain in the covenant relationship with him. Study of the Law is an important part of Jewish life.

THE SABBATH

The fifth commandment lays down that no work must be done on the seventh day of the week, the sabbath, or *shabbat*. The sabbath begins at dusk on Friday and ends at dusk on Saturday. Jewish families welcome the sabbath with the best food, clothes, singing and celebration. Saturday may be spent visiting friends and family, relaxing or reading the Torah. The synagogue holds services on Friday night and Saturday morning.

A ceremony called *havdalah* (separation) marks the end of the sabbath on Saturday evening. The family gathers round, a candle is lit, and a box of sweet-smelling spices is passed around.

As darkness falls the mother and daughters of the house light the sabbath candles and set out a festive meal which has been prepared earlier, for no cooking is done on the sabbath.

Meeting, Study and Worship in the Synagogue

TYPES OF SYNAGOGUE

Synagogues vary in how they are decorated. Many are very plain, but others are decorated according to local taste and culture. There are not usually any images of people or animals, in obedience to the Second Commandment (see page 29).

Twentieth-century East European

Traditional wooden.

After the destruction of the Temple in Jerusalem in CE 70 and the scattering of the Jews to all parts of the Roman Empire, the synagogue became the center of Jewish community life. Many of the features of a synagogue recall details of worship and ritual in Temple times. It fulfills three main functions: as a house of assembly, where the Jewish community can meet for any purpose; as a house of study, where the Torah and Talmud are studied and children learn Hebrew and study the Torah; and as a house of prayer, where services are held on the sabbaths and festival days. Public congregational prayers are said at the synagogue every weekday, but this can only take place if ten adult Jewish males are present. It is therefore every Jewish man's duty to attend prayers as often as possible to help form a *minyan*, or quorum.

Members of the congregation carry new Torah scrolls into the synagogue.

INSIDE A SYNAGOGUE

In Orthodox and traditional synagogues, men and women sit separately. In most non-Orthodox synagogues men and women may sit together. Many of the prayers in the service are sung, and there is a rich heritage of Jewish music from different traditions. The singing may be congregational, led by a single cantor or by a choir. In Orthodox synagogues no instrument other than the human voice is used.

MEMORIAL

Members of the community who have died are remembered every year on the anniversary of their death with special prayers for their surviving friends and family. Their names are often recorded on a board, and a lamp is lit on the anniversary of their death.

PERPETUAL LAMP

In the Temple in Jerusalem, and now in every synagogue, there has always been a light before the ark called the Perpetual Lamp or Eternal Light. In the Temple the menorah was a seven-branched candlestick in which six lamps were only lit at night but the central one was never extinguished.

THE TORAH SCROLLS

Every synagogue has a set of parchment scrolls on which the Torah is hand-written. This is an extremely skilled and laborious job, performed as an act of devotion itself and done by a specialist scribe. It often takes a year to write a full Torah.

Each scroll has a belt to hold it when rolled, a breastplate and a crown, together with a silver pointer used when reading to avoid finger contact with the parchment—both as a sign of respect and to preserve a costly item for as long as possible.

There is a Torah reading set for every sabbath in the year, making a complete reading in the course of the year. It is the privilege and responsibility of every adult male to take a turn at this reading, which requires training and practice since the

Torah scrolls are written with no indication of the vowel sounds. When a boy does this for the first time, it is an important occasion in his life.

PROTECTING THE SCROLLS

The Torah scrolls are "dressed" in velvet coverings and silver ornaments, as below. This is done mainly to protect the valuable parchment, but the decorated mantle also recalls some of the ritual clothing worn by priests in Temple times.

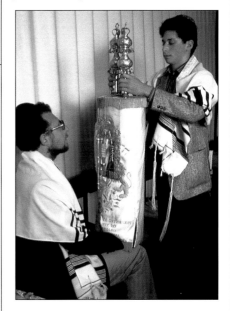

TORAH SCROLLS

Every synagogue has a set of hand-written Torah scrolls, which are treated with great respect, and kept in a special cupboard or alcove (called the ark) in the wall of the synagogue which faces Jerusalem.

BIMAH

Most synagogues have a raised platform, the *bimah*, near the center of the room where the Torah and prayers are read, and a sermon may be preached. Seating is usually arranged round three sides of the bimah.

THE ROLE OF A RABBI

No rabbi (literally "teacher") or other qualified person is necessary for the existence or operation of a synagogue, but in practice there is usually a rabbi employed by the congregation to have authority over the running of the synagogue and to attend to the religious needs of the congregation. He or she teaches the study of the Torah to both adults and children, and may also be called upon to settle matters of dispute about interpretations of the Law, especially in Orthodox synagogues.

Rituals, Beliefs, Customs and Symbols

E**very aspect of Jewish life, from birth to death and in the normal round of everyday life, is marked by actions performed in obedience to the Commandments and serving as reminders to the Jew to be constantly aware of God and of his Laws.

Birth

The Torah lays down that as a sign of the Covenant between God and the Jews, every boy baby must be circumcised. This operation is performed at home by a specially trained person, a *mohel*, on the eighth day after birth. The mohel recalls the Covenant, and recites a blessing while cutting off the foreskin. The baby's name is announced at this time. For girls there is a blessing at the synagogue. After the ceremony there is a meal, the "feast of the fulfilment of a commandment."

Bar mitzvah

At the age of thirteen a Jewish boy is considered old enough to take responsibility for himself and his observance of the Law. He is in religious terms an adult, a "son of the commandment," *bar mitzvah* in Hebrew. He can take an active part in services and be counted in the minyan, the quorum for public prayer. One of the privileges and duties of a Jewish man is to be called to read a passage of the Torah in Hebrew in a synagogue service. It is a special occasion when he does this for the first time. Friends and relatives attend the synagogue to hear the boy read, after saying a prayer in which he promises to keep God's commandments. At this age, too, the boy may put on the *tefillin* for the first time. In Reform Jewish congregations girls also celebrate their coming of age at thirteen years with a *bat mitzvah* (daughter of the commandment) ceremony.

Orthodox Jews have a *bat hayil* service for twelve-year-old girls on a day other than the sabbath, often Sunday afternoon, because girls and women do not take part in services.

Marriage

Marriage and the raising of children is an important part of Jewish life. In many Jewish communities the role of the matchmaker is still important; celibacy is not encouraged.

The celebration may be in a synagogue, but in many countries it is often held in the open air. The bridegroom places a gold ring on the bride's forefinger. The marriage contract (the *ketubah*) is read out, and the rabbi recites seven marriage blessings. At the end of the ceremony the bridegroom breaks a wineglass under his foot. There are different explanations for this: some say that, even at a time of joy, it recalls the destruction of the Temple in Jerusalem.

Death

Jews believe in the resurrection of the dead, but there are different beliefs about what happens to the body, and consequently about burial or cremation. Orthodox Jews do not cremate their

A Jewish couple stand under the hupah, a canopy decorated with flowers that symbolizes the new home the bride and groom will make together. The wedding takes place on any day other than the sabbath or festivals.

REMINDERS OF THE LAW

The first commandment for the Jews is also the most important: "You shall love
the Lord our God with all your heart, soul and strength."
This is called the Shema, from the Hebrew for "hear." The Torah says:
*You shall therefore lay these words of mine upon your heart and your soul; and you shall
bind them as a sign upon your hand, and they shall be as frontlets between your eyes. And you
shall teach them to your children, talking of them when you are sitting in your house, and when
you are walking by the way, and when you lie down, and when you rise up. And you shall write
them upon the doorposts of your house and upon your gates.*
(Deuteronomy 11:18-20)

TEFILLIN
A scribe writes the words of the Shema in
Hebrew, sometimes with other words
from the Torah, on tiny scrolls. These
words are then placed in small boxes
called *tefillin*, with straps or tapes attached.
During weekday prayers a Jewish man or
boy wears the tefillin bound to his
forehead and to his left arm and hand.
On his forehead the words of the Shema
are close to his mind, and on his arm they
are close to his heart and the straps fasten
them to his hands.

MEZUZAH
Once Jews used to carve the words of the
Shema in Hebrew into the doorposts.
Today tiny scrolls written with the words
of the Shema are put into small boxes
called *mezuzah*, which are nailed to the
doorpost while saying a blessing.

TALLIT
*Speak to the people of Israel, and bid
them to make tassels on the corners of
their garments throughout their
generations, and to put upon the tassel
of each corner a cord of blue; and it shall
be to you a tassel to look upon and
remember all the commandments of
the Lord.* (Numbers 15:38-39)
In obedience to this commandment,
male Jews wear a fringed cloak or shawl
during prayer, and some wear a fringed
undergarment at all times.

YARMULKE
Orthodox Jews wear head coverings to
show submission to God. For men these
are often small caps called *yarmulkes*.
Some Orthodox women cut their hair and
wear a wig. All except liberal Jews wear
head coverings for services.

MEZUZAH
There is usually a mezuzah on
every doorpost in a Jewish
home except outside the
bathroom and toilet. This
reminds everyone to keep
God's laws every time they
enter or leave a room.

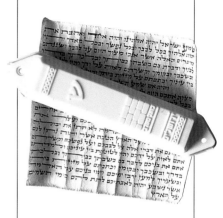

*The valley of Kidron, outside
Jerusalem, is one of the most
ancient Jewish burial
grounds. Here, Hassidic Jews
visit some of the graves.*

dead, seeing this as a denial of belief in bodily
resurrection, but non-Orthodox Jews sometimes do so.

The body must be buried as soon as possible
after death (usually within twenty-four hours),
in Jewish consecrated ground. The body is
washed, anointed with spices and wrapped in a
white sheet.

The rituals of mourning help the bereaved to
come to terms with their loss. For a week after
the death, close relatives sit at home, wearing a
torn or cut upper garment, taking no part in
ordinary life. Friends and relatives have a duty
to visit, bringing food and succor. For eleven
months after the death a prayer is recited every
day at the synagogue, and thereafter every year
the anniversary of the death is remembered.

Celebrations, Remembrance and Symbolic Events

THE LUNAR CYCLE
The Jewish calendar is lunar, but every few years a thirteenth month is added to keep in step with the solar year. The new day begins at nightfall, so festivals begin in the evening. The years are counted from the traditional Jewish dating of the creation of the world, thus CE 2000 is the Jewish year 5760.

A Purim tableau at a Jewish school. Jewish children love to dress up for Purim and re-enact the dramatic story of Queen Esther's bravery.

Almost the whole of Jewish history and teaching is embodied in its festivals, in which traditions are passed on from one generation to the next by means of stories, actions, symbolic food and singing. Most festival celebrations are based on the home and family, with the events of the past being re-enacted in a way that makes them meaningful to present-day life. So, for example, at Hanukah Jews remember the religious persecution of the past, but also that in the modern world.

In the Jewish calendar festivals are officially divided into "major" and "minor" categories. The five major festivals are those laid down in the Torah: the two Days of Awe, Rosh Hashanah and Yom Kippur, and three joyful festivals, Pesach (Passover), Shavuot and Sukkot (Feast of Tabernacles). Many of the minor festivals have also become popular, and some, such as Hanukah, are celebrated more widely than some of the major festivals.

ROSH HASHANAH
This is the Jewish New Year. It begins a ten-day period of repentance leading up to Yom Kippur. Jews prepare for Rosh Hashanah during Elul, the month before, with reflection and self-examination. A ram's horn, the *shofar*, is blown every day in Elul to call the people to repent and to start the New Year afresh.

YOM KIPPUR
The Day of Atonement is the major fast of the year, when Jews seek forgiveness from anyone they have wronged. The *kol nidrei* is sung, in which the congregation ask for absolution from religious vows they have failed to keep in the past year.

SUKKOT
Sukkot commemorates the time when the Israelites lived in temporary shelters in the desert in their journey to the Promised Land. Families build shelters in the open air and fill them with greenery. For seven days the family eats there. Sukkot also celebrates the end of the harvest.

SIMHAT TORAH
This comes at the end of Sukkot and marks the end of the annual reading of the whole of the Torah. The Torah scrolls are carried in procession around the synagogue, with singing and dancing.

HANUKAH
In the second century BCE, the Israelite Judah Maccabee defeated the Greek tyrant who had forced the Jews to abandon their religion. The Temple was rededicated, but there was only enough oil for the Temple lamp to last one day, and it would take eight days to prepare a fresh supply. The lamp was lit nonetheless, and miraculously it kept burning for eight days.

An eight-branched candlestick is lit for the festival, one candle burning on the first day, two on the second, and so on for eight days, celebrating the survival of the Jewish faith in adversity. Hanukah is especially popular with Jews in Europe and the United States, because it falls at winter holiday times and is celebrated as a children's festival.

TU B'SHEVAT

The New Year for Trees is increasing in importance as an environmental festival. Families around the world may plant trees in their own locality, or they may prefer to give money for reforestation projects in Israel, where schoolchildren plant trees.

PURIM

This celebrates the story of Esther, the Jewish queen of the Persian king Xerxes, who saved her people from destruction at the hands of the king's minister Haman. People dress up in odd clothes for the synagogue service. The scroll of Esther is read aloud, and every time the villain's name "Haman" is spoken, people attempt to drown out the sound by making loud noises.

The Jewish calendar is lunar, but seven times in nineteen years a thirteenth month, *Adar Sheni*, is added to keep in line with the solar year.

PESACH

The festival of Passover (Pesach) celebrates God's deliverance of the Israelites from captivity in Egypt. The Israelites had to depart so quickly from Egypt that they had no time to bake ordinary bread, but made unleavened bread for the journey. Only unleavened bread (*matzoh*) is eaten during the eight days of the festival.

The high point is the seder meal eaten in the home on the first evening of the festival. Families try to come together for the meal. The seder meal recalls in words and symbols the departure of the Israelites from Egypt. The youngest child present asks a series of questions, and the answers tell the story of the Exodus.

A seder plate, matzoh, and wine.

Blowing the shofar for Rosh Hashanah.

SHAVUOT

Also known as Pentecost or the Feast of Weeks, Shavuot combines a festival for the wheat harvest in Israel with thanksgiving for the gift of the Torah to Moses on Mount Sinai. Children may begin their study of the Torah at this time of year, and the Book of Ruth is read aloud. Ruth is celebrated because she was a foreigner who was willing to take on a commitment to the Torah.

1 **Rosh Hashanah** 1 Tishri
2 **Yom Kippur** 10 Tishri
3 **Sukkot** 15-23 Tishri
4 **Simhat Torah** 24 Tishri
5 **Hanukah** 25 Kislev-3 Tevet
6 **Tu B'Shevat** 15 Shevat
7 **Purim** 14 Adar
8 **Pesach** 15-22 Nisan
9 **Shavuot** 6-7 Sivan
10 **Tishah B'Av** 9 Av

TISHAH B'AV

A number of disasters have befallen the Jewish people on the ninth day of Av. Both the first and the second Temples in Jerusalem were destroyed on this day, and it is the anniversary of other persecutions. It also provides an opportunity to remember and mourn the six million Jews murdered in the Nazi Holocaust. It is a day of fasting and mourning.

Jewish Traditions, Lifestyle and Identity

It is possible to be Jewish without being religious. The term *Jew* refers to an ethnically distinct group as well as to those who follow Jewish religious laws and teachings. In Jewish law and thought it is possible to convert to Judaism, but it is impossible to stop being a Jew if you are born Jewish, even if you convert to another religion. Whether or not a Jew is religious is the individual's choice.

There are three main forms of contemporary Judaism, especially in America: Orthodox, Conservative (known as Reform in the UK) and Reform (Liberal in the UK).

Orthodox Judaism

Orthodox Judaism sees itself as the upholder of traditional Judaism. Hebrew is the language used at all services, and traditional Jewish law (*halakhah*) is observed concerning food and behavior (see opposite).

Among the most Orthodox of the Orthodox

The Western Wall in Jerusalem is all that remains of the last great Temple, destroyed in CE 70. It is a center of pilgrimage and prayer for Jews from all over the world, both for private prayer which is said facing the wall, and for public services and bar mitzvahs.

are the Hassidic Jews, whose dress and lifestyle is that of eighteenth-century Eastern Europe, particularly Poland, where the Hassidic movement began. They are distinguished by their black clothing, long coats, and tall or wide hats.

Conservative (Reform) Judaism

Conservative Judaism is primarily an American expression of Judaism. It seeks to observe the traditional Jewish laws (*halakhah*), but also allows modifications, so long as these are seen to be loyal to the Law and to developments of the laws over the centuries. For example, in 1960 the Conservative Jews agreed to the use of electricity on the sabbath and to using a car to travel to the synagogue—something Orthodox Judaism would not permit.

Reform (Liberal) Judaism

This arose in the early nineteenth century as an attempt to make Judaism a more modern faith, unencumbered by what its founders saw as outdated dietary laws and the exclusive use of Hebrew in worship. It also embraced modern biblical scholarship; for example, it does not teach that Moses wrote the five books of the Torah.

Reform and Liberal Jews worship primarily in the language of their own country. They observe some dietary laws, but not nearly as many as those observed by the Orthodox. While many Orthodox Jews play a role in social and political issues, Reform and Liberal Jews are particularly active.

Judaism at home

While the synagogue is important in Jewish life, the home is of greater importance because this is where many of the festivals take place, and where the sabbath is celebrated. The details of the Law of Moses are observed in the home in all sorts of everyday details.

Hospitality is a very important aspect of Jewish life. The Torah describes how Abraham and Sarah entertained strangers who turned out to be angels, and their example is important to Jewish families. Strangers will often be invited home for the sabbath, and travelers can be assured of a warm welcome during festivals.

Private time for study of the Torah and for prayer is also often a feature of Jewish family life, in addition to worship at the synagogue.

Judaism beyond the home

Concern about maintaining Jewish identity means many families encourage their children to join Jewish clubs and organizations, attend Jewish schools and seek marriage partners within Judaism. Some Jewish men attend a *yeshiva*, a Talmudic college where the Torah and rabbinic literature are studied and debated. Traditionally the yeshiva is open only to men. For many Conservative and Reform or Liberal Jews, interfaith dialogue, especially with Christians and Muslims, has grown to be of considerable interest since the Holocaust.

Kibbutz

It is common for young people not living in Israel to spend some time studying or working in Israel, often on a *kibbutz* (plural *kibbutzim*). These farming communities were first set up in 1909 by small groups of twenty or thirty people who began to cultivate desert areas in Palestine. Today thousands of people live on kibbutzim. Some spend all their working lives in these communities, others come to live or work there for a few months or years. There is no individual ownership on a kibbutz: the land, factories, houses and animals belong to the community.

Some kibbutzim are open to people of all nationalities and religions. Others are religious kibbutzim that follow Jewish laws.

LAWS OF FOOD AND DIET

Jewish food laws (called *kashrut*) relate to what may be eaten, and to how animals are slaughtered, prepared, cooked and eaten. Food is *kosher* (permitted) or *terefah* (forbidden).

The only land animals that are kosher are those that both chew the cud and have a cloven hoof. The prohibition of pig products is widely known, but other animals that are terefah include the rabbit, the hare, the camel and the rock badger. Fish must have both fins and scales, so shellfish are terefah.

Animals and birds must be ritually slaughtered in the correct manner by an adult Jew, and certain parts of the animal may not be eaten. Meat must be drained of blood before being cooked.

Meat products and dairy products may not be eaten together or at the same meal, and great care is taken in Orthodox Jewish households to keep them separate at every stage of preparation. A completely different set of utensils is used for the two types of food. There are different storage areas, and utensils are washed separately.

A Jewish butcher at work. All blood is removed from the meat by salting.

Kashrut law affects Orthodox lifestyle in that it makes it impossible to eat out except in kosher restaurants, or to accept hospitality from non-Jews. It is one of the issues over which the Reform and Orthodox are most divided, for Reform Jews have a much wider definition of what is kosher.

Harvest festival celebrations on a kibbutz.

The Diaspora: Spread all Over the World

A Hassidic Jew—one of many Orthodox Jews who have recently emigrated to Israel from all parts of the world.

T he Jewish people have undergone many periods of exile from their original lands. Their history and development down the centuries have been affected by the tolerance, or lack of it, with which they were treated. The first major Jewish exile was in the sixth century BCE, when Jerusalem was conquered by the Babylonians and the Jews were taken away to Babylon. While some returned, many stayed and went even further into central Asia.

Judaism under the Greeks and Romans

The coming of the Greeks under Alexander the Great in 332 BCE shattered the Jewish state and many Jews migrated to new Greek cities such as Antioch and Alexandria. Under the Roman Empire, Jerusalem was sacked twice, in CE 70 and again in CE 124. Both times, Jews were scattered abroad.

By CE 200 the Roman Empire enclosed the areas of Jewish settlement around the Mediterranean, although there were still concentrated Jewish communities beyond the Roman border in Babylonia. By CE 400 the Roman Empire had become largely Christian, and Jewish settlement had extended into Spain and northern France. With the rise of the Arabs and Islam in the seventh century, and their rapid expansion during the following centuries, many of the areas that had previously been Christian came under Muslim rule.

Although most Jews lived under Christian and Muslim governments, there were scattered communities in India, China and Africa. The only African group to have kept its Jewish identity through the centuries are the Falashas of Ethiopia (see page 41).

The Middle Ages

During the Middle Ages the long-established Jewish communities in Europe were affected by the cultures in which they settled, and two groups developed with different religious customs. Those who lived in Germany and then spread further into central and eastern Europe were called *Ashkenazim* (singular *Ashkenazi*); those who had settled in Spain and Portugal were called *Sephardim* (singular *Sephardi*). The Sephardim were expelled from Spain in 1492. Some traveled to Europe and others to North Africa, but the majority migrated to Turkey and lands under Ottoman rule in the eastern Mediterranean.

MIGRATIONS THROUGH HISTORY
In 300 BCE (near right), Jewish population was still concentrated in Judaea and Babylon, but settlements began to appear along important trade routes and in the eastern Mediterranean.

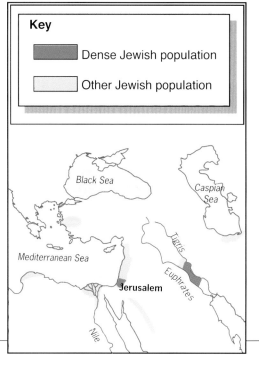

Key

▨ Dense Jewish population

☐ Other Jewish population

Black Sea

Caspian Sea

Mediterranean Sea

Tigris

Euphrates

Jerusalem

Nile

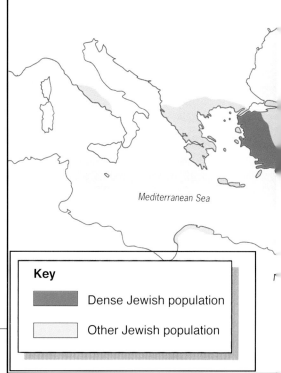

Mediterranean Sea

Key

▨ Dense Jewish population

☐ Other Jewish population

Modern times

By 1800 the majority of the world's Jews lived in Europe, but the nineteenth and twentieth centuries saw the largest ever displacement of Jews. Between 1881 and 1914 more than 2.75 million Jews left Eastern Europe, mainly for the Americas, South Africa, Australia and New Zealand. Anti-Semitism grew worse in Europe and more than 500,000 Jews left between 1932 and 1939, with over 46% traveling to Palestine.

With the beginning of the Second World War in 1939, Jewish freedom of movement was severely controlled. In the war years 6 million Jews lost their lives in Europe. After the war, hundreds of thousands of Jews were displaced and many sought a new life in the State of Israel, which was established in 1948.

A sculpture in the Holocaust Museum in Jerusalem.

THE HOLOCAUST

Soon after coming to power in 1933, Hitler's extreme right-wing and anti-Semitic National Socialist (Nazi) Party brought in severe restrictions on the Jewish communities of Germany. Their rights as German citizens were taken away and they were forced to wear yellow badges as a public sign that they were Jewish.

As increasing pressure was put on the Jews, 300,000 left Germany in the years leading up to 1939. The Nazi invasion of Poland that year marked the beginning of the Second World War. The Jews remaining in Germany, and the millions of Jews living in Poland and other countries that came under Nazi occupation, could not escape.

THE CONCENTRATION CAMPS
In 1940 the systematic rounding up of Jews began, and mass death camps known as concentration camps were established. Between 1940 and 1945, 6 million Jews were killed by the Nazis and their collaborators. This number was more than a third of the total number of Jews in the world at the time. Millions of Jews and non-Jews were murdered in these camps, while others died from disease or starvation. This period is known as the Holocaust, a word from the Greek version of the Hebrew Bible referring to a sacrifice consumed by fire.

HOLOCAUST MEMORIALS
The tragedy of this period is remembered by Jews in their prayers and on days such as Tishah B'Av which are set aside for remembrance. In Jerusalem the people and places of the Holocaust are remembered at a site called Yad Vashem, which means "a place and a name." The place of this memorial is an empty room lit by a candle. The name refers to the list of concentration camps inscribed on the floor of this room. The avenue of trees outside is called the Avenue of the Righteous: It is planted in remembrance of Gentiles who helped Jews during the Second World War.

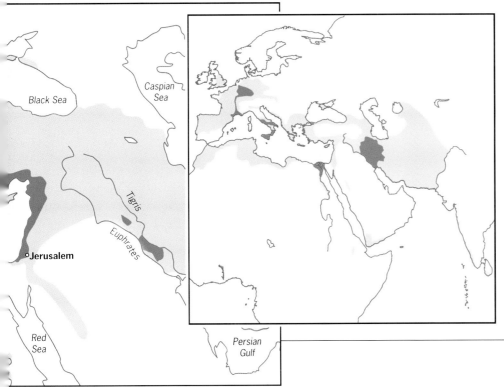

MIGRATIONS THROUGH HISTORY
By CE 100 (center map) there were probably more than 8 million Jews in the world, nearly 6 million of them beyond Judaea. The expansion of the Roman Empire and its accompanying trade led to the establishment of Jewish communities in Europe, North Africa, and the Middle East (map immediate left).

Facing Old and New Challenges

The Israeli flag flying in Jerusalem.

 constant theme in the history of Judaism is the challenge of a world in which Jews are a small minority. Estimates of the present world Jewish population give a total of about 13 million. For nineteen centuries, until the foundation of the modern State of Israel, there was no country in the world with a Jewish majority. Currently, three fifths of world Jewry lives outside Israel. Judaism today is very much shaped by the experience of living within changing societies the world over and by having had one third of its adherents killed during the Nazi Holocaust. The twenty first century brings new challenges.

Zionism

Mount Zion is the hill on which Jerusalem was originally built. Zion is used throughout the Hebrew Bible as a symbol of a lost homeland or a future state in which Jews will live in peace with all people. Some prophets also used Zion as the symbol of the place where all nations will bow down before God.

Political Zionism grew from two themes, one ancient and one modern, in the late 19th century. The first was the desire, expressed in traditional Jewish prayer and literature to be "next year in Jerusalem". The Jewish diaspora, known in Hebrew as galut or exile was considered to be a temporary phenomenon, so that Jews longed to return to their homeland. However, when countries offered full citizenship to Jews, many Jews ceased to idealise the "ingathering of exiles" once they could fully participate in the life of their home nations.

The second theme was that having endured so much persecution many Jews wanted their own state where they could defend themselves and their way of life. Zionism was a form of nationalism. Jews began to immigrate to Palestine in large numbers from the end of the nineteenth century, swelling the pre-Zionist community of a few tens of thousands to many hundreds of thousands by the time that the State of Israel was founded in 1948. At this time the land was part of the British Mandate, taken over from Ottoman control at the end of the First World War. The creation of a "national home for the Jewish people" had been encouraged by the Balfour Declaration on behalf of the British government in 1917 with the proviso that none of the peoples already settled there would be adversely affected.

Though the state of Israel has achieved a modern infrastructure and a rich cultural life in part due to its population drawn from Jewish communities around the world, its existence has been precarious ever since 1948. The state has been involved in conflicts on several occasions with neighboring countries and has been affected by the development of a Palestinian national consciousness.

Political Zionism was mostly driven by secular Jews. The majority of Israel's Jews are themselves secular, but the religious right wing also has much power and influence in the Israeli government.

Hassidic Judaism

Hassidic Judaism arose in Poland and Eastern Europe as a pious, poor people's movement. It began moving to North America in the early 20th century and survived there when its original centers were destroyed in the Holocaust. In North America and then later in the State of Israel, Hassidic Judaism not only recovered but saw itself as having a specific role to call Jews back to "true" Judaism.

Centered upon charismatic leaders, the appeal of the Hassidic is based on longing for the old ways, on the desire for strong religious leadership and the need for a defense against secularism, particularly in North America and Israel. The Lubavich are part of the Hassidic movement and are extremely active in trying to bring Jews back to their faith. In public places, in Jewish quarters on Friday nights, in camps and clubs, the Lubavich try to re-activate the divine spark that they believe is within all Jews.

Who is Jewish?

In Orthodox Judaism, anyone born of a Jewish mother is Jewish. Non-Jews can convert to Judaism on marriage, but one of the biggest problems facing Judaism today is the loss of numbers caused by marriage between Jewish men and non-Jewish women. Children born of such marriages are not strictly considered Jews.

In Britain, the number of Jews has fallen from 500,000 thirty years ago to fewer than

300,000 today, mostly as a result of inter-marriage. Increasingly, Jewish communities outside Israel are seeking to find ways of amending the rules to allow a broader definition of who is a Jew, or to find ways of helping Jews marry other Jews – including setting up Jewish dating agencies on the worldwide web . Many Jewish leaders see this as the most difficult challenge currently facing Judaism.

JEWISH POPULATION

In 1800 there were approximately 3 million Jews worldwide, distributed as shown below. By 2000 the balance had shifted dramatically: of around 13 million Jews worldwide, the distribution was as shown below right. These numbers represent individuals who have identified themselves as being religious Jews.

There are over 4.8 million Jews in Israel, where they make up over 80% of the population, although the largest Jewish group lives in North America (5.8 million). The third largest Jewish population is in France (650,000) followed by Russia (440,000), Canada (362,000), and then Great Britain (267,000).

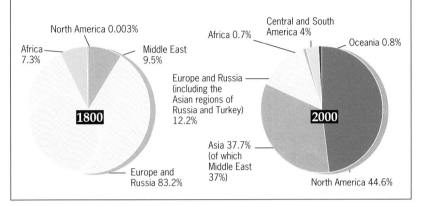

The native Jews of Ethiopia call themselves Beta Yisrael *in preference to their old name* Falashas *which refers to their status as foreigners. Many of them lived near the border with Sudan. For centuries they have been isolated from the Jewish world and they use a language called* Ge'ez *(ancient Ethiopic) for religious ceremonies. In 1975 the Falashas were given the right to settle in Israel and a steady stream of them emigrated. Then in 1991 Sudan was struck by civil war, and in a dramatic airlift 20,000 Falashas were flown to Israel, most of them in the course of a single day.*

CHAPTER TWO

CHRISTIANITY

Christians are followers of Jesus Christ, who was born a Jew in the Roman province of Palestine (present-day Israel, Palestine and Jordan) probably just before the first century CE. At the age of about thirty, he spent three years as an itinerant preacher and healer near his home town of Nazareth and in Jerusalem.

Jesus Christ, as portrayed in a mosaic in Kykko Monastery, Cyprus. The halo and cross behind his head are symbols of his holiness. His hand is held in a traditional gesture of blessing.

The Cathedral in Siena, Italy, is typical of many great European churches, with its elaborate carving depicting saints and angels, and its rich decoration.

Whereas many people of other faiths recognize Jesus as a great teacher, Christians believe that he is God, or "the Son of God," who chose to take on human form in order to reconcile humanity to God, and to restore the relationship that had been broken by human disobedience. His mother, Mary, is said to have conceived by the power of God, not by a human father, and most Christians teach that Jesus was fully God and fully human. They believe that he was executed by crucifixion, but rose from death and still lives today as Lord of all creation.

Although Christianity arose out of Judaism, it rapidly developed as a faith with a separate identity. Today it is numerically the largest faith in the world, with adherents in every continent and a total membership of nearly 2 billion worldwide.

There are many different traditions (churches or denominations) within Christianity. These have arisen over time with disagreements about teaching or different ways of worshiping. The variety of forms of Christianity is often bewildering, and it can be difficult to recognize the same faith in, for example, the ornate cathedrals of Europe and the "base communities" worshiping in the slums of South American cities. Nearly all, however, agree on the central teachings described in this chapter, and in the last fifty years there has been more dialogue between differing traditions.

Early Roots: The Life of Jesus of Nazareth

Christianity takes its name from the Greek word *Christ*, a translation of the Hebrew word *Messiah*, meaning "the Anointed One"—a ruler chosen by God. Christians believe that Jesus, born a Jew in first-century Palestine, was the Christ.

The birth of Jesus

Jesus was born to a Jewish couple, Mary and Joseph, who lived in Nazareth, in Galilee. The whole of Judaea was under Roman rule, and at the time of Jesus' birth, according to accounts in the New Testament, Mary and Joseph had traveled to Bethlehem, near Jerusalem, in response to a Roman census. Jesus grew up as a Jewish boy, following Jewish traditions.

Jesus' public life

At the age of about thirty he left his quiet life in Nazareth and began three years of traveling and teaching throughout Judaea. He taught a new way of fulfilling the Law of Moses, beginning with the words of the prophet Isaiah:

> *The Spirit of the Lord is upon me, because he has anointed me to preach good news to the poor. He has sent me to proclaim release to the captives and recovering of sight to the blind, to set at liberty those who are oppressed, to proclaim the acceptable year of the Lord.* (Luke 4:18-19).

He called this the Kingdom of God, and proclaimed that this hope for captives and the oppressed was near at hand.

The disciples

Jesus traveled throughout Judaea, healing the sick and performing many miracles. He gathered a special group of twelve men who went everywhere with him, now known as the twelve disciples or the twelve apostles, and many other friends and followers (the Bible mentions a special group of seventy), including several women. They looked after him and listened to his teaching. At first Jesus taught only Jews, but gradually he broadened his teaching to include non-Jews, known as Gentiles.

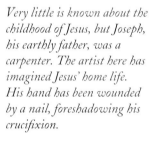

Very little is known about the childhood of Jesus, but Joseph, his earthly father, was a carpenter. The artist here has imagined Jesus' home life. His hand has been wounded by a nail, foreshadowing his crucifixion.

The arrest and death of Jesus

Jesus' actions soon aroused opposition. The Roman rulers suspected that he was planning a rebellion of the Jews. Some religious leaders believed that his words were blasphemous and that he was teaching people to ignore Jewish law. Although it was clear that the authorities wanted to kill him, Jesus continued to draw large crowds, and he preached even more forcefully. On the night before he was arrested, he gathered his close friends for the Passover meal (see *Judaism*, page 35). Christians call this meal the Last Supper.

The authorities plotted with Judas Iscariot, one of Jesus' disciples, to have him arrested and brought to trial before Pontius Pilate, the Roman governor. Pilate could find no evidence against Jesus, but a large crowd demanded his execution, and Pilate agreed. He sentenced Jesus to be crucified, the standard Roman method of execution for serious criminals.

Jesus died, and one or two of his friends asked the Roman governor for permission to bury him. They laid his body in a cave that they closed with a heavy stone. This took place on a Friday, the day before the sabbath.

The Resurrection and Ascension

On the following Sunday, when the sabbath rest was over, some women followers of Jesus came to embalm his body. They discovered that the stone had been rolled away, and there was no body in the cave. An angel appeared to them and told them that Jesus was alive. Over the next few weeks, more and more of Jesus' friends saw him alive, and believed that he had been raised from the dead. They came to understand that he was a new kind of Messiah: not an earthly king, but ruler of the universe.

Forty days after his resurrection, the disciples saw Jesus lifted up into heaven; this was the last time they saw him. But before he left, he promised that he would send them a "helper," the Holy Spirit of God, and so they waited. One day when they were all together, they heard the sound of a strong rushing wind, and saw what looked like flames resting on each one of them. They were filled with a new

---

PETER AND PAUL

Among the accounts we have of the growth and spread of Christianity in its early years, two very different men stand out. One was Peter, originally called Simon, a fisherman from Galilee who had been one of the first to be chosen by Jesus as a disciple. The second was Paul, whose original name was Saul. He was a highly educated Jew, skilled in both Greek and Jewish thought.

PETER

There are many stories in the Gospels revealing Peter's impetuosity and fallibility, but Jesus saw his underlying strength and renamed him Peter, which means "Rock." After Jesus' arrest Peter three times denied knowing him, but later became one of the most courageous and outspoken Christians. He was imprisoned several times by the Romans, and according to tradition he was eventually executed for his faith. Although he had very little education, he was one of the main leaders of the early Christians.

PAUL

At first Paul had helped to arrest many of Jesus' followers, but after an overwhelming vision of the Risen Christ on the road to Damascus he became a leading Christian. He traveled the Mediterranean world, preaching and establishing communities of Christians. Paul encouraged non-Jews to convert to Christianity, teaching that those who followed Christ need not become Jews. It was Paul who first wrote down the most important aspects of Christian belief, writing to new churches offering advice and encouraging their faith.

---

enthusiasm, and rushed out into the streets to tell people that Jesus was the Son of God, that he had been raised from the dead by the power of God, and that through baptism, all who would recognize Jesus as the Messiah could be saved from their sins.

This Greek Orthodox icon shows Jesus, indicated by his halo, descending to Hell after his death, breaking down the gates and raising up all the good men and women of the past, giving them eternal life in Heaven. This "Harrowing of Hell" illustrates the belief that Jesus' triumph over death at his resurrection is for all people, at all times, not just for Jesus or those who came after him.

The Bible and Other Christian Writings

A Romanian painting of the Last Supper. One of the central stories in the Gospels tells of the meal that Jesus shared with his disciples just before his arrest and death. John's Gospel relates that Jesus took the part of a servant and washed his disciples' feet before the meal (lower picture). John also tells of "the disciple whom Jesus loved," who was leaning close to him during the meal (upper picture).

The Christian holy book is the Bible, a diverse collection of traditional teachings written down by different people at different times. It is divided into the Old Testament and the New Testament. The word *testament* means "witness," and Christians believe that the Old Testament contains the witness of God originally to the Jews, and the New Testament the witness of people who knew Jesus or were closely associated with events in the early church.

The Bible is described as "inspired by God" or "the word of God," and there is disagreement about what this means. Some believe that it is literally the words of God uttered through the mouths of the different writers, and that therefore every word is true. Others believe that the writings are a distillation of insights influenced by the time and context of the individual writer, but which embody truth.

The Old Testament
The Jewish roots of Christianity mean that it shares the Hebrew Bible with Judaism, but Christians call it the Old Testament. They say that the history of the Jews as described in the Hebrew Bible is part of God's plan to bring the world back to himself, and that the writings of the prophets anticipate the coming of Jesus.

The New Testament
The second part of the Christian Bible is called the New Testament. This consists of books and letters written soon after the life of Jesus. There are four accounts of Jesus' life, death, and resurrection, known as the Gospels. (The word *gospel* means "good news.") These are followed by the Acts of the Apostles, which relates events that took place during the twenty or so years after the Resurrection. It particularly describes the journeys of Paul. Then there are twenty-one letters, or "epistles," written by early leaders of the church to teach or encourage groups of Christians in different parts of the Mediterranean world. Many of these were written by Paul. They vary in length: some are just a page or so, others consist of many chapters of complex argument. They were addressed variously to large groups of people or to individuals. The final book in the New Testament is the Revelation of St. John. Traditionally said to be written by John, one of Jesus' closest friends, this describes his vision about the end of time (the Apocalypse) and Jesus' return.

The writings now included as the New Testament in the Christian Bible were gradually chosen by the early church and agreed around CE 380. Many other books were not finally included in the agreed New Testament because of questions about their validity. Indeed, there was a great deal of discussion before the Book of Revelation was finally included.

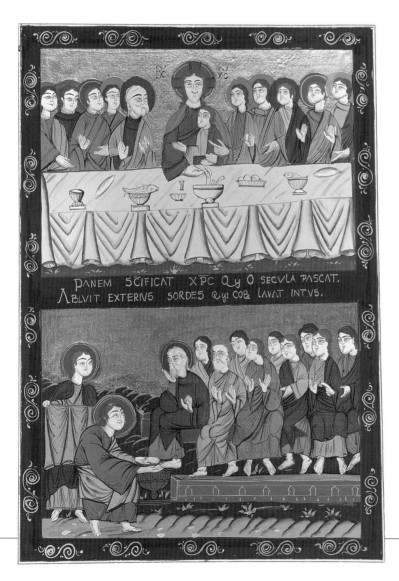

PANEM SCIFICAT XPC Qy O SECVLA PASCAT.
ABLVIT EXTERIVS SORDES Qyi COR LAVAT INTVS.

Other writings

Most Christians draw their inspiration from the Old and New Testaments. However, other writings have been used over the centuries for teaching and meditation. Although the Bible is at the heart of Christian teaching, there is a worldwide tradition of interpreting, analyzing and producing new material that can be used for Christian reflection and discussion. The scope of Christian literature includes lives of the saints, reflection and teaching by other Christians and accounts of visions, as well as prayers and hymns of praise.

Translating the Bible

The Old Testament was originally written in Hebrew and the New Testament in Greek. Before the Christian era, the Hebrew Bible had been translated into Greek, and the early Christians knew the Greek version. By the end of the second century CE there were translations of the Bible into Syriac and Latin and since then translations have appeared in many languages. The first complete Bible in English appeared late in the fourteenth century.

FROM THE NEW TESTAMENT

THE BEATITUDES

This list of those who can be called happy is referred to as "the Beatitudes," from the Latin word beatus—"happy" or "blessed."

*How happy are the poor in spirit:
theirs is the kingdom of heaven.
Happy the gentle:
they shall have the earth for their heritage.
Happy those who mourn:
they shall be comforted.
Happy those who hunger and thirst for what is right:
they shall be satisfied.
Happy the merciful:
they shall have mercy shown them.
Happy the pure in heart:
they shall see God.
Happy the peacemakers:
they shall be called sons of God.
Happy those who are persecuted in the cause of right:
theirs is the kingdom of heaven.*
(Matthew 5:3-10)

THE LORD'S PRAYER

The prayer taught by Jesus to his disciples has become one of the central Christian prayers, uniting Christians from different denominations. It is familiar in several slightly different English versions.

*Our Father in Heaven,
may your name be held holy,
your kingdom come,
your will be done,
on Earth as in Heaven.
Give us today our daily bread,
and forgive us our debts,
as we have forgiven those who are in debt to us.
And do not put us to the test,
but save us from evil.*
(Matthew 6:9-13)

The Lord's Prayer is sometimes called the Paternoster, after the Latin for "Our father." This tablet, found in Cirencester, England, and dating from Roman times, contains the word Paternoster *in a hidden form, and may be a secret Christian sign.*

In the Orthodox church, the book of the Gospels is treated with great respect because it is seen as an icon of Christ, and so is kept in finely decorated covers. Before it is read, it is usually carried in procession around the church for the congregation to venerate.

The Christian Declaration of Belief

Ever since the early church, Christians have attemped to agree on statements of belief, called creeds, which inevitably attempt to express something that is beyond words. Most Christians say that God is three persons in one, traditionally expressed as God the Father, God the Son (Jesus) and God the Holy Spirit: the Holy Trinity. Saint Patrick, the fifth-century saint who brought Christianity to Ireland, used the shamrock, a plant whose leaf has three equal parts, to illustrate the idea of the Trinity—three in one and one in three. Probably the oldest and simplest credal statement is the one known as The Apostles' Creed, first recorded in CE 390.

An Ethiopian icon of the Virgin Mary. All Christians give great honor to Mary, because God chose her to be the mother of his son, and because she accepted this calling humbly and willingly. Some give her great titles, such as "Queen of Heaven," "Mother of God," and many Christians pray to her for help.

1 Like Jews and Muslims, Christians believe in one all-powerful creator, God. Genesis, the first book in the Bible, tells how he created the universe in six days. He created human beings on the sixth day, and on the seventh he rested. The most important thing for Christians is that the world and everything in it is an expression of God's power and love.

2 Most Christians believe that Jesus was both divine and human—hence the Son of God.

3 Luke's gospel tells how the angel Gabriel came from God to a young girl named Mary, who was promised in marriage to Joseph, and told her that she would conceive and bear a son:
He will be great, and will be called the Son of the Most High; and the Lord God will give to him the throne of his father David, and he will reign over the house of Jacob for ever; and of his kingdom there will be no end. (Luke 1:32-33)
Mary questioned this since she was a virgin, but the angel told her that the child would be conceived by the power of God, not by a human father.

4 The story of Jesus, Pontius Pilate and the Crucifixion is told on pages 44-45. Christians believe there is no doubt that Jesus was really dead. (See *Abrahamic Faiths*, pages 20-23, for the Muslim view). Many pilgrims go today to see what are pointed out as the remains of his tomb in the Church of the Holy Sepulcher in Jerusalem.

5 On the sabbath, after Jesus died, he is believed to have descended to Hell, broken down the gates and raised up all the good men and women of the past, giving them eternal life in Heaven.

6 The belief that Jesus rose from the dead and still lives today is central to Christianity.

7 In Roman times, the heir to the emperor sat on his right-hand side. The Creed, in using this image, says that Jesus shares authority over the universe with God the Father. At some time known only to God, this world will pass away, Jesus will return to earth in glory, and everyone who has ever lived will be judged. Christians disagree about exactly how this will happen, and what the judgment will be. Some believe that judgment happens to each person when they die, others that there will be a Day of Judgment at the end of time. One story that Jesus told (Matthew 25:31-46) shows that he will judge whether people cared for those in need.

8 The third aspect of God is the Holy Spirit whom Christians believe was present as the world was created, and who is God's power at work in the world today.

9 The word *catholic* means "universal," and "church" means all Christians. Christians believe that all Christians form one community, one family. Paul wrote to a group of early Christians, "There is neither Jew nor Greek, there is neither slave nor free,

there is neither male nor female; for you are all one in Christ Jesus."

Today, Christians disagree about the membership of this family. In common usage, the word "catholic" is often limited to the Roman Catholic church (see page 51). Some Christians limit true Christianity to their own particular group, while others believe that the many different churches and denominations are authentic expressions of the faith and should become one again.

THE APOSTLES' CREED

1 *I believe in God, the Father Almighty, creator of heaven and earth.*
2 *I believe in Jesus Christ, his only Son, our Lord.*
3 *He was conceived by the power of the Holy Spirit and born of the Virgin Mary.*
4 *He suffered under Pontius Pilate, was crucified, died, and was buried.*
5 *He descended to the dead.*
6 *On the third day he rose again. He ascended into heaven,*
7 *and is seated at the right hand of the Father. He will come again to judge the living and the dead.*
8 *I believe in the Holy Spirit,*
9 *the Holy Catholic Church,*
10 *the communion of Saints,*
11 *the forgiveness of sins,*
12 *the resurrection of the body, and the life everlasting.*

A seventh-century monk's cross from Cappadocia, modern Turkey. The face of Christ has been replaced with a cross. The fish is an early Christian symbol.

10 This is another way of saying that Christians are all one community, but also emphasizes continuity with those who have died and those to come. Originally, *saint* meant any Christian, but later came to mean someone who was especially holy, or who was used by God in an outstanding way. Some Christian traditions officially recognize saints, and there might be an investigation into whether a person is worthy of sainthood. Others use the word more informally, to mean a very good person.

11 Christians believe that Jesus died for our sins. This is interpreted differently by different traditions. Some believe that Jesus' crucifixion stands for the consequences of human sin—disobedience to God—for sin led humanity to kill God's son. Others see Jesus as being a substitute for us, taking the punishment which should be ours for our sins. Yet others see Jesus as showing all who can follow him that good must sometimes make the ultimate sacrifice of death to defeat evil. Almost all Christians believe that God's love has the strength to overcome the worst of human sin and depravity, and that God forgives the sins of anyone who repents and wishes to lead a new life.

12 Christians believe that after death, although the body decays, a person lives on in some way. Many believe that at some time in the future, everyone will have a new body that will never decay, and that life will go on forever. Many different people have tried to imagine what this might be like, and no one knows for sure. What is important is that Christians believe life does not end when a person dies.

Christian Divisions and Denominations

F rom its earliest days, Christianity has had groups within it with very different ideas. Over the centuries, the differences became divisions and various traditions of Christianity came into being. The divisions were at first over how to describe or define Jesus. This is what separated the various Orthodox traditions and the Orthodox from the Western Catholic tradition. These traditions are usually called churches. In the sixteenth century, Martin Luther and others "protested" against faults they saw in the Catholic church, and the Protestant denominations began to be formed. This is known as the Reformation. Today there are attempts to bring the traditions closer together, and some have reunited. Meanwhile, however, new and indigenous traditions are arising in many parts of the world.

The choir of a Spiritual Baptist church in Barbados, West Indies.

THE NESTORIAN CHURCH
Also known as the Assyrian church, separated in CE 431 due to disagreements over the title given to the Virgin Mary. Active in Asia and the Far East during the Middle Ages, later dwindled due to persecution and opposition. Now consists of a few groups in Middle East, India and the United States known as the Thomarist Christians.

ORTHODOX
In CE 320 the capital of the Roman Empire moved to Constantinople and Eastern Christianity established its headquarters there. From here Christianity spread east to Bulgaria and Russia. In each country the Orthodox church is self-governing and independent, but they respect the patriarch of Constantinople as "the first amonst equals"; he is also the head of the Orthodox church in North America.

WALDENSIAN
Formed in 1184 by Peter Waldo, a traveling preacher expelled from the Catholic church. He preached the giving up of wealth, and he and his followers were persecuted. The Waldensians were given full civil rights in Italy in 1848 after centuries of marginal existence. It is considered the earliest reformed church.

AMISH
The Amish church, named after a seventeenth-century Mennonite bishop remain a very insular and conservative community of people who shun modern living styles.

METHODISTS
Developed in eighteenth-century England by Charles and John Wesley, who were traveling preachers. The name derives from the "methodical" way they studied the Bible. Starting as an Anglican evangelical movement, by the end of the eighteenth century the Methodists had separated to form their own churches.
UNITED STATES METHODIST CHURCHES
Split in 1844 over slavery and clerical issues. This led to Methodist-based churches, including the Methodist Episcopal Church South and the three large black churches—the African Methodist Episcopal, the African Methodist Episcopal Zion and the Colored (later Christian) Methodist Episcopal Church.

INDIGENOUS CHRISTIANS
In many areas such as Africa and Latin America, Christianity has merged with existing traditional beliefs. Many of the churches that have appeared reflect this combination of tradition and Christianity.

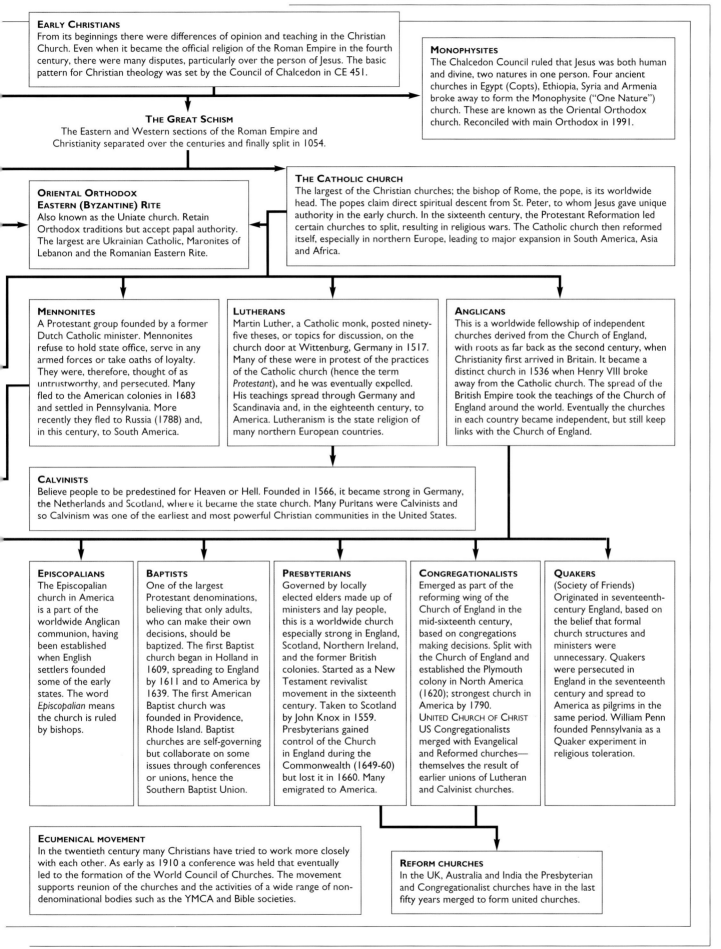

EARLY CHRISTIANS
From its beginnings there were differences of opinion and teaching in the Christian Church. Even when it became the official religion of the Roman Empire in the fourth century, there were many disputes, particularly over the person of Jesus. The basic pattern for Christian theology was set by the Council of Chalcedon in CE 451.

MONOPHYSITES
The Chalcedon Council ruled that Jesus was both human and divine, two natures in one person. Four ancient churches in Egypt (Copts), Ethiopia, Syria and Armenia broke away to form the Monophysite ("One Nature") church. These are known as the Oriental Orthodox church. Reconciled with main Orthodox in 1991.

THE GREAT SCHISM
The Eastern and Western sections of the Roman Empire and Christianity separated over the centuries and finally split in 1054.

ORIENTAL ORTHODOX
EASTERN (BYZANTINE) RITE
Also known as the Uniate church. Retain Orthodox traditions but accept papal authority. The largest are Ukrainian Catholic, Maronites of Lebanon and the Romanian Eastern Rite.

THE CATHOLIC CHURCH
The largest of the Christian churches; the bishop of Rome, the pope, is its worldwide head. The popes claim direct spiritual descent from St. Peter, to whom Jesus gave unique authority in the early church. In the sixteenth century, the Protestant Reformation led certain churches to split, resulting in religious wars. The Catholic church then reformed itself, especially in northern Europe, leading to major expansion in South America, Asia and Africa.

MENNONITES
A Protestant group founded by a former Dutch Catholic minister. Mennonites refuse to hold state office, serve in any armed forces or take oaths of loyalty. They were, therefore, thought of as untrustworthy, and persecuted. Many fled to the American colonies in 1683 and settled in Pennsylvania. More recently they fled to Russia (1788) and, in this century, to South America.

LUTHERANS
Martin Luther, a Catholic monk, posted ninety-five theses, or topics for discussion, on the church door at Wittenburg, Germany in 1517. Many of these were in protest of the practices of the Catholic church (hence the term *Protestant*), and he was eventually expelled. His teachings spread through Germany and Scandinavia and, in the eighteenth century, to America. Lutheranism is the state religion of many northern European countries.

ANGLICANS
This is a worldwide fellowship of independent churches derived from the Church of England, with roots as far back as the second century, when Christianity first arrived in Britain. It became a distinct church in 1536 when Henry VIII broke away from the Catholic church. The spread of the British Empire took the teachings of the Church of England around the world. Eventually the churches in each country became independent, but still keep links with the Church of England.

CALVINISTS
Believe people to be predestined for Heaven or Hell. Founded in 1566, it became strong in Germany, the Netherlands and Scotland, where it became the state church. Many Puritans were Calvinists and so Calvinism was one of the earliest and most powerful Christian communities in the United States.

EPISCOPALIANS
The Episcopalian church in America is a part of the worldwide Anglican communion, having been established when English settlers founded some of the early states. The word *Episcopalian* means the church is ruled by bishops.

BAPTISTS
One of the largest Protestant denominations, believing that only adults, who can make their own decisions, should be baptized. The first Baptist church began in Holland in 1609, spreading to England by 1611 and to America by 1639. The first American Baptist church was founded in Providence, Rhode Island. Baptist churches are self-governing but collaborate on some issues through conferences or unions, hence the Southern Baptist Union.

PRESBYTERIANS
Governed by locally elected elders made up of ministers and lay people, this is a worldwide church especially strong in England, Scotland, Northern Ireland, and the former British colonies. Started as a New Testament revivalist movement in the sixteenth century. Taken to Scotland by John Knox in 1559. Presbyterians gained control of the Church in England during the Commonwealth (1649-60) but lost it in 1660. Many emigrated to America.

CONGREGATIONALISTS
Emerged as part of the reforming wing of the Church of England in the mid-sixteenth century, based on congregations making decisions. Split with the Church of England and established the Plymouth colony in North America (1620); strongest church in America by 1790.
UNITED CHURCH OF CHRIST US Congregationalists merged with Evangelical and Reformed churches—themselves the result of earlier unions of Lutheran and Calvinist churches.

QUAKERS
(Society of Friends) Originated in seventeenth-century England, based on the belief that formal church structures and ministers were unnecessary. Quakers were persecuted in England in the seventeenth century and spread to America as pilgrims in the same period. William Penn founded Pennsylvania as a Quaker experiment in religious toleration.

ECUMENICAL MOVEMENT
In the twentieth century many Christians have tried to work more closely with each other. As early as 1910 a conference was held that eventually led to the formation of the World Council of Churches. The movement supports reunion of the churches and the activities of a wide range of non-denominational bodies such as the YMCA and Bible societies.

REFORM CHURCHES
In the UK, Australia and India the Presbyterian and Congregationalist churches have in the last fifty years merged to form united churches.

Worldwide Spread and Diversification

F ollowing the crucifixion and resurrection of Jesus, an increasing number of people came to believe in him as the Messiah. The original apostles traveled widely, teaching and making converts. These converts then set up local Christian groups. Soon there were groups of Christians—churches—all around the Mediterranean. The new faith was attacked by the Roman authorities, since it refused to recognize the Roman emperors as gods, or to worship the Roman gods. Many Christians were executed for their beliefs, but the numbers continued to grow.

At first, Christians expected the speedy return of Jesus from Heaven to judge the world. But when this did not happen, they came to believe that Jesus lived in and among them, and that they must not simply wait for him to return, but must actively work toward the Kingdom of God on earth—the kingdom described by Isaiah and spoken of by Jesus.

The Roman Empire and beyond

By around CE 60 Christianity had spread to many parts of the Roman Empire. In around CE 300 Armenia became the first officially Christian nation. Beyond the Roman Empire, Christianity was a large minority in the Persian Empire, especially from around 450 when a distinct tradition—the Nestorian church—arose there. This tradition spread through to China and into Afghanistan and India.

Street scene outside a church in China.

CHRISTIANITY IN CE 615
Christianity was the official religion of the Roman Empire. By CE 615, Ethiopia, Sudan and Egypt were Christian.

CHRISTIANITY IN 1453
Christianity had shrunk to almost its smallest ever area. North Africa was lost by the ninth century.

1453

AD 615

Key

■ Predominantly Christian

■ Strong minority Christian presence

■ Small Christian communities

Retreat and advance

In 615 the Persians sacked Jerusalem, and although the Christian Byzantine Empire recaptured it soon after, it fell to the Arab Muslims in 638. With the exception of a brief period (1099-1187) during the Crusades, it has never been under direct Christian control since.

In 1453 Constantinople, the capital of the Byzantine Empire, fell to the Turkish Muslims and thus ended the last vestige of the ancient Christian Roman/Byzantine Empire. Most of the ancient Christian communities in central Asia had been wiped out by the Mongolians, especially under Tamerlane (1336-1405), and in China they had withered away.

By the eighteenth century the invasions of the Islamic Turks into Europe had ceased. The ferment of economic and religious changes in Europe gave rise to a period of European expansion into the Americas, Asia and Africa, and the emigrants took Christianity with them. By the time of the first International Missionary conference in 1910, Christian missionaries had penetrated to many areas of the world, often traveling the trade and conquest routes of the Western powers. The Americas were predominantly Christian, as was southern Africa. Much of central Africa was well on its way to forming majority Christian countries. European colonization had also created Christian majorities in Australia and New Zealand.

Patriarch Alexy II, head of the Russian Orthodox church. When the eastern Mediterranean came under Muslim rule, Russia became the major center of Orthodox Christianity. It was repressed by the Soviet regime, but is now making a recovery.

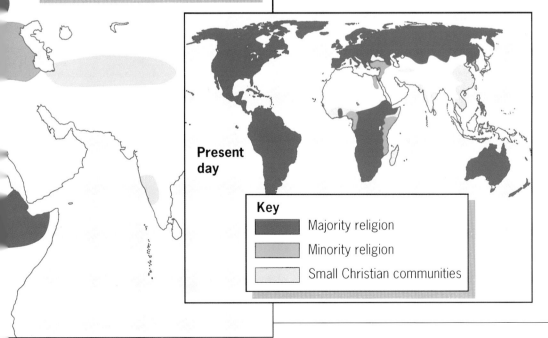

Key

- Majority religion
- Minority religion
- Small Christian communities

Present day

Key

- Majority religion
- Minority religion
- Small Christian communities

By 1453 the Middle East was largely Muslim. However, Christianity had spread into northern Europe: Russia became Christian in 988; Finland was largely Christian by the late thirteenth century. The Mongol invasion had pushed Christian Russia back to Moscow but by 1453, the Russian kingdom was regaining lands.

THE PRESENT DAY
Christianity has now spread to almost all parts of the world.

Community, Prayer, Celebration and Worship

OTHER CHURCHES

Most churches are built to meet the needs of the local Christian community, so the architecture varies with climate, resources and denomination. Great cathedrals are built as a celebration of faith and might also reflect the power and influence of a wealthy sponsor.

Greek church

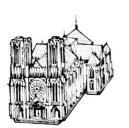

Catholic cathedral

Worshiping together with others as a group is an important part of Christian life, although "going to church" is not a necessary form of Christian worship. The essential meaning of the word *church* is a "group of believers," although it is frequently used to mean "a place of worship." Buildings specially set aside for worship range from enormous, richly decorated cathedrals to simple huts. But a church may also meet in a private house, or out of doors. The important element is the shared sense of community and celebration. Christians usually meet for worship on Sunday, the first day of the week, as that is the day when Jesus rose from the dead.

Most churches hold a service known as the Eucharist, Mass, the Lord's Supper or Holy Communion. Based on the Last Supper (see page 46), it celebrates the death and resurrection of Jesus by the sharing of bread and wine. This service varies in frequency in different churches. Other services may include prayers, Bible reading, a sermon and music.

Sometimes Christians gather in a circle or informal group to underline the idea that Jesus came to be part of a human community.

CHURCH DESIGN

Churches can be any shape, but traditionally they are built in the form of a cross, the top of which points toward Jerusalem, where Jesus lived and died. Orthodox churches take the form of an orthodox cross and are more square in shape, often with a domed roof.

MEMORIAL

The Christian community includes, not only the living, but all Christians throughout the ages. Many churches contain memorials to those who have died—often a simple tablet, sometimes a statue or ornate chapel.

THE CROSS

This is the universal symbol of Christianity, emphasising the central belief that Jesus died for the sake of humanity. When first adopted by the early Christians, it was a paradoxical symbol, as it was the sign of a shameful, criminal death, and yet Paul told Christians to "glory in the cross." Some churches use a crucifix: a cross with the figure of Christ crucified on it.

STAINED GLASS

Some churches are richly decorated with paintings, statues and stained glass. For some Christians, beautiful things inspire prayer and celebrate the beauty of God. Others believe that such objects are a distraction from devotion.

THE PULPIT OR LECTERN

Most church services include a sermon or talk by the priest or minister. Christian services include reading from the Bible. A special lectern may be used for both purposes.

THE ALTAR

Some denominations have a High Altar which is richly decorated and divided from the church by a screen or rail. Some Protestant churches have a much simpler table that recalls the disciples gathered at the Last Supper.

HYMNS AND PRAYERS

Christians worship in many different ways. Hymns might be sung by the entire congregation or by a choir, or might alternate between them, and can be in any style of music. The psalms are a collection of poems in the Bible and are often said or sung, as well as being the inspiration for many hymns. Christians throughout the ages have written new hymns and poems.

The leadership of the service depends on the denomination. Some churches have an appointed minister, and in others members of the congregation take turns to lead.

Prayers may be read from a book or spoken by different people according to the needs of the moment, and are said kneeling, sitting or standing. Silence is also an important part of prayer, especially among the Quakers (Religious Society of Friends). One of the central Christian prayers is the one Jesus taught his disciples, known as The Lord's Prayer, or the "Our Father," from the first words (see page 47).

THE PRIEST

In Orthodox, Roman Catholic and Anglican churches, only a priest can perform certain ceremonies. A priest may wear ornate robes or a simple preaching robe, or ordinary clothes. Here an Anglican priest consecrates wine at the Eucharist.

Rites and Sacraments: The Stages of Life

I n Christian teaching, a sacrament is both a means of obtaining a spiritual blessing and an outward sign of an inward reality. Baptism, for example, is a means of becoming a Christian and accepting God's forgiveness, but the act is also a sign of that forgiveness. Different traditions give varying weight to the various rites. In general, Roman Catholic and Orthodox use more formal ritual than most Protestant churches. Baptism and Holy Communion are two sacraments that are almost universal in Christianity in some form, since they are recorded in the Gospels as acts of Jesus.

The Mass or Eucharist

At his last meal with his disciples, Jesus broke bread among them, saying, "Take, eat, this is my body which is given for you. Do this in remembrance of me." Then he passed around a cup of wine, saying, "Whenever you drink it, do so in remembrance of me." Christians ever since have shared bread and wine in remembrance of Jesus' death and resurrection.

Confession and absolution

In many traditions a priest has the authority to hear a confession of wrongdoing and to grant forgiveness, or absolution, in the name of God. This is one of the rites of the Roman Catholic Church and many Catholics will ask a priest to hear confession on a regular basis.

Baptism

For most believers, baptism marks the start of life as a Christian. It involves being immersed completely in water, or being sprinkled with water. In some traditions babies are baptized as a sign of belonging to God; in others, adults are baptized only when old enough to make their own choice. Being dipped in water and raised out of it is a sign of death and resurrection as well as of cleansing from sin.

Adult baptism in a river in Jamaica. Candidates for baptism usually wear a simple white robe, and will be held completely under the water for a moment. Baptism by full immersion may be performed in a river, lake or the sea, or, especially in colder climates, in a specially built indoor pool.

Confirmation

In many traditions this is the next rite after infant baptism. In the Orthodox church confirmation immediately follows baptism. In other traditions it is seen as a confirmation of vows that people, as infants, could not make for themselves at baptism. This often takes place at adolescence or in adulthood.

Marriage

Marriage and family life are not a necessity for all Christians, and in some traditions there is respect for those who choose not to marry—monks and nuns, and Roman Catholic priests. Christians regard marriage as a serious commitment, and marriage vows are made before God. Some traditions, such as the Roman Catholic church, do not recognize divorce.

Death

In the New Testament there are references to anointing the sick with oil in the name of Christ. Known as unction, this is continued in some traditions. In particular, the Roman Catholic church offers extreme unction to the dying, praying for forgiveness for sins committed in life.

The funeral service in many churches begins with these words from the Gospel of John:

> Jesus said, I am the resurrection and I am the life; he who believes in me, though he die, yet shall he live, and whoever lives and believes in me shall never die.

Christians believe that death is not the end of life. There are different beliefs about exactly what happens to an individual after death, but all Christians believe that Jesus has promised eternal life for those who believe. A service is held that commemorates the dead person, offers comfort to the bereaved and commits the deceased to God's care. Following this the body is either buried or cremated, depending on the particular tradition.

A newly married French couple leaving the church.

All Souls Day, Chugchilan, Ecuador. On this day, November 2nd, Christians pray for the souls of all who have died, often lighting a memorial candle.

ORDINATION

In the New Testament there are various accounts of how specific people were appointed, or ordained, to go and preach in the name of Jesus, and given authority to forgive sins. Gradually the churches evolved a hierarchy of those appointed or ordained to exercise authority in the church, ranging from deacons (helpers) to bishops, archbishops and patriarchs, who exercise authority over entire churches or areas. Ordination usually involves anointing or blessing the person, and in many traditions is done by the bishop. Apostolic churches (for example Orthodox, Roman Catholic and Anglican) claim a direct line of blessing and authority through the bishop to the first apostles.

Celebrations: The Birth of Jesus to the Birth of the Church

This celebrates Jesus' birth in Bethlehem. The story is retold in songs, stories, pictures and drama. Christians meet for worship, often at midnight, and celebrate at home with feasting and presents. For many Christians the festival of Easter is of equal if not greater importance, but Christmas is the one best known to the wider world.

Mary and Joseph traveled from Nazareth to Bethlehem, to comply with the orders of the Roman governor that everyone should return to their home city for a census. While they were there, Mary's baby was born. Because of the number of visitors to Bethlehem there was no room for them in the inn, so they took shelter in the stable, where Mary gave birth to Jesus and laid him in a manger. That same night, some shepherds were out looking after their sheep, when an angel appeared, telling them to see the Savior born that night. Then they saw angels singing "Glory to God, and on Earth peace, goodwill toward men!"

No one knows the date of Jesus' birthday, but most Christians celebrate it on December 25. When Christianity spread into northern Europe, believers thought that the coming of Jesus was like a light coming into a dark world, so they celebrated his birth at the darkest and coldest time of year. In the Roman Empire, December 25 was the feast day of the Sun.

ASSUMPTION OF THE BLESSED VIRGIN MARY

This major celebration in the Roman Catholic church is held on August 15. It stems from the belief that Mary, the mother of Jesus, did not die but was taken up into Heaven at the end of her earthly life. This belief is not shared by Protestant churches.

A church procession in Lesachtal, Austria. Many churches hold processions through their local area at festival times, often carrying statues and shrines.

The festivals in the Christian calendar primarily commemorate the events in the life of Jesus and the beginnings of the Christian faith. The main festivals are universally celebrated, while others, such as saints' days, have much more local or personal appeal and some, such as harvest festivals, depend on particular traditions.

The Christian calendar

The system of numbering years that is most familiar in the Western world is based on the year when it was thought that Jesus was born: AD stands for Anno Domini—Latin for "year of the Lord"—and BC stands for "Before Christ." But more recent research shows that Jesus was probably born in 4 BCE, not 1 CE. The "Christian" dating system only became widely used from the eighth century onward. Before that the church used the date of the foundation of Rome—753 BCE—as the start of its counting system.

EPIPHANY

Some time after Jesus' birth "wise men from the East" came looking for a newborn king. They had followed a bright star in the east that led them to Jesus, Mary and Joseph, and they brought gifts of gold, frankincense and myrrh. At that time these gifts would have been very valuable, so a tradition arose that the "wise men" were kings, and that there were three of them because there were three gifts.

At Epiphany (meaning "manifestation"), twelve days after Christmas, many Christians celebrate the arrival of the wise men. The festival also celebrates the "manifestation" of Jesus as the son of God when he was baptized in the River Jordan.

LENT, HOLY WEEK AND EASTER

The events surrounding Jesus' death and resurrection are remembered during **Holy Week**, which leads up to **Easter Sunday**, regarded by many as the most important festival in the Christian calendar.

The date of Easter for the Protestant and Roman Catholic churches varies between March 23 and April 24. The Orthodox church uses a different dating system.

Six weeks before Easter, Christians begin the period of **Lent**, during which they prepare for the solemn remembrance of Jesus' death. Lent starts with **Ash Wednesday**. Ashes were an ancient symbol of sorrow and repentance, and many churches hold a service in which each person is marked on the forehead with ashes. Lent is a time of reflection and repentance, and recalls the forty days that Jesus spent fasting and praying in the desert.

During Holy Week, Christians remember the events of the last week in Jesus' life: his entry into Jerusalem on **Palm Sunday**, the Last Supper on **Maundy Thursday**. Jesus was crucified on a Friday, and this is called **Good Friday** because Christians believe that when Jesus willingly went to his death it showed God reaching out to human suffering and taking it on himself.

Easter Sunday recalls the disciples' discovery that Jesus was alive (see page 45), a time of great rejoicing. Many church communities keep a vigil throughout Saturday night in order to greet Easter Day with singing and feasting.

ASCENSION DAY

Forty days after Easter Day, the disciples saw Jesus lifted up into Heaven, and this is commemorated on Ascension Day.

PENTECOST OR WHITSUN

This is celebrated on the seventh Sunday after Easter. When Jesus left his disciples for the last time, after his resurrection, he promised them a "helper," or a "comforter" who would be with them forever. On the Jewish festival of Pentecost they were all gathered together when they heard a sound like rushing wind, and saw flames of fire resting on each of them (see page 45). They also found they could speak in other languages and heal the sick in the name of Jesus. Christians believe that all this is the work of the Holy Spirit, who is ever-present within them and is God's power active in the world.

1 **Christmas Day**
December 25
(preceded by the 4 weeks of Advent)
2 **Epiphany**
January 6
3 **Ash Wednesday**
(start of Lent)
4 **Palm Sunday**
(start of Holy Week)
5 **Easter Sunday**
6 **Ascension Day**
7 **Pentecost**
8 **Assumption of the Virgin Mary**
August 15
9 **All Hallows Eve**
October 31
10 **All Saints' Day**
November 1

Outer and inner blue-gray segments compare the earliest and latest periods for Lent, Holy Week and Easter.

SAINTS' DAYS

Every day of the year has at least one saint associated with it. Among the major saints' days are those of Saints Matthew (September 21), Mark (April 25), Luke (October 18) and John (December 27). All Saints' Day, November 1, was once called All Hallows Day, and the night before was called All Hallows Eve or Halloween.

In many parts of Europe it is customary to paint elaborate decorations on eggs to celebrate Easter. Eggs and flowers symbolize new life, and eggs are one of the foods not eaten during Lent, and so particularly enjoyed once Easter comes.

To Be a Christian: the Body of Christ

Nuns and children from a Christian school at an open-air Mass in Zimbabwe.

The monastery of St Martin de Canigou in southern France. Many medieval monasteries were built in remote and mountainous regions to encourage detachment from worldly life.

 hristians believe that the worldwide church—that is, the whole body consisting of all the Christians in the world—is Christ's body on earth, guided by the power of the Holy Spirit.

Christians try to put this into practice in everyday life. They believe that the Holy Spirit will help them to be more like Christ through prayer and Bible study, and many of them devote some time each day to reading the Bible, praying and meditating on God. Roman Catholic and Orthodox Christians often have icons or statues that help them to focus their prayer. Protestant homes may have verses from the Bible or short prayers written up around the home. Christian families might pray together, and many give thanks to God before each meal and ask for his blessing.

Jesus was once asked which is the greatest commandment and his reply was:

> You shall love the Lord your God with all
> your heart, and with all your soul, and with
> all your mind. This is the great and first
> commandment. And a second is like it. You
> shall love your neighbor as yourself.
> (Matthew 22:36-39)

Many Christians care for the homeless or people who are rejected by society. Others work for peace and justice for all.

Monasticism

Before he began his public teaching, Jesus spent forty days alone in the desert, fasting and praying. This example of retiring from the world and giving up family relationships has been followed by thousands of men and women in different Christian traditions. Some have become hermits, living alone and devoting themselves to prayer. Others have lived as communities of monks and nuns, usually in single-sex monasteries, although occasionally in mixed communities. Such religious communities vary in the amount of contact they have with the outside world. Some are "enclosed," and devote themselves to prayer and to the work needed for self-sufficiency. Others exist in order to provide a service to those around them, such as teaching, nursing or missionary work. Many government-run schools and hospitals all over the world were originally founded by monks and nuns.

Pilgrimage

Many Christians from very different traditions undertake pilgrimage for a variety of reasons. In the Middle Ages a pilgrimage was a common way of atoning for sins or expressing repentance, but might also be undertaken as a means of revitalizing one's faith, in a search for physical healing, or simply for enjoyment.

PILGRIMAGE SITES

Today, pilgrimage is important for many people in celebrating a shared faith, finding time for reflection and prayer, recalling more vividly the events of Jesus' life, or as an act of devotion. Some pilgrimage sites are specific to a local community and some are internationally known.

THE HOLY LAND

This is the name given by Christians to the land associated with the life and death of Jesus, now divided between Israel, Palestine, Jordan and Syria. The main focus of a pilgrimage to the Holy Land is Jerusalem and the Via Dolorosa ("Street of Sorrows"), the route believed to have been taken by Jesus to his crucifixion. Other important sites in the Holy Land are Bethlehem, where Jesus was born, Nazareth, where he grew up, and the River Jordan, where he was baptized.

CONSTANTINOPLE (ISTANBUL)

Constantinople (modern Istanbul) was named after Constantine, the first Roman emperor to become a Christian. For centuries it was the center of Christianity in Eastern Europe. The Patriarch of Constantinople is still the leading figure of the Orthodox church. The great church of Santa Sophia is now a museum.

ROME

Both Peter and Paul were executed and buried in Rome. Peter was the first leader, or bishop, of the Christians in Rome. His successors were recognized for centuries as leaders of the whole Christian church, and today the pope is the head of the Roman Catholic church, the largest single Christian group. Christians, especially Catholics, make the pilgrimage to Rome to visit the great basilica under which Peter is buried.

SANTIAGO DE COMPOSTELA

A city in northern Spain, Santiago is believed to be the burial place of St. James, one of Jesus' disciples. It was especially popular as a pilgrimage center in medieval times, and thousands of pilgrims still walk all or part of the pilgrim route to Santiago.

LOURDES

In 1854 a young girl named Bernadette had a series of visions of the Virgin Mary, in the course of which a spring of water appeared. Ever since that time there have been many healings associated with this spring. Thousands of people make the pilgrimage to Lourdes, some seeking healing, some to take care of the sick, and others to give honor to the Virgin Mary. While only a few cases are claimed as truly miraculous, many thousands of people believe their illnesses have been helped by a visit to Lourdes, and many more have found comfort and strength.

Pilgrims at Lourdes in southern France.

Modern Developments in Christianity

Modern Christianity is as much the product of the nineteenth century as it is of the rest of its history. The nineteenth century saw the greatest expansion of Christianity ever, through the hundreds of missionary movements founded by churches of European and US origin. This missionary drive continues today and Christianity is numerically the fastest-growing religion in the world.

There are today thousands of missionaries working in the world, especially in areas which were formally Communist such as Eastern

A Christian rally in Washington. The "Sons of God" are former Hell's Angels who aim to spread the Christian message among bikers.

Europe and countries in Asia. Probably the most famous of all evangelists is Dr. Billy Graham, who has preached to hundreds of millions in his ministry. Television evangelism is still primarily a US phenomenon associated with evangelical movements, but the use of television and radio as means of reaching the unconverted is just one of the ways modern technology is used by Christians to spread the Gospel, even if some of the showmanship that goes with television evangelism is not seen as appropriate by all Christians.

Liberal or Conservative

The missionary movement produced two distinct streams in the older traditions. The first is a liberal stream, open to critical studies of the Bible and keen to modernize the church and to engage in dialogue with other religions. The second stream sees other religions and ideologies as essentially misguided, and seeks to convert them to Christianity. These evangelical groups tend to read the Bible in a literal manner and reject modern biblical criticism and theories such as evolution, which seem to them to contradict the biblical account of creation. Groups with an even more literal tradition are sometimes described as "fundamentalist." The struggle between literal and liberal streams has characterized recent Christian history and crosses all traditions.

Movement toward unity

Many missionaries, disturbed by the divisions of Christianity, felt it hindered their message to those who knew nothing of Jesus. From this disquiet arose the call, first clearly expressed in 1910 at the International Missionary Conference at Edinburgh, for reunion of the divided body of Christ—the church.

Since 1910, some denominations have reunited—especially the Congregationalists and Presbyterians. Many hoped to see the churches reunited by the end of the twentieth century, but this has not happened. The ecumenical movement (from a Greek word meaning "household") has increasingly focused on helping churches to work together while retaining their distinctive identities. The World Council of Churches is the main body for Protestant, Orthodox, Lutheran and Anglican traditions. A new concern is the decline of institutional Churches in Western Europe and Australasia leading to closure of churches, loss of members and shrinking finances. While Christianity is expanding elsewhere, secularism is affecting the traditional European bases of Christianity.

In the Catholic church

The Second Vatican Council (1962-65) revolutionized the church by taking seriously modern biblical scholarship, the ecumenical movement and other religions. It also revitalized the monastic orders and instituted the use of local languages rather than Latin in church services. The liberalism that the Second Vatican Council symbolized has been under attack in recent decades but a new openness in the church is here to stay.

The role of women

Sexuality and women's rights have also affected the church. The issue of women's rights has challenged all traditions. Some still bar women from any significant role, but in many others women have been given greater power. In the Lutheran and Anglican traditions, women can

now be priests and bishops. In the Catholic church, the ordination of women is going to be one of the most contentious issues for the coming decades. Many traditions retain their ban on homosexuality, but some have changed, even to the extent of ordaining openly homosexual clergy and of blessing same-sex marriages. This issue is increasingly dividing liberals from more traditional believers.

An in-vitro fertilization (IVF) specialist studies a human egg under a microscope. Sexuality, health issues and scientific developments such as cloning raise serious challenges for many Christians. HIV/AIDS has made many reconsider traditional attitudes and in many areas the Churches are key partners in combating this disease. Questions about when human life begins and the unique nature of each life lie behind much unease over abortion, cloning and other areas of medical and scientific research.

An evangelical crusade in Seoul, Korea. Christianity is growing very fast in Southeast Asia.

Movements Arising Out of Christianity

While many new groups have arisen within Christianity, some that claim to be Christian are not recognized as such by the other traditions. These groups often take a Christian idea or teaching but develop it in ways that differ so greatly from traditional Christianity as to make them new religions.

The Church of Jesus Christ of Latter-day Saints

This church, commonly known as the Mormons, holds to the revealed nature of the Bible but also to the Book of Mormon. This book is supposed to be a lost sacred text written down by the prophet Mormon around CE 420. It tells that the Native Americans were one of the lost tribes of Israel who became degenerate and fell from grace. The Book was reputedly rediscovered by Joseph Smith (1805-44) in 1823, engraved on plates of gold in a form of Egyptian language and buried on a hillside near New

York. Smith also had a revelation in which he was told that all existing Christian traditions were corrupt and that he was to found a new Church of last day saints (Latter-day Saints), who were to take over responsibility for keeping the true word of God alive and bringing people to salvation. Smith's teachings brought great persecution and he was murdered by a mob. His followers, led by Brigham Young, trekked away from the East Coast of the United States to unclaimed land in the West, and founded Salt Lake City and the State of Utah. Other groups did not accept Young's leadership; the largest of these is in Missouri. Membership is about five million worldwide.

Latter-day Saints believe that human beings progress from a spiritual state prior to birth to a mortal life and then to an afterlife where salvation depends on membership of the Mormon community. The church lays great emphasis on genealogical research, so that the ancestors of the members may be baptized by proxy.

Jehovah's Witnesses

This is another group originating in the United States, also claiming that other Christian traditions are wrong and that they alone bear true witness to God, whom they title Jehovah, using

RASTAFARIANS
This is almost entirely a black church, particularly popular among West Indians both in the West Indies and elsewhere. Its title comes from Ras Tafari—the title for the last Ethiopian emperor, Haile Selassie, the Lion of Judah. Many West Indians looked to Ethiopia as a homeland because it was Christian from the sixth century onward and had fought against European domination. When Haile Selassie was crowned in 1930, he was seen to be the Messiah, sent from God (Jah). The language of Rastafarianism draws heavily upon biblical imagery—so Ethiopia is the Promised Land, Rastas are the Chosen People and everywhere else is Babylon. One of their traditions, based on Leviticus 21:5 in the Bible, is never to cut their hair, which they often wear in "dreadlocks."

the seventeenth-century version of the Hebrew name of God. Their founder, Charles Taze Russell (1852-1916), founded the International Bible Students Association, the formal name of the Witnesses. Members of the church believe that they will be the only ones whom Jesus will rescue when the Second Coming takes place. Russell predicted that Jesus would return in 1914. When this did not happen, the church claimed other dates. Now they simply say that Jesus will return very soon.

The Unification Church

Founded in 1954 by the Korean businessman Sun Myung Moon, known as the Reverend Moon to his followers, this church claims that God has constantly sought to create the perfect family but has been thwarted by Satan. Thus Adam and Eve fell, and Jesus was killed before he could produce a family. Believers hold that the Reverend Moon and his wife are the new godly family, and that through belonging to the church, they can become members of the Divine Family. The core book is Moon's *The Divine Principle*. The "Unification" title comes from Moon's claim that his group unifies all churches. His followers are frequently known as Moonies.

Christian Scientists

The main teaching of Christian Scientists is that all physical aspects of life, especially illness, are illusory and that all one requires to be rid of them is to understand this. They reject belief in Christ's death on the cross. Their founder was Mary Baker Eddy (1821-1910) whose book *Science and Healing with a Key to the Scriptures* is read alongside the Bible at meetings. There are about 3,000 Christian Science churches and organizations in more than 50 countries.

Interior of the Mormon Tabernacle, the headquarters of the Mormons, in Salt Lake City, Utah.

Members of the Unification Church in Seoul, South Korea, participate in a mass wedding ceremony, overseen by their leader Reverend Sun Myung Moon and his wife. This ceremony inaugurates them into the Divine Family.

CHAPTER THREE

ISLAM

Muslims believe that Islam is the faith of all God's prophets from Adam onward, and therefore is the original religion. They see the formal creation of a distinct religion in the seventh century CE as the final form of the religion, explicitly revealed in the Qur'an.

A carved wooden panel on the grounds of the Great Mosque in Xian, China. The Chinese character means "to seek," or "to pray."

At a mosque in Lahore, Pakistan, Muslims gather for prayers at Eid ul-Fitr, the end of the month of fasting.

Islam is an Arabic word meaning "to submit," and a Muslim is "one who submits"—that is, one who lives life in the way God intends. Islam is a total way of life, not just concerned with spiritual matters. Muslims believe that from time to time God has sent prophets such as Moses, Abraham (*Ibrahim* in Arabic) and Jesus to enshrine this way of life in human society, but that their message has often been mistaken, forgotten or distorted. They believe that Muhammad was the last of these prophets, and that because his message was written down almost as soon as it was revealed, it has been passed on as God intended in the words of the Qur'an. Muslims give Muhammad deep love and respect. They regard him as God's final prophet, and seek to follow his example. After the Qur'an, the words and actions of Muhammad are the second highest authority in Islam, but worship belongs only to God. Muslims recognize the revealed nature of the Hebrew Bible and of the New Testament but claim that the texts have become corrupted over the centuries, and that they have lost their original message. Muslims worship one God (*Allah* in Arabic), who is the creator and ruler of the universe, all-powerful and with no equal.

Today there are over a billion Muslims worldwide, especially in the Middle East, North and West Africa, southeastern Europe, and Malaysia. There are two main branches of Islam: Sunni, who comprise eighty percent of all Muslims, and Shi'a, who are found mainly in Iran, Iraq, Yemen and Bahrain.

Origins, Developments and Divisions

The extraordinary speed of the growth and spread of Islam in its first fifty years is unique in religious history. Undoubtedly part of its appeal lay in the clear teaching of belief in one God and the daily practices of prayer.

Arabia in the seventh century CE was a place of many religions. Christianity was well established in the lands bordering the Byzantine Christian Empire and in areas such as the Yemen. In the lands on the borders of the Zoroastrian Persian Empire, Zoroastrian ideas were highly influential, together with Manichaeism, which combined elements of Zoroastrian, Christian and Buddhist teaching. Judaism was strongly represented in all the cities and had followers among the tribes. Muhammad studied with a Syrian Christian monk and had many contacts with Jews.

Many of the Arab tribes were polytheistic: They worshiped a wide range of deities. Makkah was a major pilgrimage center for the

ISLAM'S HEARTLAND
From the holy cities of Makkah and Medina the Arab conquests spread out to the north and west, conquering Palestine, Jerusalem, Syria, Egypt and the rest of North Africa and penetrating into Spain. In the east, Islam conquered the Persian Empire and its armies were fighting the Chinese by the early eighth century. Damascus, Baghdad and Cairo soon rose as major social, political and religious centers of Islamic power.

A man interrupts his journey through the mountains of Baluchistan to pray in the direction of Makkah.

people whom the Qur'an calls pagans, and the Ka'ba (see page 72) was full of statues of various deities.

Although Arabia had long been surrounded by the two great empires—Byzantium and Persia, by 630 both had become exhausted by their wars.

Muhammad the Prophet

Muslims believe that Muhammad was God's final prophet and that the revelation given to him has never been corrupted, so there is no need for further revelation. When Muslims speak or write the name of Muhammad, they add "Peace Be Upon Him" as a mark of respect.

Muhammad was a respected and successful trader in Arabia in the seventh century. Muslim texts tell how, in 610, at the age of forty, he was meditating in a cave at Hira outside the city of Makkah when he had a vision of the angel Jibra'eel (Gabriel). The angel told him, "Recite!" but Muhammad refused three times until at last the angel said: "Recite in the name of thy Lord who created!" The words that were then given to Muhammad declared the oneness and power of God, to whom worship should be made.

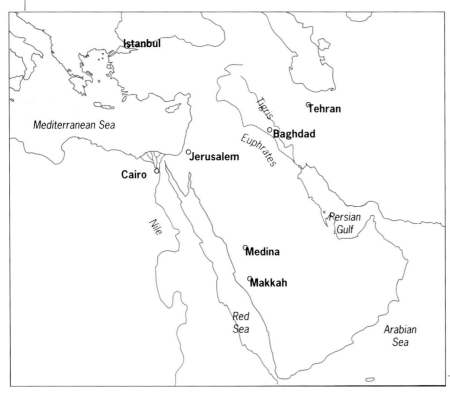

Muhammad began to teach the oneness of God in the city of Makkah, but here he met with opposition. He and his followers retreated to Medina, where the first Islamic community was founded. Muslim dates are all calculated from this journey (the Hijrah) in 622 CE, which is therefore year 1 AH (After Hijrah). A period of missionary, political and military activity then followed, so that by the time of the Prophet's death in 632, Islam was established in most of the Arabian Peninsula, including Makkah itself.

The development and spread of Islam

After the death of Muhammad the leadership of the Muslim community passed to a succession of caliphs ("deputies"), under whom Islam continued to spread. Large areas came under Muslim religious and political rule through the Arab conquest. Followers of other religions were usually tolerated provided they did not fight against Islam, and conversion was usually gradual in these areas.

In 711 Muslim forces crossed the Indus River into India in the south and entered Spain in the north. Their farthest northward expansion was reached in 732, when a Muslim army was defeated near Tours in France. But Christian forces from northern Europe fought back over many centuries. They slowly regained control of Spain, finally expelling the Muslims in 1492. In the fourteenth century, Ottoman Turks crossed into eastern Europe from Anatolia and took over most of the Balkans.

Meanwhile, under the Abbasid Caliphate in Baghdad (750-1258), Muslim control spread eastward through northern India to the bay of Bengal. From 1526 onward, the Mughal Empire in India controlled most of the Indian subcontinent but gradually lost control of the outlying areas before being deposed by the British in 1858.

SUFISM
From about the eighth century CE, a more mystical tradition arose in Islam, emphasizing the inner spiritual state of love and devotion to God. This tradition became known as Sufism, and many different Sufi orders arose, some of which still survive. In contrast to other forms of Islam, they developed the use of music, drumming and dance in worship. The Turkish Mevlevi order, better known as the "Whirling Dervishes," performed a dance, each stage representing ascent towards union with the Divine. In recent years Sufism has experienced a considerable growth, not least in the West. There the poems of the greatest Sufi poet, Rumi (thirteenth century), have touched the hearts of many, just as they have been doing down the centuries in Islam.

DIFFERENCES IN ISLAM
The fourth caliph, Ali, was Muhammad's son-in-law. Islam split during his caliphate in the mid-7th century since some believed that because of his family relationship, he was Muhammad's first true successor, and that leadership of the Muslim community should be on a hereditary principle. These became known as the *Shi'a* ("partisans") of Ali and of his sons Hassan and Husseyn. The majority held that caliphs should continue to be democratically chosen in the same way as the first four, and are known as *Sunni* ("majority").

There are four schools of Sunni Muslims, with only minor differences between them. The Shi'a are divided into a number of smaller groups with differing beliefs.

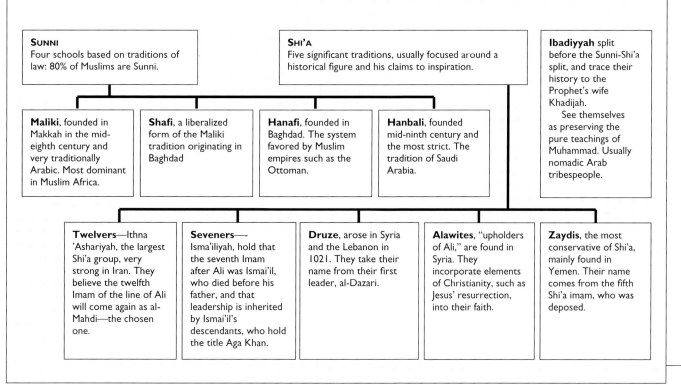

SUNNI
Four schools based on traditions of law: 80% of Muslims are Sunni.

SHI'A
Five significant traditions, usually focused around a historical figure and his claims to inspiration.

Ibadiyyah split before the Sunni-Shi'a split, and trace their history to the Prophet's wife Khadijah.
See themselves as preserving the pure teachings of Muhammad. Usually nomadic Arab tribespeople.

Maliki, founded in Makkah in the mid-eighth century and very traditionally Arabic. Most dominant in Muslim Africa.

Shafi, a liberalized form of the Maliki tradition originating in Baghdad

Hanafi, founded in Baghdad. The system favored by Muslim empires such as the Ottoman.

Hanbali, founded mid-ninth century and the most strict. The tradition of Saudi Arabia.

Twelvers—Ithna 'Ashariyah, the largest Shi'a group, very strong in Iran. They believe the twelfth Imam of the line of Ali will come again as al-Mahdi—the chosen one.

Seveners—Isma'iliyah, hold that the seventh Imam after Ali was Ismai'il, who died before his father, and that leadership is inherited by Ismai'il's descendants, who hold the title Aga Khan.

Druze, arose in Syria and the Lebanon in 1021. They take their name from their first leader, al-Dazari.

Alawites, "upholders of Ali," are found in Syria. They incorporate elements of Christianity, such as Jesus' resurrection, into their faith.

Zaydis, the most conservative of Shi'a, mainly found in Yemen. Their name comes from the fifth Shi'a imam, who was deposed.

Foundations of
the Faith

Detail of a Qur'anic inscription from el-Goun Mosque.

A decorative 15th-century Ottoman Qur'an. Copies of the Qur'an are always treated with great care, often wrapped in a clean cloth and kept on a high shelf. A stand is used to hold the book open for reading. Before handling the book, Muslims always make sure that they themselves are clean.

Muslims believe that the Qur'an was written by God and revealed to Muhammad at intervals from the time of his first vision at the age of 40 until he died aged 62. He memorized these himself and taught them word for word to his followers. The revelations were recorded in writing and collected into one volume soon after the Prophet's death. As the words are regarded as a direct communication from God, the Qur'an is read and studied in the original Arabic and translations are never used in worship. It is written in a poetic style and contains teachings about God, justice and daily life as well as Islamic versions of stories also found in the Bible. Muslims consider the Qur'an to be the foundation of all other knowledge.

The beauty of the Arabic of the Qur'an is often cited as one proof of its divine nature.

Because of its poetry and style it is considered by Muslims to be a greater work than any other written text.

In Muslim countries, learning to read and recite the Qur'an is an important part of a child's education. Elsewhere, Muslim children often attend classes in the mosque to learn to read Arabic and recite the Qur'an. Muslim children living in the West, and increasingly also in traditional Muslim areas such as Malaysia, are often learning two languages: their mother tongue and Arabic.

Hadith

Muhammad is believed to have interpreted the word of God by his actions (*sunna*). Stories of his life and his sayings that do not form part of the Qur'anic revelations were handed down and collected for more than two hundred years. They were carefully examined for authenticity by scholars who checked the reliability of the line of transmission. These stories and sayings are known as *Hadith*, and are a source of guidance for Muslims where there is no specific guidance in the Qur'an. The combination of

the Qur'an and Hadith forms the basis of Islamic law (*Fiqh*). An example is the Hadith related by Bukhari:

Anyone drawing pictures will be punished
by Allah until he blows the spirit into that
picture, and he will never be able to blow the
spirit into it…draw things that have no spirit.

BASIC BELIEFS

A Muslim is one who can say with understanding and sincerity:
There is no god but God and Muhammad is his prophet.
These two linked ideas—the oneness of God and the prophethood of Muhammad—form the basis of Islamic belief.

THE ONENESS OF GOD

The Qur'an forbids the worship of idols, and therefore Muslims do not make images either of God or of the Prophet. Many Muslims object to any form of representational art because of the danger of idolatry. This is why mosques and other Muslim buildings are often decorated with geometric patterns: the beauty of the patterns reflects the beauty and unity of God's creation. One of the greatest sins in Islam is *shirk*, or blasphemy—that is, associating anything or anybody with God, who is unique and transcendent.

In the Qur'an and the Hadith, God (*Allah* in Arabic) is spoken of with ninety-nine names, each one saying something of his character (for example, Revealer, Sustainer, Judge, the All-wise, the All-Compassionate). However, Islam also teaches that there is a hundredth name that has never been revealed. This emphasizes that God has a dimension that is unknowable.

PROPHETHOOD

The names of twenty-five prophets are mentioned in the Qur'an, including Noah, Abraham and Jesus. Muslims believe that earlier prophets were given messages that were relevant for their time, but that these were incomplete or only partially understood. Muhammad received the full, complete and final revelation, and is loved and honored as God's final prophet.

As pilgrims circle the Ka'ba in Makkah they try to come close enough to kiss the black stone that is set into the outer wall of the Ka'ba. An Hadith tells how Umar, one of the early Muslims, explained why he kissed the black stone: "I know you are a stone which has no power to do me harm or good. If I had not personally seen the Prophet Muhammad kiss you, I wouldn't do it."

Prayer and Community in the Mosque

Muslims pray five times a day, at specific times, wherever they happen to be. On Fridays all Muslim men are expected to gather at the mosque for the after-midday prayer. Friday is not a "holy day" in the way that Jews or Christians understand the Sabbath. Business may go on before and after the midday prayers, and in all other respects it is like any other day. Nor is the mosque a consecrated place: Islam teaches that the whole world is a mosque because one can pray to God anywhere. The building is simply a convenient place for the Muslim community to meet. The story of how Muhammad chose the site of the world's first mosque in Medina illustrates this. Many people vied to offer their house or their land. But Muhammad simply let his beloved camel wander around, and noted where it stopped. This turned out to be a piece of wasteland and here Muhammad settled and led communal prayers.

Islam teaches that there is no distinction between the sacred and the everyday—Islam is a way of life rather than a "religion." In many parts of the world one can see travelers resting or sleeping in the mosque, because it is for the general use of the community.

Djenne mosque and market, Mali. In many Muslim towns and villages the mosque is at the center of activity, and prayers in the mosque form part of everyday life.

INSIDE A MOSQUE

Mosques always have a minaret for the call to prayer, and a public hall for prayer—but these can be in almost any style. In China the minaret is often shaped like a pagoda, while in modern mosques in countries such as Dubai or Kuwait the minaret is in a modernistic style. Islam often adopts the local architecture and uses the best of modern design as well.

MINARET
In Muslim countries the call to prayer is sounded five times a day from the top of the minaret.

WUDU AREA
Every mosque has an area supplied with water where *wudu* (washing) can take place before prayer. (See page 77)

IMAM, MUEZZIN AND KHATIB

There are three public functions in a mosque: the muezzin, who calls people to prayer, the imam, who leads the community prayers, and the khatib, who preaches the Friday sermon.

In many Muslim communities the imam is also the khatib, and may also be the muezzin. The imam is not a priest, and there are no rites which only he can perform, although he usually conducts marriages and funerals. The imam normally acts as leader of the local Muslim community, giving advice about Islamic law and customs. He is chosen for his wisdom and qualities of leadership.

In Muslim countries the times of prayer are announced by a muezzin calling from the minaret.

A translation of the call is as follows:

God is most great
I bear witness that there is no
god but God
I bear witness that
Muhammad is the
messenger of God
Hasten to Prayer
Hasten to success
Allah is most great
There is no god but God.

Traditionally, the muezzin used just the power of his voice, and the design of the minaret helped the sound to carry, but today the call is often amplified by loudspeakers.

WOMEN'S AREA
Women may attend prayers in the mosque but this is not a requirement for them. They sit in a separate area, often in a gallery upstairs.

MIHRAB
All Muslim prayer takes place facing in the direction of the Ka'ba, the house of God in Makkah (see page 72). Muslim homes mark this direction in some way, and in the mosque it is marked by a niche in the wall and the mosque then designed around this wall.

MINBAR
At Friday prayers a sermon (Kutbah) is often given by the imam, the leader of the community; political as well as specifically religious issues may be addressed.

The call to prayer from a mosque in the United Arab Emirates.

CONGREGATIONAL PRAYERS
When prayers are held congregationally people stand in rows shoulder to shoulder with no gaps or reserved spaces, for all are equal when standing before God. At the end of prayers the people turn to greet those on either side of them.

Rites of Passage and Prayers

I n different ways, often colored by local traditions, Muslims celebrate births, marriages and mourn death as part of the greater picture of life itself and of God's will at work in the world.

Birth

As far as possible, the first thing a baby hears is the call to prayer, whispered in each ear. All boys must be circumcised, but the age at which this is done varies between seven days and twelve years.

Customs vary in different countries. In Turkey, boys of about seven are dressed in fine costumes and their circumcision is a time for a big family gathering and celebration. Other popular customs are often not, strictly speaking, Islamic. For example, in India and Pakistan it is common to shave the child's head and give the weight of the hair in silver to the poor.

Marriage

Marriage, family life and the raising of children are regarded as part of God's provision for humanity; in Islam there is no value in celibacy.

And among His Signs is that He created mates for you from among yourselves, so that you may dwell in tranquillity with them, and He has put love and mercy between your hearts. (30:21)

Parents have the responsibility of choosing a marriage partner for their children, as marriage is regarded as linking two families, not just two individuals. However, the Qur'an decrees that the girl must give her consent and not be forced to marry. Marriage is essentially a contract between two people, not a religious rite, so although the ceremony is often performed in the mosque by an imam, this is not necessary.

Nevertheless, marriage is seen as a state blessed by God. The Qur'an points to the fact that most of the prophets were married and that marriage is how one learns restraint and responsibility. The Qur'an uses a lovely image of the relationship between husbands and wives. Surah 2: 187 says:

Permitted to you on the night of the fasts is the approach of your wives, they are your garments and you are their garments.

Divorce is permitted but is vigorously discouraged. A Hadith of Muhammad says, "Marry and do not divorce, for the throne of

A village wedding procession in Eritrea. In most Muslim cultures, a marriage is as much the joining of two families as of two individuals.

Allah is shaken when divorce happens." In Islamic law it is allowable for a man to have more than one wife, and in traditional Islamic societies this is a way of making sure that every woman can have the protection of family life. But the Prophet Muhammad advised that a man who felt unable to treat several wives with equality between them should marry only one.

Death

One of the articles of faith of a Muslim is that there will be a Day of Judgment on which all the dead will be raised and judged by God. Those whose good outweighs their bad will go to Paradise and the others to the Fire.

After death the body is ritually washed and wrapped in a white shroud, and should be buried as soon as possible. Because there will be a bodily resurrection, bodies are not cremated. Prayers are said by the community, affirming God's power over life and death. Death is believed to be predetermined by God as part of his design and thus is not to be feared. Excessive grief is discouraged as it is presumed that someone who dies as an observant Muslim will go to Paradise. To overdo mourning seems to show mistrust in God's love and mercy.

For you know you were without life, and He gave you life; He will cause you to die, and will again bring you to life, and again to Him you will return. (2:28)

A funeral passing through Cairo, Egypt.

PRAYERS

So give glory to God when you reach evening and when you rise in the morning. Yes, to Him is praise in the heavens and on earth and in the afternoon and when the day begins to decline. (30:17-18)
...celebrate the praises of your Lord before the rising sun, and before its setting. Yes, celebrate them for part of the night and at the sides of the day, so that you may have spiritual joy. (20:130)

These passages of the Qur'an are the basis for the five daily times of prayer. These are a few of the words and positions of prayer, which is always said in Arabic.

Through wudu, the ritual washing, Muslims prepare for prayer in mind, body and spirit.

God is most great.

O God, glory and praise are for You, and blessed is Your name, and exalted is Your majesty; there is no god but You.

God is most great.

Glory to my Lord, the Highest.

God is most great.

All prayer is for God and worship and goodness. Peace be on you, O Prophet, and the mercy of God and His blessings.
O Lord, make me and my children steadfast in prayer. Our Lord, accept the prayer. Our Lord, forgive me and my parents and the believers on the day of judgment.

Peace and mercy of God be on you.

Celebrations and Festivals of Islam

The main festivals in Islam are few and far between, with some months completely clear of any festivities. However, local traditions and festivals often fill up the year's cycle, depending upon where the Muslim community is. Certain groups also have their own festival days. For example, Sufis celebrate the day of death of their holy man Abd al-Qadir in the month of Rabi al-Thani, while Shi'a celebrate the martyrdom of Imam Husayn in the month of Muharram.

A procession celebrating Eid ul-Fitr in Katsina, Nigeria. The end of the month of fasting is a time of festivities and rejoicing throughout the Muslim world.

The Islamic calendar is entirely lunar, and unlike most other lunar calendars, is not adjusted to keep in step with the solar year. Since the lunar year is ten or eleven days shorter than the solar year, Muslim dates change constantly in relation to the Western, solar calendar. Years are counted from the Prophet Muhammad's move to Medina in CE 622. The year 1426 AH began in February 2005 AD.

MUHARRAM

The first month of the year. New Year's Day is not a major festival, but the 10th of Muharram is the festival of Ashura. This was originally the Jewish festival of Passover and its theme is still the celebration of the escape of the Israelites from Egypt. This is also celebrated as the day when Noah's ark touched ground and he stepped on to dry land again. Muslims fast for two days before Ashura. In Shi'a Islam, Ashura is also the celebration of the martyrdom of Hussein, son of Ali, when young men in particular subject themselves to extreme physical testing.

RAMADAN

The ninth Muslim month, Ramadan, is laid down as a month of fasting: an adult Muslim refrains from eating, drinking, smoking and conjugal relations from dawn to sunset. This is in obedience to the Qur'an:

O you who believe, fasting is prescribed to you as it was prescribed to those before you, so that you may learn self-restraint. (2:183)
Ramadan is the month in which the Qur'an was sent down as a Guide to mankind, full of clear signs of guidance and judgment between right and wrong. So every one of you who is at home during that month should spend it

Ramadan and the Night of Power are times for prayer and reflection.

in fasting, but if anyone is ill or on a journey the prescribed period should be made up later. God desires your well-being, not to put you in difficulties. He wants you to complete the prescribed period and to glorify Him and to be grateful for His guidance. (2:185)

Children under the age of puberty are exempt, but may undertake a more limited fast. The early breakfast before daylight and the meal after dark take on a special quality for Muslims during the month.

THE NIGHT OF POWER— LAILAT UL QADR

It is not known exactly which night it was that the Qur'an was given to Muhammad, but it was one of the last ten nights of Ramadan. Many Muslims, following the example of the Prophet, spend the last ten days of Ramadan in the mosque, so as to be at prayer during the Night of Power (usually thought to be around the 27th), which the Qur'an describes as "better than a thousand months" (97:4).

EID UL-FITR

This celebrates the end of the month of fasting and is heralded by the sight of the new moon. Congregational prayers are offered and special foods prepared. New clothes are often bought for the festival and presents may be given. Sending cards wishing *Eid Mubarak* (a happy or blessed festival) is a growing custom.

8-13 DHU-L-HIJJA

The time of the pilgrimage events in and around Makkah (see page 72).

EID-UL ADHA

(10th Dhu-l-Hijja) This celebrates the willingness of the prophet Ibrahim (Abraham) to sacrifice his son Ishmael when God asked it of him. On God's command, a lamb was sacrificed instead of Ishmael, so the sacrifice of a lamb or goat is an important part of the festival.

BIRTHDAY OF THE PROPHET MUHAMMAD—MAULID AL NABI

Celebration of this varies locally. For example, the island of Lamu, off the coast of Kenya, attracts thousands of visitors from the whole of East Africa and other parts of the Indian Ocean for processions, speeches and prayers in the many mosques on the island.

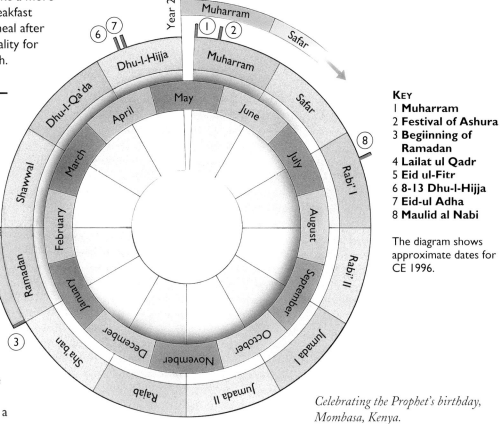

KEY
1 **Muharram**
2 **Festival of Ashura**
3 **Begiinning of Ramadan**
4 **Lailat ul Qadr**
5 **Eid ul-Fitr**
6 **8-13 Dhu-l-Hijja**
7 **Eid-ul Adha**
8 **Maulid al Nabi**

The diagram shows approximate dates for CE 1996.

Celebrating the Prophet's birthday, Mombasa, Kenya.

To be a Muslim: A Total Way of Life

A veiled woman, Sudan. There is no specific Islamic dress but both men and women are required to dress modestly. For many women this means covering the whole body in public, except for the face and hands (some women cover the face as well). Clothing should be loose and not reveal the shape of the body.

aily life is the arena where Islam is put into practice. Islam is about how to live, day by day as well as on a larger scale. *Shari'ah*—"the clear path"—is based on the Qur'an, the Hadith and the consensus of scholars, giving guidance for all aspects of life. The structure of five daily prayers helps form the basis for daily life.

Islam recognizes five categories of human activities: forbidden; disapproved of but not forbidden; neutral (it is not important one way or another whether one does them or not); good and rewarded by God; and obligatory (to neglect these is a sin).

Law and the state

Islamic law is founded upon shari'ah, which arises from the Qur'an, the Hadith (the sayings and actions of Muhammad) and the interpretations of scholars. God is the supreme lawgiver and his laws are for the whole of creation, not just for human beings. Shari'ah is both a personal rule of life and a system of law that confirms the rights and duties given by God.

The extent to which shari'ah is applied in countries with a Muslim majority varies. In some countries the system is purely secular, while others have a hybrid system that combines European legal structures with elements of shari'ah. Others apply shari'ah as the legal code for the country.

Education

The Prophet Muhammad is reported to have said: "Seek knowledge from the cradle to the grave." Using one's God-given intelligence to find out more about the world is seen as a

UPHOLDING THE COMMUNITY

Let there arise among you an ummah advocating all that is good, enjoining what is right and forbidding what is wrong. They are the ones to attain peace and prosperity. (3:104)

The word *ummah* is central to Muslim life. It can be translated as "community," but also includes the concepts of brotherhood, nation and way of life. Family life is an essential part of being a Muslim, and every member of a family should care for the others. The Prophet Muhammad was especially emphatic that a man should take care of his mother.

This concept of community extends to animals too:

There is not an animal that lives on the earth, nor a being that flies on its wings, but forms part of communities like you (6:38)

Human beings are enjoined not to treat animals in a way that violates their life in communities.

Within a local community there is a shared sense of responsibility and all members should try to care for each other in practical ways, such as by visiting the sick or bereaved, and giving hospitality freely.

JIHAD

The word *jihad* means "to strive" or "struggle," and has frequently been translated as "holy war," although its meaning is far wider. It includes armed struggle to defend the Muslim community if attacked, but also encompasses "inner jihad"—the struggle to make Muslim society and one's own life more truly Islamic, developing greater understanding and commitment to Islam.

An imam preaching in a mosque in London. The imam gives guidance on matters of life and faith.

religious activity, but knowledge comes from God, and it is important to subject all learning to the will of God as revealed in the Qur'an.

Food and drink

Any meat eaten must be slaughtered in the correct way, including invoking the name of God. This is called *Halal* meat. Pig meat is very strictly forbidden and is regarded with revulsion by most Muslims. The Qur'an also outlaws alcohol.

Use of money

The Qur'an specifically forbids usury and the charging of interest but encourages trade and making a fair profit. This can be difficult to put into practice and Muslim banks aim to bring prosperity to all by investing in new projects and products. Trade and business is described

in the Qur'an as "seeking the bounty of God," and any wealth acquired is to be used first for the support of one's family and then given to those in need.

The Qur'an also forbids gambling, since it encourages people to trust to luck rather than to God's provision and one's own honest work.

Girls learning to read the Qur'an in Britain. Many mosques hold classes in the evenings or at weekends.

Modern Developments in Islam

he developments in modern Islam have their origin in two very different sources: the first is the spread of Western colonialism and imperialism into traditionally Muslim cultures over the last two to three hundred years; the second is the reawakening of conservative Islam.

The colonial legacy

Muslim India, Muslim North Africa, the remnants of the Ottoman Empire, Muslim Indonesia and Malaysia have all experienced in some form the control or erosion of their social and political life by Western powers. The resulting attacks on Islamic identity led at first to the subduing of Islam in these places and then, as the independence movements began to grow, to a revitalized and reinvigorated Islam.

Conservative movements

The reawakening of conservative Islam is often described in the West as "fundamentalist." It

ISLAM AND TECHNOLOGY
Muslims believe that Islam is capable of taking the best from modern Western culture and fusing it to Islamic ideals, but are wary of the materialist or secular values that are seen to accompany this. It is significant that Islam, whether literal or liberal, does not reject modern discoveries so long as they are put to good uses. Computers and modern communications, for example, are seen as fields within which Islam can be put into practice. Islam's scientific heritage and love of knowledge and its belief that all knowledge ultimately comes from God give it freedom to embrace modern knowledge and technology.

A procession through the streets of Cairo, Egypt, commemorating a local religious figure.

Women at the Islamic University, Gaza.

has its roots in the Arabic opposition to the Ottoman Empire and in particular in the fiercely independent and traditionalist interpretation of Islam by the Wahhabis in the region of modern Saudi Arabia. This movement, which dominates Saudi Arabia today, was founded by Muhammad ibn Wahhabi (died 1787). He accused the Ottoman caliphate of having become pagan and corrupt, and launched a purification movement that was Arab and traditional in its ideology.

The revolt of the Wahhabis inspired others ruled by the Ottoman caliph to seek their independence. The caliphate has been the ruling spiritual authority in Islam since the time of the Prophet, although its line of descent is disputed between the Sunnis and the Shi'a. For over five hundred years the leadership had resided with the Ottoman caliph in Istanbul. But when the Ottoman Empire was overthrown in the early years of the twentieth century the caliphate was abolished, leaving Islam without a clear political or religious authority.

This vacuum has been filled by movements emanating from many traditions of Islam. One of the most powerful and influential was launched by a charismatic religious leader called Hasan al-Banna, who in Egypt in 1929 founded the al-Ikhwan al-Muslimum—known in English as the Muslim Brotherhood. They

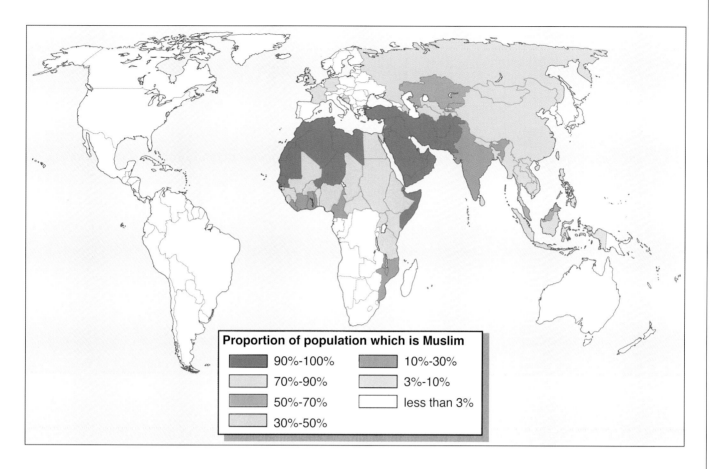

Proportion of population which is Muslim

- 90%-100%
- 70%-90%
- 50%-70%
- 30%-50%
- 10%-30%
- 3%-10%
- less than 3%

set out to reject the secular laws and structures imposed on Egypt by the British.

The Muslim Brotherhood, which has spread throughout Islam, has been very influential in the drive to create purely Islamic legal systems for Muslim states.

Political developments

Tensions between a certain Islamic vision of society and secular western influenced governments in Islamic areas have become a focus for extreme action by those claiming to represent true Islam. Hard-line groups see western influence and, in particular, that of the United States as undermining Islam and they are now responding with a militant form of Islam.

Perception of Islam has been affected by the terrorist attacks in New York, London, Bali, Spain and other places. These have been carried out by groups claiming justification from their Islamic beliefs. For most Muslims these actions have no place in Islam and they are resisting the move to extremism. At the same time, they often encounter a widespread misunderstand-ing of the complexity of contemporary Islam, and this may give rise to increased assertion of their Muslim identity.

Economic developments

One of the signs of Western appeal to Islamic cultures has been the dominance of Western interest-based banking, and the acceptance of bodies such as the International Monetary Fund to dictate how a nation should conduct its affairs. While many Muslims have abandoned their traditional ban on usury, many others see overturning the standards of Western banking as one way of resisting Western domination and reasserting Islamic identity. As a result a number of countries now have Islamic, non-interest-based banking, while in almost all Muslim communities, alternative banking structures are arising to provide usury-free banking facilities. This movement is also linked to the creation of new local economic structures which, through local cooperative industries and finances, free people from the debts incurred by international banking.

There are now sizable Muslim communities in Europe and in North America. Most of these are migrants from traditional Islamic lands, but converts are growing, especially in the United States, where Black Muslim groups, such as the Nation of Islam, are a significant force, converting many African Americans. It remains to be seen what the result of growing up in the West will be on Muslims of the twenty-first century. They could provide a vital bridge between these two great cultures that may well dominate the social, religious and political scene for decades to come. Or they could become partisan, either for or against Western values. Their future role will be crucial as the rise of Islam continues and the power of the West increases.

*A wandering Hindu holy man (*sadhu*) in the grounds of a temple at Vrindavan, northern India. This sadhu has renounced material attachments and follows a strict ascetic path. The cows he is leading, like all cows in India, are protected, since they play an important religious and economic role in traditional Hindu life.*

The Vedic Faiths

The term *Vedic* is often used to describe the three faiths that arose historically in India and that share a common root in the Vedic culture of ancient India. These faiths are Hinduism, Buddhism and Jainism. The word *Veda* means "sacred knowledge" or "learning" in Sanskrit, the oldest surviving written language of India. The Veda is the title of the collection of the oldest extant sacred texts from India. The Veda consists of four sections: the *Rig-Veda* (Veda of praise, the oldest text), *Sama-Veda* (a collection of readings for chanting), the *Yajur Veda* (prose text for the liturgy), and the *Atharva Veda* (chants, songs and spells). These Vedas formed the first clear written tradition of religion in India.

Early Hinduism arose from the common stock of Vedic teachings. It emphasized reincarnation and the release from rebirth, known as *moksha*. By the sixth century BCE, these teachings and their associated practices had attracted criticism, both philosophical and practical. Philosophically, there was a great deal of debate about the nature of the soul and about release from the wheel of reincarnation. Practically, the domination of religious life by the priestly caste meant most people were left out of religious practice in temples and shrines.

Both Buddhism and Jainism emerged in the sixth to fifth centuries BCE in reaction to this early Hinduism. Each stressed different areas of disagreement with Hinduism: Buddhism centered on the exclusiveness of the official priestly caste and the teachings about the soul (*atman*) and moksha, while Jainism looked to a more austere and disciplined self-regulation as a way to seek release and enlightenment.

Karma

Karma means "action" or "deed" and has also come to mean the results of such an action or deed, the fruits of which can create good or bad karma. Thus killing an animal creates negative karma, but releasing a captive animal is good karma. The production or development of karma is what binds the soul, or sense of self, to this physical world and to the cycle of rebirth and reincarnation. Only when all karma has been removed or eroded or balanced out can the soul be freed from rebirth. In Hinduism certain acts produce certain forms of karma, and the effect is carried as the soul migrates from life to life, but it can finally be worked out and karma ceases.

In Buddhism the goal is to free oneself from the effects of karma so that all desires and attachments cease. When there is a sense of self there is something for the individual to identify with, whether it is an object, mood or feeling. These attachments arise out of ignorance and cause endless wandering from life to life, but when the sense of self disappears there is nothing to be reborn.

Karma also forms one of the major foci for Jain teaching. Jains believe that bad karma makes the soul literally heavy, while good karma lightens it. This leads to Jain ascetic practices, designed to reduce the heaviness of the karmically afflicted soul.

A Buddhist making offerings at a Chinese temple in Ho Chi Minh City, Vietnam. There are joss sticks burning before the shrine and incense cones hanging from the ceiling. Positive karma is accumulated through acts of devotion.

The Cyclical Nature of Existence

All three Vedic faiths view life, indeed all material existence, as cyclical. They see the universe as being without beginning or end, but caught up instead in repeating cycles of birth, growth, decline and death, leading to birth again. This is related in particular to the personal journey through life, but also explains how creation, all life, all universes that ever have existed or will exist, come into being. Even the buddhas, gods or deities are subject to this cycle of rebirth. There is no one Creation, nor will there ever be one final day of judgment. Instead, each cycle of life or of a universe has its beginning, middle and end, only to be superseded by the next life.

A world cycle lasts for millions of years. A traditional Buddhist description imagines a mountain five kilometers high and five kilo-

meters wide. Just once every hundred years a man comes and rubs the mountainside once with the softest cloth. The whole mountain will be rubbed away in a shorter time than that taken for a world cycle to run its course. That world declines as it is filled with greed, anger and hatred, and when it is finally destroyed, then another world will take its place.

Reincarnation

The cyclical nature of existence at a personal level is expressed in the idea of reincarnation. This is the belief, held by all three Vedic faiths, that the soul or the essence of the individual is reborn time after time, in different bodies or forms. In classical Hinduism, each soul (*atman*) goes through countless reincarnations, rising slowly from the most basic life forms, through insects to humans and on to demigods before finally achieving reunion with the Ultimate Nature of all existence.

Whatever state of being one remembers when he quits his body, ... that state will he attain without fail. (*Bhagavad Gita* 8.6)

In other words, the focus of the soul at the time of death will affect the next existence: a consciousness focused on mere animal existence and the satisfaction of animal desires will produce a subsequent life in an animal body.

All three faiths seek to find release from the cycle of reincarnation. Reincarnation is caused by karma, but is also the means by which karma can be worked off. In Jainism, for example, the soul or the illusion of a soul can be released from this cycle of birth, death and rebirth by austere practices and total nonviolence. In Buddhism it is the attachment to self that creates karma; when this attachment ceases, reincarnation also ceases.

Moksha and nirvana

The state of being free or liberated from the cycles of death and rebirth is termed *moksha* in Hinduism and Jainism and *nirvana* in Buddhism.

Moksha means "release," and this captures its sense in Hinduism and Jainism. It is the point of release from the wheel of reincarna-

Some of the incarnations of the Hindu deity Vishnu. Hindus believe that Vishnu has appeared in times of need in ten main incarnations.

tion. Once the soul is released, it reunites with the Ultimate and thus has its existence within the ultimate source of all life.

In Buddhism, release is from suffering and illusion, it is the letting go of the sense of self and the realization of wisdom and compassion. The word *nirvana* originally meant "blowing out"—as when a candle flame is blown out.

In Mahayana Buddhism, with its salvationary buddhas and bodhisattvas, nirvana becomes a specific place or state of continued existence, beyond the reach of the laws of karma and reincarnation. In some traditions it becomes even more clearly named as the Pure Land, a place of supreme happiness where the soul dwells without fear of rebirth.

Atman

One of the areas of greatest difference between the Vedic faiths is on the issue of whether there is a soul. The Sanskrit word is *atman*, originally meaning "breath" but later expanding to mean the true and eternal "soul" of each being.

Hindus believe that what passes from incarnation to incarnation is this atman, around which karma accrues. The atman originates from, and is an expression or breath of, the Ultimate. In the end, after all the reincarnations, it is the pure atman which is reunited with the Ultimate.

> *This is the truth; as from a blazing fire there spring forth thousands of sparks like little fires, so, my fellow seeker, from God, the Imperishable, diverse life forms are produced and indeed go back again to Him.*
> (*Mundakopanishad* II, 1.1)

In Buddhist teachings the soul is impermanent, it has no surviving or enduring personality or breath. Thus Buddhism seeks to overcome the illusion of a soul or sense of self that moves from incarnation to incarnation. When this illusion is destroyed, the hold of karma and the illusion of permanence disappears, and thus Nirvana—the ultimate peace—is possible and reincarnation ceases.

Buddhist pilgrims making devotions at a Tibetan temple in Dharamsala, northern India.

FINAL RELEASE

There are many paths in the Vedic faiths that lead to release or liberation from reincarnation. Depending on the path followed, the final release can be described as union with God, returning to the world-soul, supreme peace or the quenching of all desires.

The Vedic faiths recognize the difficulty of using language derived from this world to describe the world of moksha or nirvana. This is expressed in the Buddhist story of the turtle and the fish:
A turtle and a fish lived side by side in the sea. One day the fish asked the turtle to go out of the sea onto the land, to travel around and come back and tell him what life was like out there. So the turtle crawled out of the sea. He waddled across the hot dry sand. He waded through a shallow stream and tried climbing a tall tree. After a while he returned to the sea and his friend the fish. "So," said the fish, "tell me all about it."
"Well," said the turtle, "dry sand is not like wet sand. Breathing in the open air is not like breathing under water. Walking across grass is unlike anything in the sea..."
The fish broke in impatiently. "Don't tell me what it isn't like, tell me what it is like."
The turtle replied "How can I? Nothing you know is like what is out there. All I can do is tell you what in your world is unlike that in the other world."

CHAPTER FOUR

HINDUISM

Hinduism is the religion followed by more than 800 million people in India and up to 50 million in the rest of the world, and it encompasses a huge variety of beliefs and rituals. Over the centuries this religious tradition has slowly evolved to be practiced and understood in many different ways, but it is intricately woven into the land and culture of India. Although religious beliefs may vary, they are not exclusive of one another and are accepted by Hindus as part of the wide body of Hindu tradition.

This symbol represents the sacred syllable "Aum" (sometimes spelled "Om"), which is spoken at the beginning of Hindu prayers and worship. According to the scriptures, Aum was the first sound, out of which the rest of the universe was created.

A Hindu holy man (sadhu) beside the river Ganges. For Hindus the Ganges is one of the great sacred rivers of India.

"Hinduism" is not the name that the people of India gave to this spiritual tradition, but was a name given later by outsiders to describe the people who lived east of the river Indus. Hinduism came to be the term used by foreigners to describe the religion of India, although Hindus refer to their religion as *sanatana dharma*, the "eternal truth" or "ancient religion." The word *dharma* is rich in meaning: it can refer to the natural, unchanging laws that sustain the universe and keep it in balance, or it can be translated as "law" or "social duty."

In the Hindu holy books there are traditional laws and duties that have been handed down from generation to generation. For Hindus it is a religious responsibility to carry out the duties that are associated with each stage of life and with the family and part of society into which they are born. These include the duties of a mother to her children, of a son to his father, of a teacher to his students, and other spiritual and devotional duties. Members of families and communities also carry a responsibility to participate in important rites of passage such as birth, marriage and death. For many Hindus, secular and religious life are not separate, since faith plays a vibrant part in everyday life.

Hindu Roots and Beliefs

It is impossible to be precise about when Indian civilization began, but archaeologists have found evidence in North India of a thriving culture based around walled cities from at least five thousand years ago. However, there is evidence that at some time during the second millennium BCE, a people called the Aryans came from the north or west to conquer and settle in northern India. They brought with them the Vedic teachings that over time contributed to what we now know as Hinduism. Their teachings were recorded in an early form of Sanskrit.

Karma

There is great diversity in Hindu belief and practice, but the idea of reincarnation based on *karma* is almost universal in Indian religion. In Hindu teachings, all actions produce effects in the future—this is the law of karma.

People who carry out their religious duties faithfully and behave righteously in ordinary life will be rewarded with a desirable rebirth, perhaps into a high-caste family. Those who

Offerings made to the Shiva lingam. The lingam is the most common manifestation of Shiva and is one of the oldest forms in which he is worshiped. The lingam embodies Shiva's creative force.

neglect their religious duties, who cause suffering or act immorally, are liable to feel the effect of these actions in the status and condition of their next life. They may be reborn into a lower caste, into a life of poverty, suffering or pain, or outside the caste system altogether.

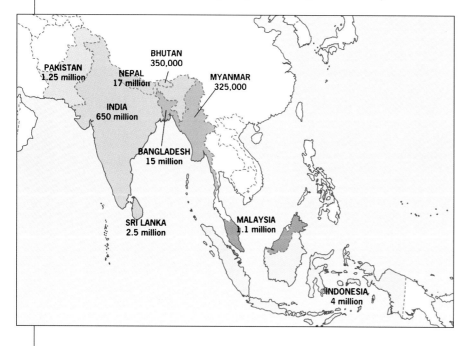

Members of a Brahmin family performing a morning puja at a shrine built in the garden of their home.

Map labels:

PAKISTAN 1.25 million

NEPAL 17 million

BHUTAN 350,000

MYANMAR 325,000

INDIA 650 million

BANGLADESH 15 million

SRI LANKA 2.5 million

MALAYSIA 1.1 million

INDONESIA 4 million

Atman and moksha

Since the law of karma states that every action, good or bad, will have its consequences, it seems that the cycle of birth, death and rebirth must be endless. However, release is possible and the *atman*, or soul, can be freed.

The atman is the fundamental, unchanging essence of the individual living being. According to Hindu thought, people are born over and over again into a state of suffering because they misunderstand atman. As long as the belief persists that the individual atman is separate from the universal brahman, or "world-soul," this cycle of suffering will continue. Release, or *moksha*, is made possible by the realization that the inner atman and the universal brahman are identical. This relationship between atman and brahman is most famously expressed in the Chandogya Upanishad in the words *tat tvam asi*, or "you (atman) are that (brahman)."

Attaining moksha is one of the main aims of Hindu spiritual practice. The atman may pass through hundreds if not thousands of rebirths before this final liberation is achieved. If the individual is hampered by karma, this will cling to the atman and together they will be transferred into a new body. But if the individual has broken free from karma and achieved moksha, the atman is free to reunite with brahman and there will be no further rebirth.

DEVELOPMENT OF THE CASTE SYSTEM

In early Hindu scriptures, society was divided into interdependent groups, each of which had a specific role and place in society. The *Brahmins* were the priests, the *Kshatriyas* were the warriors, the *Vaishyas* were the merchants, and the *Shudras* were the craftspeople.

INHERITANCE OF CASTE

Over the centuries, an individual's caste was inherited and it was extremely difficult to move from one caste to another. Hundreds of divisions developed within each of these castes, leading to further separation between the groups. Each caste also has its own set of rules and traditions, and these can affect occupation, diet and contact with members of other castes. Marriage, in particular, usually takes place within the same caste.

In small rural communities the distinctions between the castes are often more noticeable than in the towns and cities, where the boundaries between castes are less sharply defined. While the caste system can be rigid and divisive, it has also offered a strong sense of belonging and identity. Being a member of a particular caste can prevent access to certain professions, places or people; however, it also provides a social and professional network of support.

THE 'SCHEDULED' CASTES

There is a fifth group, who call themselves *Dalit* (downtrodden). They do the most menial work in society, such as street cleaning or clearing away the dead bodies of humans and animals. They formed the "untouchable" castes, now officially known as the "scheduled" castes. A law passed in 1950 outlawed the practice of "untouchability," but this group remains the most socially and economically underprivileged section of society.

A stall selling religious artifacts for the festival of Divali. The businesses that Hindus run or the occupations they follow often depend on the caste into which they were born.

Hindu Deities: The Manifestations of God

H indus believe in one ultimate Supreme Being who has unlimited forms. Some of these forms, such as Vishnu or Shiva, display the full power of God, while some of them, such as Brahma, are only partial aspects of God. Ultimately, all living beings, both human and animal, are tiny parts of God.

In Hindu teachings there are male and female counterparts at every level in the universe: the god Vishnu is accompanied by the goddess Lakshmi, the god Brahma by goddess Saraswati, and in the human world there is man and woman. But in the eternal spiritual realm the parts of God are beyond the duality of male and female—they exist as perfect beings in full freedom, knowledge and bliss. Everything in the material realm experiences the sufferings of birth, disease, old age and death.

In order to create and maintain the material world God assumes the three forms of Vishnu the Preserver, Brahma the Creator and Shiva the Destroyer. To protect truth and goodness, and to help people learn who they really are and free them from material illusions, God enters this world as *avatar*, "one who descends." The best known avatars are the ten incarnations of Vishnu, among whom are Krishna and Rama.

VISHNU, LAKSHMI AND BRAHMA

Vishnu is a full manifestation of God. He creates each universe from his breathing, then enters it to create Brahma, the first living being. Vishnu is known as the Preserver of the Universe—Hindus believe that if he were to withdraw even for an instant the whole world would be destroyed. He also sustains the universe, giving guidance and protection. He is loved by Lakshmi, the Goddess of Fortune. She awards wealth and good fortune to her worshipers. Vishnu blesses his devotees with love and freedom from material desires, which releases them from the cycle of reincarnation. Brahma works under Vishnu's direction to create the planets and to fill them with created beings.

Ganesh is honored as a wise demigod and a son of Lord Shiva. He can remove obstacles from the path to success. Businessmen are fond of him and his picture is often found in shops and offices.

To obtain assistance in the running of the universal affairs, Brahma creates demigods such as Indra the rain god, Agni the fire god and Surya the sun god.

Krishna and Radha

Krishna is the most popular avatar of Vishnu. In his childhood he played with his friends in the forest, herded cows, and danced with the cowherd girls. The love between him and

THE TEN FORMS OF VISHNU

Kalki

Krishna

Narasimha

Kurma

Matsya

Parasurama

Radha symbolizes the divine love between the soul and God. The image of God as a child who dances and plays the flute, and who is in love with Radha, has inspired generations of poets, musicians and artists and is the focus of the Hindu *bhakti* movement of devotion.

When he grew up, Krishna taught the *Bhagavad-Gita*, the "Song of the Lord" (see page 95), to his close friend Arjuna. The song contains the message that has become the best known spiritual teaching of Hinduism.

Rama and Sita, and Hanuman

As Rama, the avatar of Vishnu, God set the example of the perfect king, who loved his people and who showed honor, courage and love for his queen, Sita. The tragic story of the *Ramayana* tells how Sita and Rama were banished to the forest and how Sita was kidnapped by the wicked Ravana. The festival of Divali celebrates the homecoming of Sita after Rama rescued her and killed Ravana. But the story ends with the forced separation of Sita and Rama. This represents the tragedy of life in this world where the love of the soul for God is constantly tested.

Hanuman, Rama's faithful servant, is the most popular character in the *Ramayana*. He carries messages of love between Rama and Sita and eventually helps free her. Although he is a monkey, he is also the divine son of Vayu, the god of the wind, so he has superhuman powers. In the service of Rama he is able to do anything, even lift mountains. He symbolizes faith

Boys resting by a roadside shrine to Hanuman, who symbolizes loyalty to the service of God. In the Hindu epic, the Ramayana, *he is the faithful and devoted servant of Rama.*

and loyalty in the service of God, and the inner strength that this inspires.

Sarasvati

Sarasvati is the goddess of learning and music and the consort of Brahma. She is invoked by scholars, poets, artists and musicians to inspire them in their work.

SHIVA AND PARVATI

Shiva is the form of God who takes care of the dark side of nature—destruction, suffering and death. When the universe must be destroyed it is Shiva who does it with his dance of destruction, which reduces everything to ashes so a new universe can arise. He is associated with the Himalayas, where he lives and performs austerities, and where he caught the Ganges River as she fell to earth. He is worshipped by the yogis who fast and meditate to gain mystical powers. To them he represents the death of material desires and brings release from the cycle of birth and death. He is kind and merciful to his followers and benevolent to those who need protection. His consort Parvati is worshipped as the Divine Mother under many names, including Durga and Kali. She is believed to be the force of nature and the womb of the universe from which all life springs.

Buddha   Vamana   Rama   Varaha

Hindu Sacred Literature

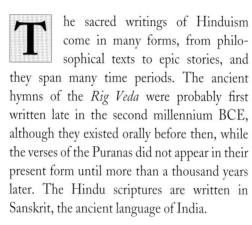

The sacred writings of Hinduism come in many forms, from philosophical texts to epic stories, and they span many time periods. The ancient hymns of the *Rig Veda* were probably first written late in the second millennium BCE, although they existed orally before then, while the verses of the Puranas did not appear in their present form until more than a thousand years later. The Hindu scriptures are written in Sanskrit, the ancient language of India.

The Rig Veda

The four collections of scriptures that make up the Vedas are the most ancient sacred texts of India. The oldest and best known of these is the *Rig Veda*, which is a collection of hymns.

Hindus gathered for worship before a shrine. The priest and some of the worshipers are reading hymns from the Hindu sacred scriptures.

> *Who truly knows? Who can declare it?*
> *Whence it was born, whence is this manifestation?*
> *On this side of the manifestation are the gods.*
> *Who then knows where it has arisen?*
> *Whence has this manifestation arisen*
> *Whether created or not?*
> *Only He who is its overseer in the highest abode*
> *Knows or Knows not.*
> *Rig Veda* X.129.6-7

The *Rig Veda* is concerned with the Hindu pantheon of gods and divine beings (known as *devas*), and with the earliest form of Hindu ritual, which involved huge public ceremonies. During these, Brahmins offered sacrifices and the juice of a plant called Soma was drunk.

The original sacrifice, according to the *Rig Veda*, was the self-sacrifice of Purusha, the "cosmic man," whose body became the universe. The public sacrifices of early Hinduism echoed this primal sacrifice.

The central gods of the *Rig Veda* are Varuna, god of water and oceans; Indra, the powerful god of storm and war; Agni, god of the sacrificial fire; and Soma, god of the sacred plant. Despite their importance during Vedic times, however, none of these gods is worshipped today apart from Indra, who survives in the role of a weather god. On the other hand, two gods who are not prominent in the *Rig Veda*—Rudra (later known as Shiva) and Vishnu—would later become the central deities of Hinduism.

The Upanishads

These are a later group of writings that reflect a decline in the importance of the sacrificial rituals and a shift toward a more personal, internal style of religious practice.

> *This then is the truth: As from a blazing fire there spring forth thousands of sparks like little fires, so, my fellow seeker, from God the Imperishable diverse life forms are produced and indeed go back again to Him.*
> *Mundaka Upanishad* II.1.1

The Upanishads introduce certain extremely important Hindu concepts—it is here that the idea of reincarnation in particular is developed. In a sense, the outlook of the Upanishads is pessimistic: it presents ordinary life as an endless cycle of birth, suffering, death and rebirth. The Vedic sacrifices are no solution to this problem. The goal of the Upanishads is to find a means of release, or moksha, from an unsatisfactory existence.

The Puranas

The word *purana* means "ancient history," and the eighteen Puranas, which have been passed down and developed from ancient times, show another stage of Hinduism. Rather than being philosophical or mystical books, these are mythological epics describing the exploits of Vishnu or Shiva; here, the emphasis on abstract philosophy and ascetic practice that was so vital in the Upanishads is giving way to the idea of devotion to a personal god.

One of the most famous and influential of the Puranas is the *Bhagavata Purana*, which tells the story of Krishna's early life and which became a focus of the popular cult of Krishna. This took shape in southern India and spread across large areas of the country.

The Ramayana

One of the two great epics of Hinduism, the *Ramayana* was a popular folk story before it was written down as a Sanskrit text. The final version is thought to have been completed around 2,000 years ago. It tells the story of King Rama, another famous and popular avatar of Krishna. Whereas the *Mahabharata* is said to express the entire scope of Hinduism, the *Ramayana* offers, in the character of Rama, a model for the ideal Hindu life. In his struggles to rescue his queen Sita from the demon Ravana, Rama is seen as an example of honor, strength in the fight against evil and obedience to social duty, while the moral values that Sita upholds are seen as the ideal model of womanhood. For many Hindus the *Ramayana* is a source of religious inspiration and its story is familiar through readings, re-enactments, plays, films and works of art that depict scenes from the epic.

An Indian fan depicting Rama and Sita, whose story is told in the Ramayana. *Hanuman, the loyal servant of Rama, is sitting at their feet.*

THE BHAGAVAD-GITA

I am the Atman seated in the heart of all beings. I am the beginning, I am the middle, I am the end of all beings.
Bhagavad-Gita 10:20

Within the *Mahabharata* is a section called the *Bhagavad-Gita*, or "Song of the Lord," which is the most famous and popular of all Hindu religious writings. The *Bhagavad-Gita* records a conversation between the hero Arjuna, who is preparing to go into battle, and his charioteer, Krishna. Arjuna is unwilling to participate in the horrors of war but Krishna gives him hope and teaches him the meaning and purpose of life. Krishna points out that, even though Arjuna may kill the bodies of his enemies, their souls are immortal and indestructible. Furthermore, he explains, if Arjuna accepts that it is his duty (*dharma*) to fight, and if he seeks no reward from fighting, then despite the chaos of the battle around him, his mind will remain as calm and detached as that of a yogi in meditation. Krishna then describes his own nature as God, and reveals himself to Arjuna in his divine form. Finally, the doctrine of the love (*bhakti*) between God and humanity is explained, as a more desirable goal even than moksha.

The *Gita* is a very complex piece of philosophical writing, and it has influenced almost all later developments in Hindu thought. The present text is thought to be over 2,000 years old.

A Hindu Temple— Worship and Ritual

The diversity of Hindu beliefs is reflected in the style and size of the millions of temples and shrines throughout India. Some temples can accommodate hundreds of worshipers in their grounds, others are simple village shrines. Hindu temples often date back a thousand years or more and are little changed, while others are new. In India today there is a boom in temple construction to serve the needs of the rapidly expanding population. Beyond India, older buildings have been converted into temples but increasingly the Hindu community is building new temples in cities and towns.

Throughout the day people visit temples to make offerings, pray, sing, and listen to teachings. The *parikrama*, a circumambulatory path around many temples, allows worshipers to walk around the shrines as they offer their prayers. Trees are also honored by Hindus as givers of life and shelter. Near most temples are to be found ancient trees, such as banyan or peepal (also called the Temple Tree), which are included in the daily round of worship.

Holy men chanting hymns in the doorway of a temple. The marks on their foreheads are a sign that they are devotees of Vishnu.

A VILLAGE TEMPLE
The temple shown here is a typical village temple in India dedicated to Shiva or Vishnu and has several shrines in an open courtyard shaded by a few trees. It is a place for prayer, petition, and celebration and somewhere to congregate for village meetings.

SHRINE ROOM
One or more deities are worshipped in the main shrine-room. Only Brahmin priests can enter here to perform the puja, in which the image is woken, bathed, dressed, fed, and put to sleep. The sanctified food, and other offerings from the puja, are distributed to all who come. Visitors bow before the deity and offer prayers and small gifts. The act of seeing the sacred form of God, called darshan, is itself sufficient to give blessings and purification.

MEMORIAL SHRINE
Most temple compounds have memorial shrines to locally revered saints, beneath which their bodies are often interred. Although Hindus usually cremate their dead, the bodies of saintly people who have inspired devotion are sometimes preserved because they are recognized as having achieved a state of physical purity.

TULASI PLANT
In all temples where Vishnu is worshiped the sacred tulasi plant, also called Sacred Basil, is kept, usually in a special container. The leaves are needed in the worship of Vishnu and his avatars such as Krishna and Rama, and are valued by the community for their medicinal properties.

BHAKTI AND PUJA

CEREMONIAL CHARIOT

Most temples possess a ceremonial chariot, called a *rath*, which is like a small temple on wheels. A smaller version of the main deity is placed upon the rath and taken out on procession at festival times, allowing everyone the benefit of *darshan*, or seeing the deity.

BHAKTI

Bhakti is the devotional path of Hinduism, the adoration of one or more deities who in return will release the worshippers from their karma. Service to God through thought and action is the basis of bhakti. It is an exchange of love between worshipper and deity, an exchange which brings the worshipper closer to God. Bhakti is expressed through chanting, hymns, music and dancing, and bhakti devotees try to bring the same sense of religious commitment to every aspect of their lives.

PUJA

Most Hindu worship takes place in the home, and almost every Hindu home has a household shrine with images of the gods and goddesses. Daily puja or worship involves offerings such as flowers, fruit, rice, incense, sandalwood paste, milk, water and the flame of the arti lamp that burns ghee (clarified butter). All these items are usually kept on a puja-tray near the shrine. Before the midday meal, food is also offered at the shrine. On the festival day of any of the major Hindu deities, a special, extended puja may be performed. For most Hindus, puja is the basic daily expression of devotion to the deities, at home or in the temple. The word puja can also mean the respect due to one's parents and teachers.

A husband and wife offer morning puja at a shrine in their home.

SECONDARY SHRINE

There may be several of these. Usually, if the temple is dedicated to Lord Vishnu, this shrine will be for Shiva, and if the temple is dedicated to Lord Shiva, this shrine will be for Vishnu. There may also be a separate shrine for the female consort of the main deity— Lakshmi for Vishnu and Parvati or Durga for Shiva, or for the deity's mount—Garuda the eagle for Vishnu and Nandi the bull for Shiva. Other deities who may be present are Hanuman and Ganesh.

NANDI

The figure of Nandi the bull is usually found alongside shrines to Shiva since he is Shiva's personal attendant and mount. The bull is an ancient and important symbol in Hindu culture. He is revered as a father in village communities because of his strength in ploughing fields and pulling carts.

Rites of Passage: Birth, Marriage and Death

There are many rituals that surround each rite of passage in Hinduism. These rituals, called *samskaras*, begin before a child is born and end at death with cremation. They are major celebrations in the life of a Hindu family and also strengthen the bonds that exist within the wider community.

Birth

There are traditionally sixteen samskaras and eleven of them are connected with the birth of a child, although some families may not follow all of them strictly.

When parents want to conceive a child they may consult a Hindu priest to find the best days for sexual intercourse in order to generate good karma for the baby's new incarnation. While the mother is pregnant she reads and recites from the Hindu scriptures so that their positive influence will protect the baby. During the eighth month of pregnancy the parents may make offerings of cooked rice to Vishnu so that his sustaining powers might be transmitted to the unborn baby.

The hair-cutting ceremony is one of the samskaras, or rites, associated with the birth of a child. It takes place at one, three, or five years old, and it signifies the elimination of negative karma that has been carried through from a previous life.

SACRED THREAD RITUAL
Upper-caste Hindu boys must undergo the rite of the Sacred Thread before they can marry, and before they begin to study the Sanskrit prayers that will allow them to represent their family in worship. This ceremony takes place when the boy is twelve years old and marks his passing from childhood into adult life. After a series of blessings and ritual baths, the boy stands facing west. His guru, or teacher, stands opposite him and gives him a loop of cotton thread, made sacred by being sprinkled with water. After the thread has been placed around his right shoulder and the left side of his waist, the guru says, "May this sacred thread destroy my ignorance, bring me long life, and increase my understanding." The boy repeats this as he arranges the sacred thread. He is then taught the ancient Gayatri hymn from the *Rig Veda*, and finally the guru offers the boy advice on his duties and obligations to his family and teachers.

The naming ceremony usually takes place on the tenth or twelfth day after birth, although this can be deferred. At birth the family will record the time and the day, which enables a Hindu priest to cast a horoscope and suggest which syllables would be most suitable for a name. The detail and formality of the naming ceremony varies between families but is always a time of celebration, and a sanctified food called *prasadam* is shared out.

The baby is taken on a first outing at the same time as the naming ceremony. After the family have bathed in the morning, the father performs puja at the home shrine and the baby, dressed in new clothes, is taken outside for a short time. Sometimes, particularly in rural areas, the baby is also taken by the mother to visit the shrine of the local deity.

The baby is given his or her first solid food during morning puja, usually five months after birth, although this may be later depending on the child's health. Special prayers are offered and the father then gives the child a small spoonful of boiled rice mixed with yogurt, ghee and honey, or sometimes the rice is simply mixed with milk.

When the child is one, three or five years old the head is shaved, leaving boys only a small tuft of hair. Shaving the hair symbolizes the removal of negative karma that has been carried through into this birth, and also marks the wish that the child will lead a good life. On the same day that the hair is cut the child may also be initiated into knowledge of the scriptures, with one of the parents guiding the child's hand to write three mantras from the Hindu scriptures. Finally the child's earlobe may be pierced on the day the hair is cut, although nowadays this usually only happens to girls.

Death

The final samskara is carried out for the departed soul. Where possible, just before the soul leaves the body, a few drops of Ganges water, the leaves of the sacred tulasi plant and a piece of gold are placed in the mouth of the dying person. The body is cremated, since it is only the continuation of the atman, or soul, that is needed for reincarnation. The body is bathed, dressed, wrapped in a new cloth and laid on a stretcher, which is carried in procession to the funeral pyre. In places where it is not possible to build a funeral pyre, the body is taken in a coffin to the crematorium.

Before the cremation on the pyre, the eldest son drops pieces of kindled wood into the mouth of the deceased, while others place small pieces of wood on the pyre. At this time a mantra is chanted: "This lump of food is served to you, O departed one. Let this be your satisfaction and let this be your liberation from all bondage." When the pyre or furnace is lit, prayers from the Hindu scriptures are recited to give the soul peace. After the cremation the ashes, flowers and bones are collected and, if possible, some are scattered on the river Ganges or on another river or sea.

The body of a man is prepared for cremation on the banks of a river in Kathmandu, Nepal. When families cannot cremate their deceased by a sacred river they will try to spread the ashes over water.

HINDU WEDDINGS

In traditional Hindu culture, as in Indian culture generally, it is normally considered the responsibility of the parents and family to find suitable spouses for the sons and daughters of the family, either by word of mouth or through classified advertisements in newspapers. The family astrologer will often be asked to examine the couple's horoscopes, and if they are compatible, to choose a suitably lucky day for the ceremony to take place.

THE CEREMONY

The bride's parents begin the wedding ceremony by offering a traditional welcome to the groom, including various symbols of happiness, fertility, good life, food and safety. While this is happening the bride herself may make private prayers to the goddess Parvati. She then joins the bridegroom and, after songs of blessing have been sung, the bride's father formally gives her away. The couple's union is marked when their right hands are symbolically bound together with a piece of cotton thread dyed with yellow turmeric, and water sprinkled over them. They then walk around the sacred fire three times, offering grains of rice. The marriage ceremony is not complete until the couple has taken seven steps, making a vow at each step. The seven steps represent food, strength, prosperity, well-being, children, happy seasons, and harmony in their marriage and friendship. The couple is now married, and after blessings and prayers, friends and family share the wedding feast.

A bride and groom wearing a garland at their wedding in Jaipur, India. A Hindu wedding is one of the most important stages of life: It not only marks the union of two people, but of two families.

Major Festivals in the Hindu Calendar

HINDU CALENDAR

Hindu festivals are based on a lunar calendar of twelve months, with an extra month added every five years to keep in line with the solar calendar. Each month is divided into a "bright fortnight," when the moon is waxing, and a "dark fortnight," when it is waning. However, slightly different calendars have traditionally been used in different parts of India. In most the month ends with the full moon, and in areas where the month begins with a new moon the dates of festivals may differ by as much as fifteen days. The year is also divided into six seasons that correspond to weather conditions in India.

The celebration of festivals, like so much else in Hinduism, can vary enormously between different parts of India, and between India and the rest of the world. There are many local festivals, often associated with pilgrimage sites or shrines, which are not known outside their own area. Festivals also depend on the particular manifestation of God that the worshipers follow. For example, the devotees of Krishna celebrate his birthday at Janmashtani, and on that occasion thousands of pilgrims will gather at Vrindavan, Krishna's birthplace. Other festivals, such as Divali and Holi, are universally celebrated, although customs may vary from place to place, and different stories, songs and dances appear in different areas.

Hindus celebrating Holi as they follow one of the pilgrimage routes around the town of Vrindavan, India. Their clothes are stained red with the colored water and powder that is showered on people at this festival.

MAHASHIVARATRI

(13th or 14th day of dark half of Magh) The new moon night of every month is *Shivaratri*—"night of Shiva." *Mahashivaratri* means "great night of Shiva." Hindus honor the image of Shiva with his consort Parvati and their child Ganesh. Before the new moon appears, offerings of flowers, grain, water and milk are made to Shiva between midnight and sunrise, and the twenty-four hour fast that the worshipers have been keeping is broken as the new day dawns.

SARASVATI PUJA

(First day of Spring season) The goddess Sarasvati is the patron of the arts and learning. On her festival people wear bright yellow clothes, a symbol of royalty and of the warmth of spring, and groups of musicians play. This festival is particularly popular among Bengalis.

HOLI

(Full moon day of Phalgun) This festival celebrates the grain harvest in India, but more importantly recalls the pranks that Krishna played as a young man. The festival takes its name from a story about a prince called Prahlad who was a worshiper of Vishnu. His father, the king, tried to make him abandon Vishnu, but each time Prahlad was in danger Vishnu protected him. Finally, the king's sister, a demon called Holika, led Prahlad into a fierce fire, hoping to destroy him. But Prahlad was protected by Vishnu's power, and Holika perished in the fire. The festival is high-spirited, with bonfires, tricks, good fun and dancing.

RAMA NAUMI

(9th day of the bright half of Chaitra) Celebrates the birthday of the god Rama, hero of the *Ramayana* (see page 95). During the eight days leading up to this festival, people fast for various periods of time and there is a continuous recital of the *Ramayana*. On the day of the festival the main stories of the *Ramayana* are read. A model of baby Rama in a cradle is set up in the temple, and those coming bring offerings to the cradle.

RATHA YATRA

(16th day of Asadha) This festival originates in the town of Puri on the east coast of India, where a huge image of the god Vishnu, called Jagganath, Lord of the Universe, is placed on an enormous wooden chariot and pulled through the streets. Everyone tries to take a turn at pulling the chariot and as it passes, lamps are waved before it and flowers are thrown at it.

RAKSHA BANDHAN

(Full moon day of Sravana) *Raksha* means "protection." *Bandhan* is "to tie." The main ceremony is tying a *rakhi* (a thread or band, made of silk or decorated with flowers) to the wrists of others. In some places this is done by the head of the house, in others sisters tie the threads on their brothers' wrists. Women who have no brothers give a rakhi to another male relative.

JANMASHTAMI

(8th day of Bhadra) This festival celebrates the birth of Krishna and his delivery from the demon Kansa, who wished to kill him. Krishna is said to have been born at midnight, so worshipers gather at midnight to welcome the baby. An image of Krishna is washed with yogurt, ghee, honey and milk, following which the mixture is collected and shared out. The picture or statue of the child Krishna is then placed on a swing, which people take turns to push.

Members of a Hindu temple in the United Kingdom gather for puja at Divali, when they offer the arti flame and food to Rama and Sita. Hospitality is a feature of this festival as visitors are welcomed into homes with Divali lights and patterns.

NAVARATRI (also known as DURGA PUJA) followed by DUSSEHRA

(First ten days of the bright half of Aswin) This celebrates the most important female deity, Durga, consort of Shiva, who has many forms. As Kali she destroys time, as Parvati she is the faithful wife of Shiva, as Durga she is the destroyer of evil demons. For nine nights different manifestations of the goddess are honored. In northern India the statue of Durga is immersed in the Ganges, accompanied by dancing.

At Dussehra, the day after Navaratri, a huge effigy of the demon Ravana is set on fire to celebrate his death at the hands of Rama.

1. **Mahashivaratri**
2. **Sarasvati Puja**
3. **Holi**
4. **Rama Naumi**
5. **Ratha Yatra**
6. **Raksha Bandhan**
7. **Janmashtami**
8. **Navaratri**
9. **Divali**

DIVALI

(Starts on the 13th day of the dark half of Aswin) The most widely celebrated Hindu festival, combining many elements. Divali itself falls on the third day; traders close their old accounts, debts are settled and puja is offered to Lakshmi, the goddess of wealth and good fortune. Lamps and candles are placed in windows so Lakshmi can look in, and colored patterns are made on the ground to attract her. The festival also celebrates the return from exile of Rama and Sita.

(Calendar wheel diagram with months: Magh, Phalgun, Chaitra, Adhik, Vaisakha, Jaistha, Asadha, Sravana, Bhadra, Aswin, Kartik, Agrahayana, Paus; Gregorian months: January, February, March, April, May, June, July, August, September, October, November, December; seasons: Winter, Spring, Summer, Rainy, Early autumn, Late autumn)

To Be a Hindu: The Paths and Stages of Life

KUMBHA-MELAS

Religious fairs known as Kumbha-Melas are held every twelve years at four sites in India: Allahabad, Hardwar, Ujjain and Nasik. These colorful gatherings attract huge numbers of people, running into millions, who come to bathe in the rivers at this auspicious time. It is also a chance to hear the teachings of various gurus (religious teachers and guides), and watch or join in the many processions. The pilgrims range from urban householders to wandering *sadhus*, or holy men.

I n Hinduism there are four commonly recognized religious paths or ways of living a spiritual life, all of which can be called *yogas*. They are ways of understanding and coming closer to the divine, and it is up to each individual to choose the paths appropriate to them. Many are guided along their chosen paths by a guru.

The path of bhakti (devotion)

The idea of the universal spirit, or brahman, is very abstract and philosophical, and it is therefore simpler and more direct for most Hindus to worship brahman in the form of a personal god instead of a universal force. The follower of *bhakti* devotes himself or herself to the love of one of the gods (usually Krishna, Rama or Shiva), surrendering personal will in the faith that the god will keep his devotees safe. The bhakti worshiper hopes ultimately to make the whole of life, in every respect, a loving sacrifice to God.

The path of karma (action)

Karma means actions themselves, from the most trivial to the most extreme, and it also means the results of those actions, which keep the atman trapped in the cycle of death and rebirth. Those who follow the path of karma perform good works in order to counteract the negative karma that keeps them in the cycle of birth and death; in this way, the path of karma benefits society as well as the individual's spiritual progress.

The path of jnana (knowledge)

Jnana does not really mean the kind of knowledge that can be gained from the study of books, although followers of the path of jnana do study the scriptures carefully. More importantly, it means knowing the truth that lies behind the philosophical ideas of Hinduism. This can be achieved not only by reading about it, but also by experiencing it directly for oneself. The path of jnana is perhaps the most difficult path since the follower must be guided by a guru at every step.

ASHRAMAS

Hindu thought divides the human (or at least the male) lifetime into four stages, called *ashramas*.

The first stage, the stage of the student, *Brahmacharya-ashrama* begins with the sacred thread ritual. During this period the young man learns the skills and knowledge he will need for later life. Secondly, during the *Grihashta* or "householder" ashrama that begins at marriage, his duty is to provide for his family, to take part generously in society, to perform certain rituals and especially to see his children married. When the children are grown up and have families of their own, the man then enters the third stage—the *Vanaprastha-ashrama* or forest-dwelling stage. In modern Hinduism, this means that the man retires from work, hands the running of his household over to his children and devotes himself to the study of the sacred texts.

The final, optional stage is that of the *sannyasin*, or renouncer. If a man chooses to undertake this stage, he leaves his family and possessions behind and becomes a homeless, wandering holy man.

These sadhus have taken the path of sannyasin. Those choosing sannyasin follow an austere lifestyle in order to move closer to God and moksha.

Pilgrims crossing the sacred river Yamuna on their journey to the town of Vrindavan. The Yamuna, a tributary of the Ganges, flows through Delhi and the sacred forests of Vrindavan, where Krishna spent his early childhood.

The path of meditation and spiritual discipline

This path involves spiritual discipline of many different kinds, and often involves the body as well as the heart and mind. The training is very systematic, the disciple moving from one stage of practice to the next.

Ahimsa

The word *ahimsa* means "non-killing" or "non-injury," and has sometimes been translated as "harmlessness." All life, whether human or animal, is sacred in Hinduism, and the follower of ahimsa affirms this by not eating meat and by never killing or harming any living thing. Although ahimsa forbids killing or causing harm, it does not forbid the use of force in some circumstances, such as to defend the innocent.

The sacred cow

For centuries the Hindus have honored and protected the cow, and cow-killing has been considered to be a terrible crime. According to

PILGRIMAGE

Pilgrimages are an important part of Hindu devotion, and the blessings gained on these journeys create positive karma for the pilgrim.

Throughout India there are hundreds of pilgrimage sites, from sacred mountains and rivers to temples and small shrines. Some, such as Varanasi on the river Ganges, Mount Kailas in the Himalayas, or Vrindavan (which is associated with Krishna) attract Hindus from all parts of India and beyond, while other sites have strong regional popularity. Pilgrimage takes place at all times of the year, and each site offers its own benefits. Some are associated with healing illnesses or aiding the conception of children, others are said to bring prosperity and blessing and many pilgrims make the journey simply because it brings them closer to the divine.

THE GANGES

All the great rivers of India are worshiped as female deities such as Ganga, Narmada and Kauveri. They are the source of life and energy in a land of heat and dust. For many the most sacred is the river Ganges, which flows across India from its source in the Himalayas. Pilgrims to the city of Varanasi, associated with the god Shiva, wash in the sacred waters of the Ganges so that negative karma can be released, since the goddess Ganga offers liberation from the cycles of birth and death. Varanasi is also an auspicious site for cremation and for scattering the ashes of the deceased.

Among the tributaries of the Ganges is the Yamuna. Kalindi is the goddess of this river and is believed to bestow love for God on all who bathe in her waters.

THE HIMALAYAS

The most sacred mountains in the Hindu world are the Himalayas. Hindus see this entire mountain range as the god Himalaya, the father of Shiva's wife Parvati. It is also said that Shiva himself sits in meditation on Mount Kailas in the Himalayas. One of Shiva's greatest gifts was to tame the flow of the river Ganges. The gods wished to bestow the fertility of the heavenly Ganges on the earth, but were worried in case the mighty flow of the river destroyed the earth. Shiva, on hearing this, found a solution. He uses his hair to break the fall of the river and thus it flows in many tributaries at first, only later forming one main river.

ancient Hindu writings, killing a cow is as sinful as killing a Brahmin. The importance of the cow in Indian life is economic as well as religious. Cows eat vegetable matter and from it produce milk, which in turn becomes yogurt, cheese or ghee. Oxen pull the plow, allowing the planting of grain. Indian village agriculture depends heavily on the role of the cow and bull, and they are therefore treated as mother and father.

These oxen are dressed for a local festival in the state of Karnataka, India.

The Influence of Hinduism Today

Members of ISKCON on procession through the streets of London to celebrate the festival of Ratha Yatra. A shrine holding an image of Krishna leads the procession, followed by a large chariot that contains an image of Vishnu, called Jagganath, Lord of the Universe.

Today major Hindu communities are to be found in South Africa, the United States, Canada, the United Kingdom, Australia, the West Indies, Fiji and East Africa, to name but a few. These communities, while often still strongly linked to their original areas of India, have established many traditional features of Hindu life in their new lands. Hindu temples, institutions, schools and media thrive, offering their host communities an insight into Hindu belief and practice.

However, this has not been the only way Hinduism has spread in the last hundred years. Since the late nineteenth century swamis, gurus and teachers have come from India to spread the Vedic wisdom to an increasingly appreciative West. Hand in hand with this, translations of classic Hindu texts have become more and more popular in the West. Originally translated by scholars, they are now widely read sources of spiritual inspiration. The *Bhagavad Gita* and the Upanishads have found a place

VEGETARIANISM AND HEALTHCARE

Hindu vegetarian food has spread far beyond India in recent years. Besides being compassionate to animals, vegetarianism is believed to benefit the body, the mind and the planet. According to yoga, the human digestion functions best on a vegetarian diet, which is low in fat and high in fiber. A vegetarian diet is said to pacify the mind by attuning it to more gentle rhythms and encourages spiritual awareness.

Hinduism has its own complete system of medicine called Ayurveda. It advocates prevention rather than cure, and teaches that ill health is caused by eating the wrong foods and by negative emotions such as anger or fear. Ayurvedic cures are based on herbal remedies, massage and cleansing diets, combined with yoga and meditation to calm the mind. Ayurveda is influential as part of the worldwide trend towards alternative medicine.

among the spiritual classics of Western readers. Modern devotional movements, such as the Swami Narayana Mission, which started in Gujarat in the early 19th century, spread with Gujarati settlers to Africa, Central and North America, and Britain. It is based on devotion to God through education and community service. Its temples are often elaborate works of craftsmanship wrought from marble and stone, and usually have schools attached to them.

Modern missionary movements such as the Ramakrishna Vedanta Mission or the International Society for Krishna Consciousness (ISKCON), better known as the Hare Krishnas, have followers outside the Indian community. The Hare Krishna Movement teaches devotion to Krishna through chanting his name, and operates schools, farms and vegetarian restaurants around the world.

Another international movement with a large non-Indian following is Transcendental Meditation, or TM, practiced by 5 million people worldwide. It became famous in 1965 when the Beatles travelled to India to meet its founder, Maharishi Mahesh Yogi.

Significantly such movements have spread the use of Hindu imagery and concepts, such as reincarnation, far beyond their circle of believers. Hindu motifs and symbolism have become part of the religious vocabulary of the West.

Modern Hindu reformers

During the nineteenth and twentieth centuries a number of teachers have influenced the philosophy and practice of modern Hinduism. Their effect has been felt not only in religious and cultural spheres, but also in the arenas of politics and human rights.

Perhaps the most influential Hindu figure of the nineteenth and twentieth centuries was Mohandas Gandhi (1869-1948), who was given the title *Mahatma*, meaning "Great Soul." He advocated nonviolent opposition to all social injustice, particularly the practice of "untouchability," and was a leading figure in India's progress toward political independence. His example has had a profound effect on liberation movements throughout the world.

YOGA

Yoga, with its emphasis on personal transformation, has become popular not just among Hindus. This ancient school of Hindu thought and practice is believed to enhance life through basic exercises for the body and mind and offers a simple method for anyone to improve their health and develop inner peace. It appeals to people of any religion and none, and both Christians and Buddhists have adapted yoga practices to help them on their own paths. The word *yoga* literally means 'yoke', referring to the path to union with God. It takes several forms, the most popular of which is *hatha yoga*, which concentrates on breathing and physical posture, leading to meditation. *Karma yoga* is the path of selfless service. The most universally practiced among Hindus is *bhakti yoga*, the path of devotion to God. This is the simplest form of yoga, which usually centers on repeatedly chanting a *mantra*, a prayer, as a way to spiritualize one's life and offer one's daily actions to God.

A Brahmin priest practicing yoga. Yoga is a path that leads to liberation and union with God.

A British Hindu girl praying before Krishna at her home shrine. Many Hindu homes have a small domestic shrine for daily worship, and each community has a local temple. Temples in the cities and towns beyond India often serve as a focal point for the Hindu community to worship, meet, celebrate or study.

CHAPTER FIVE

BUDDHISM

Buddha means "Awakened" or "Enlightened One" and is the title given to Siddhartha Gautama, the founder of Buddhism, who lived in northern India in the sixth and fifth centuries BCE. The Buddha is a being who is the embodiment of perfect wisdom and perfect compassion.

Most Buddhists believe that many buddhas have appeared in the past and that there will continue to be buddhas in the future. The historical Buddha is sometimes given the title Sakyamuni, meaning "sage of the Sakka people," after the people into whom he was born.

According to tradition he was brought up in his father's palace, secluded from the world outside, but began to think deeply about the nature of sickness, old age and death. Some sources say these reflections arose after the shock of seeing for the first time a sick man, an old man, a corpse and a wandering ascetic. In order to find the cause of suffering and the way to end it he left his luxurious surroundings and took the path of a wandering ascetic.

In his search Siddhartha Gautama (Siddhatha Gotama in Pali*) sought the advice of spiritual teachers and then followed his own strict ascetic path. After several years he realized that the answer lay neither in severe austerities nor in a life of luxury, so he developed the Middle Way. By avoiding extremes and calming the mind through meditation he understood the true nature of things, the *dharma* (*dhamma* in Pali*), and achieved enlightenment.

These mani stones are found near the walls of most Tibetan monasteries. They are carved in slate by lay pilgrims with Buddhist mantras, figures or symbols.

A Buddhist monk and pilgrims at Sarnath, the place where the Buddha gave his first sermon after his enlightenment. Sarnath is one of the most important sites of Buddhist pilgrimage.

*The Pali text is used in the scriptures, liturgy and scholarly commentaries of Theravada Buddhism. Sanskrit, the common sacred language of ancient India, is the language used for many of the scriptures and scholarly texts of Mahayana Buddhism. Here we have used Sanskrit for many Buddhist terms and where appropriate have given the Pali equivalent.

Early Roots and Basic Beliefs

NIRVANA
Buddhists believe there is a way to end suffering and this is by reaching *nirvana*. Nirvana is the final release or liberation from *samsara* (wandering)—the cycles of death and rebirth. They believe we pass through many births in human or other forms. Rebirth, disease, desires, suffering and death cease to exist at nirvana—a state of supreme happiness and peace.

T he Buddha attained enlightenment while meditating under a bodhi tree at a place in northern India now known as Bodh-gaya. He then gave his first sermon to a small group of disciples at Sarnath, and it was here that he first taught the Four Noble Truths and the Eightfold Path. These teachings and others that he gave later explain the nature of suffering and the way to end it in order to achieve the ultimate freedom of *nirvana* (*nibbana* in Pali).

Theravada Buddhism
Throughout his life the Buddha continued his spiritual instruction, gathering a large community of disciples who formed the *Sangha*, the community of Buddhist monks and nuns. The Sangha preserved the teachings, which spread gradually throughout India and beyond. The teachings of the Buddha and the traditions that were established at this early stage are most closely followed today by Theravada Buddhists. *Theravada* means "Teachings of the Elders."

Mahayana Buddhism
As the Buddha's teachings developed, a new form of Buddhism called Mahayana began to emerge in the first century CE. *Mahayana* means "Great Vehicle." Some of the monastic rules followed by early Buddhist monks were reinterpreted by Mahayana Buddhists in order to adapt and spread Buddhist teachings in countries beyond India.

Mahayana Buddhists also developed the idea of the *bodhisattva*, which means "one who is possessed of enlightenment." This is the term for one who is destined to become a buddha. Through countless lives filled with good deeds, bodhisattvas reach the point at which they

Offerings before a statue of the Buddha in the Temple of the Reclining Buddha in Burma. When the Buddha is shown in this position, it represents the stage at which he is about to enter nirvana.

KARMA
Buddhists believe that there are many worlds and galaxies: Some have passed away and many more will come into existence. Everything that exists in all places and at all times is subject to the law of *karma* (*kamma* in Pali)—the law of cause and effect. Buddha saw how all actions, whether thought, word or deed, are like seeds that will grow and bear fruit in this or future lives. Positive actions build up merit; negative ones detract from it. Buddhists try to free themselves from negative karma and to generate positive karma by living a morally good life and by actions such as meditation and offerings. Buddhists believe that the accumulation of karma causes one to be reborn into the cycle of death and rebirth. The ultimate goal of Buddhist practice is to be released from the law of karma altogether.

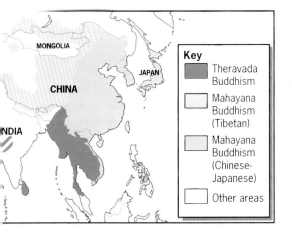

As Buddhism spread beyond India it influenced, and was influenced by, the cultures in which it became established. Many different forms are now found. Although the spread of Buddhism is sometimes associated with certain sages or monks, such as Mahinda, who brought Buddhism to Sri Lanka in 250 BCE, it also spread along trade routes and was carried by travelers.

delay their final entry into Nirvana in order to respond compassionately to calls for salvation from those trapped in the cycle of rebirth.

At all cost I must bear the burdens of all beings, in that I do not follow my own inclinations. I have made a vow to save all beings. All beings I must set free.

Vrajradhvaja Sutra, *Sikshasamuccaya* 280-81

Early Buddhist philosophy was developed in a new way by the Mahayana Buddhists. The Buddha taught that nothing is permanent. He also taught that everything depends on something else for its existence. For example, human beings depend on the Sun for light and heat, on the air for oxygen, and so on, in order to live.

At first, Buddhists expanded on this teaching, suggesting that everything was made up of basic building blocks called *dharmas* (*dhammas* in Pali). They claimed that while the particular forms that the building blocks create are not permanent, the blocks themselves are—they simply exist. A Mahayana Buddhist philosopher, Nagarjuna, noted that this contradicted the Buddha's original teaching. He argued that if dharmas existed, and if all that exists is impermanent, then the dharmas too are impermanent: in fact, there is nothing permanent or solid in anything. This teaching is called *Sunyatavada*—the Way of Emptiness.

THE FOUR NOBLE TRUTHS AND EIGHTFOLD PATH

THE FOUR NOBLE TRUTHS

The Buddha taught these in his first sermon at Sarnath. He said that to understand these truths the mind must first be at peace:
The First Noble Truth—Suffering exists.
The Second Noble Truth—There is a reason for suffering.
The Third Noble Truth—There is a way to end suffering.
The Fourth Noble Truth—The way to end suffering is through the Eightfold Path.

When the Buddha explained the nature of suffering he used a process of diagnosis and treatment that doctors may have used in his day. The suffering he spoke of parallels illness, and the Buddha recognized the cause of this illness and its cure. The cure lies in the Eightfold Path—this path, or Middle Way, leads to the end of suffering.

THE EIGHTFOLD PATH

The Buddha's path to end suffering involves discipline of both thought and action. In order to follow it many Buddhists find a teacher to guide them, and once they have listened and understood the meaning of the Eightfold Path they try to practice it. Particularly In Theravada Buddhism this is the way to nirvana.

1. *Right Views*—knowing and understanding the Four Noble Truths.
2. *Right Thoughts*—letting go of want and desire, and acting with kindness to avoid hurting anything.
3. *Right Speech*—telling the truth, speaking kindly and wisely.
4. *Right Action*—not stealing or cheating.
5. *Right Livelihood*—earning a living that does not cause bloodshed or harm to others.
6. *Right Effort*—encouraging and developing positive thought in order to keep to the Path.
7. *Right Mindfulness*—being aware of thoughts and actions that affect the world now and in the future.
8. *Right Concentration*—this is the peaceful state of mind that arises through correct practice of the Eightfold Path.

Some larger Buddhist temples have bell-shaped structures called stupas nearby, containing relics associated with a sage or a holy being. This stupa at Boudhanath, Kathmandu, Nepal, is said to hold the remains of a previous incarnation of the Buddha.

Buddhist Scriptures: Sermons, Commentaries and Poems

Painting of the Buddha's enlightenment from a monastery in Ladakh, northern India. The teachings that the Buddha gave in his lifetime have a special place in the Buddhist scriptures.

Buddhist writings fall into two main groups:—those that tradition holds to have been spoken by the Buddha, and the writings of sages and scholars. Each one of the Buddhist traditions—Mahayana and Theravada—has its own set of literature that is known as a canon.

Theravada scriptures

For several centuries the early teachings of the Buddha were passed down orally by the Sangha, the community of Buddhist monks and nuns, and in the first century BCE they were written down on palm leaf manuscripts in Sri Lanka. The teachings are recorded in an Indian language called Pali—the Buddha himself spoke a dialect of Pali.

The Pali Canon

The Pali Canon is a record of the conversations and teachings that the Buddha gave at different times to different people. This collection of texts that is gathered in many volumes is divided into three parts called the Tripitaka, meaning "Three Baskets," so named because the palm leaf manuscripts were kept in three woven baskets:

Sutta: the basket containing the discourses of the Buddha

Vinaya: the basket containing the rules of discipline

Abhidhamma: the basket containing further knowledge.

Mahayana scriptures

The earliest Mahayana scriptures were written in Sanskrit, an ancient Indian language, during the first century CE. As with the Pali Canon, many of the Mahayana scriptures record the

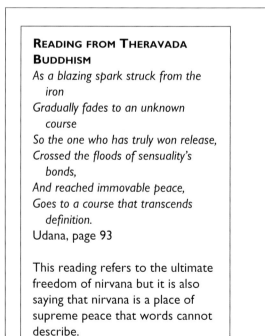

READING FROM THERAVADA BUDDHISM

As a blazing spark struck from the iron
Gradually fades to an unknown course
So the one who has truly won release,
Crossed the floods of sensuality's bonds,
And reached immovable peace,
Goes to a course that transcends definition.
Udana, page 93

This reading refers to the ultimate freedom of nirvana but it is also saying that nirvana is a place of supreme peace that words cannot describe.

Buddha's words, but new texts were also written that were attributed to the Buddha or that commented on the Buddha's teachings. As Mahayana Buddhism spread to China, Japan and Tibet the scriptures were translated and new ones written by scholars and sages. This is why the main sources for Mahayana scriptures are the Buddhist canons of Tibet and China.

Tibetan literature

Tibetan literature is divided into two large collections. The first is called the bKa"gyur, meaning the "Translation of the Word of the Buddha," and is made up of translations of Indian Buddhist writings. The second is called the bStan'gyur, or "Translation of Treatises," and this consists of commentaries on the bKa"gyur, as well as hymns and poetry.

Chinese literature

The Chinese canon is known as the Ta-ts'ang-ching or "Great Scripture Store." It is made up of a huge amount of literature, 1,662 texts in total. Most of the Theravadin works are included as well as commentaries and other

material. It is usually divided up into the three "baskets" of *sutra*, *vinaya* and *abhidharma*, but it also contains *shastras*—commentaries by non-enlightened beings.

The texts contained in the Chinese Buddhist canon are also used in the Korean and Japanese Buddhist traditions.

Novice monks studying Buddhist scriptures at a monastery in Burma. Study is an important part of monastic life and the young novices are guided and taught by older members of the community.

READINGS FROM MAHAYANA BUDDHISM

Northern Buddhism
Eveything I see and hear is a teacher that teaches me the spiritual path. The flowing of the water teaches me impermanence.... I don't need to have books made up of paper and ink. Everything I see around me teaches me the Dharma.
The Songs of Milarepa.

The songs of the twelfth-century Tibetan poet and saint, Milarepa, are still sung in Tibetan homes as families go about their everyday life. This one is a reminder that everything that happens in life is part of the spiritual path.

Eastern Buddhism I
Amitabha Buddha sees the phenomena of the three worlds as false, ceaselessly changing in a cycle, and without end, going round like a cankerworm, imprisoned like a silkworm in its own cocoon....He wishes to put the beings in a place that is not false, not ceaselessly changing in a cycle, not without end, that they may find a great, pure place, supremely happy.
T'an Luan's commentary on Sukhavativyuha

T'an Luan, a Chinese teacher (CE 476-542), wrote this commentary on a Pure Land Buddhist scripture. Those who follow the Pure Land tradition believe that this heavenly land is ruled by the compassionate Amitabha Buddha, and those who have faith in his saving power will be reborn into the Pure Land.

Eastern Buddhism II
*The mountain is the mountain
And the Way is the same as of old.
Verily what has changed
Is my own heart.*
Traditional Zen training poem

This verse was written by a medieval Japanese knight who secretly entered a Zen monastery. After twelve years there he went on a pilgrimage, during which he encountered another knight who recognized him and spat in his face. As he calmly wiped the spittle off his face, the monk realized how different his reaction to this insult would have been before he began practicing Zen, and so he returned to his monastery and wrote this poem.

Following Buddhist Teachings: Devotion and Meditation

BUDDHIST MONASTERIES

Monasteries house a community of monks or nuns who live there permanently, but they are also open to visitors, especially on festival days. The community formed by the first monks and nuns who followed Sakyamuni Buddha is known as the Sangha. In Mahayana Buddhism, the Sangha also includes bodhisattvas, and can include teachers, scholars and other Buddhists who have not been ordained as monks or nuns. The duty of the Sangha is to uphold and pass on the teachings of the Buddha.

Buddhists aim to follow the Buddha's teaching in everyday life in many different ways: through their diet, the trades they follow, through meditation, giving alms or making offerings at shrines, temples and monasteries.

In countries where Buddhism is the majority religion, devotion to a buddha or bodhisattva is a natural part of everyday life. Shrines, temples and monasteries are a familiar part of the landscape. As Buddhism has spread beyond Asia, for example into the United States, many temples and Buddhist centers have sprung up as places where Buddhists can meet for meditation, discussion or retreat.

BUDDHIST TEMPLES

Most Buddhists recognize the existence of many Buddhas. In Mahayana countries, Buddhists often make their devotions to popular figures such as Amitabha Buddha and the Bodhisattva Avalokiteshvara. They are depicted in statues and paintings, and in homes and temples there is usually a shrine room where images of such holy beings are kept. In larger temples there may be other shrine rooms, meditation and teaching halls, as well as accommodation for the religious community.

ZEN BUDDHIST PRACTICE

There are many Buddhist traditions in Japan. Zen is one of the oldest and originally came from China in the form of Ch'an Buddhism. Japanese Zen Buddhists place great emphasis on meditation, and have developed many different forms of Buddhist practice.

Zen Buddhism teaches people that words are only the surface of things and that they must get beyond words in order to understand the meaning of existence. A Zen monk may spend years meditating on a single phrase or sentence called a *koan*. A koan is often like a riddle with no solution—for example,

"what is the sound of one hand clapping?" Zen Buddhists also create and meditate on beautiful, tranquil gardens and incorporate traditional Japanese skills such as archery, flower-arranging and the tea ceremony into their meditative practice.

A Zen garden in Kamakura, Japan.

DRUM AND BELL

The drum and bell in buildings (shown in close-ups) in the courtyard of the Chinese Buddhist temple are mainly used at festival times. Smaller bells in the shrine room are rung during daily devotions.

DEVOTION

Buddhists usually begin an act of devotion before a shrine by reciting the three refuges:

I take refuge in the Buddha
I take refuge in the Dharma
I take refuge in the Sangha

They may then bow three times before holy images or objects before making offerings or chanting. The three bows are a way of paying respect to the Buddha, the Dharma and the Sangha who are also known as the Three Jewels.

THE BUDDHA

The Buddha drawn here is sitting in the lotus position. His outstretched arm is touching the earth, which symbolizes the Buddha's enlightenment.

MEDITATION AND CHANTING

Meditation is used to free the mind from passion, aggression, ignorance, jealousy and pride; and through this to allow natural wisdom to shine through. Chanting is another important part of Buddhist practice, both at the temple or monastery and in the home.

MEDITATION

It was by meditating that the Buddha reached his enlightenment, and so for many schools of Buddhism meditation is the most important aspect of religious practice, among lay people as well as monks and nuns. Meditation is normally practiced sitting down in a quiet place, with legs crossed or in the Lotus position. There are two basic types of Buddhist meditation; the first, called *samatha*, involves concentrating the mind completely on a single object or sensation— for example, the flame of a candle, or a flower. In the second type of meditation, called *vipassana*, one increases one's knowledge of self by carefully analyzing all thoughts and feelings.

Many forms of meditation have been developed by the different branches of Buddhism. Pure Land Buddhist meditation involves creating very vivid and detailed "mental pictures" of buddhas and bodhisattvas. To help create these pictures in the mind, Buddhists may use a painting or statue. Tibetan Buddhism also uses this technique combined with other methods, such as chanting or ritual gestures. The basic aim of Buddhist meditation is always to bring oneself closer to enlightenment.

CHANTING

Buddhists of many traditions chant phrases, verses or passages from the Buddhist scriptures to focus the mind. Chanting is a vital part of festivals and ceremonies throughout the Buddhist world, and in some Far Eastern schools of Buddhism, such as Pure Land and Nichiren, it is considered the most important of all forms of Buddhist practice.

OFFERINGS

In Tibetan and Chinese Buddhism, there will usually be various objects placed before the shrine:

Light from candles symbolizes understanding
A shell symbolizes sound
Food symbolizes taste
Flowers symbolize sight
Incense and perfume symbolize smell
Water—there may be several pots of water symbolizing touch, offering, healing, purification, satisfaction of thirst and of desires

Turning prayer wheels at Kyicho Temple, Bhutan. Cylindrical prayer wheels have a mantra or chant written around the face of the wheel. The wheels are spun around and with each turn the mantra is repeated.

Buddhist Rites, Rituals and Pilgrimage

Major Buddhist pilgrimage sites in India.

Buddhist pilgrims at Sarnath, India. Hundreds of sites have attracted Buddhist pilgrims, who often make long journeys to reach these destinations. Sites include temples, stupas, pagodas, mountains and bodhi-trees, which have religious and spiritual associations.

Buddhist monks and nuns play a relatively small role in the rites of passage of ordinary people. Monks generally attend celebrations of births and weddings, or a newly married couple might visit a monastery, but the role of the monks will be simply to receive *dana* (gifts) and to offer sermons or the *Paritta* ritual. The same is true of coming-of-age rituals, although in Thailand young men often spend a while in a monastery. Buddhist marriage rituals are sometimes performed today among Buddhists in the West, but this is a new development.

The exceptions to this general rule are rituals that are concerned with death. In China, where Mahayana Buddhism exists side by side with the Confucian and Taoist religions, Buddhist temples are particularly popular for funerals and anniversaries of death. Similarly, in the Theravada Buddhist countries of Southeast Asia, it is the funeral that, of all lay rites, has the greatest Buddhist content. In Tibetan Buddhism the rituals and beliefs that surround death are so important and complex that they have been described as a "science of dying." These beliefs are set out in the Bardo Thodol, the Tibetan Book of the Dead.

Paritta

Most Theravada festivals include the practice of *Paritta*, a chanting ceremony performed for protection from negative influences, or to ward off danger in any form. Paritta is performed by monks on behalf of lay people, and can take anything from an hour to several days. The monks bring with them a relic of some kind. The relic, the words that they chant and the monks themselves represent the Three Jewels (Buddha, Dharma and Sangha). The monks sit on chairs connected by threads, and pots of water are placed around the area. Often a special cloth is hung over the site of the ritual. The monks then chant relevant passages from the *sutras* (*suttas* in Pali). Finally, the threads connecting the monks' chairs are cut into short lengths and tied around the wrists and necks of the lay people; the water is also sprinkled over them, and in this way they take the blessings of

Mount Kailas in Western Tibet is a very important, and remote, destination for Tibetan Buddhist pilgrims.

the ceremony away with them. Mahayana Buddhism has a very similar ceremony, called *Dharani*, in which monks chant versions of the sutras with the words shortened to their first syllables, turning the text into a long series of apparently meaningless sounds: *du, sa, ni, ma...*

Pilgrimage

Early Buddhist scriptures mention four destinations in Nepal and India that a Buddhist pilgrim might visit. These are the Buddha's birthplace at the Lumbini Grove; Bodh Gaya, where he found enlightenment; Sarnath, where he preached his first sermon on the Four Noble Truths; and Kusingara, where, according to tradition, he died. There are also many stupas said to contain relics of the Buddha, and these, too, became early pilgrimage destinations.

Adam's Peak, or Siripada, in Sri Lanka is a special site not only for Buddhists but also for Hindu, Muslim and Christian pilgrims. At the summit of the mountain is a depression in the rock in the shape of a huge footprint. According to Sri Lankan Buddhist tradition, the Buddha left his footprint on the peak of this mountain.

In China there are four important sacred mountains (*shan*), each one associated with a particular bodhisattva. Very devout Buddhists follow a route between all four mountains. Their long journey often begins at the western mountain of Emei Shan in Szechuan Province, then continues south to the remote Jiu Hua Shan in Anhui. On the next stage the pilgrims visit the northern mountain of Wutai Shan in Shanxi Province, a particularly popular site for Mongolian Buddhists. The journey ends at Pu Tuo Shan, on an island off Zhejiang asssociated with the bodhisattva Kuan Yin.

Mount Kailas, in Tibet, is an important destination for Tibetan Buddhists. It was also sacred to Tibet's pre-Buddhist Bon religion. Milarepa, Tibet's best-loved Buddhist sage and poet, is said to have challenged a representative of the Bon religion to a race to the top of the mountain. Milarepa won by use of greater divine powers, symbolically confirming the position of Buddhism as Tibet's state religion.

ORDINATION

Ordination as a Buddhist monk means submitting to the monastic rules, drawn from the teachings of the Buddha. When a new monk is ordained, he enters into an ordination tradition or lineage, a line of teachers and disciples that is often traced back to the Buddha himself.

The new monk will take refuge in the "Three Jewels," and will accept the Five Precepts (see page 119) in their strictest form, which forbids killing, lying, stealing, alcohol and sex. His head will be shaved, and he will own nothing except his robes and his alms-bowl. However, he will not necessarily vow to remain in the monastery for the rest of his life. In Thailand, for example, it is common for young men to join a monastery for a short time.

In the Buddha's time, women were also ordained and could reach the highest levels of monastic life. However, at various times in the history of some Buddhist traditions the lineage was broken and the tradition ceased. Recently, in Theravada Buddhist countries, women who wished to join the monastic life had to remain as novices and could not be ordained. However, this situation is gradually changing, and a kind of ordination is again available to women in some Theravada traditions.

In most Mahayana schools the line of ordination was not lost, and women are ordained as nuns, but rarely reach high positions in religious life.

Buddhist monks at the head monastery of the Kadjn sect, Tibet.

Buddhist Festivals and Celebrations

In Japan the birth of the Buddha is called Hana Matsuri, the Flower Festival. This stems from a pre-Buddhist festival but since the Buddha is said to have been born in a grove of flowers, images of the young Buddha are placed in floral shrines.

T he date and the nature of Buddhist festivals vary with the tradition of the country and the indigenous culture. Many festivals celebrate the Buddha's life, teaching or enlightenment. Others celebrate bodhisattvas, teachers or events in Buddhist history. Alongside these lively and often colorful Buddhist festivals are many national or local festivals that do not have their roots in Buddhism. Some celebrate the agricultural year, ancestors or popular deities; others are rooted in traditions such as Taoism or Shintoism. Festivals are often marked by temple fairs and temple visits, alms-giving and offerings at shrines. Most festivals follow a lunar calendar, but this is not identical in all Buddhist lands.

SOUTHERN BUDDHISM

NEW YEAR FESTIVAL
(Beginning of Citta) In preparation for the festival, images of the Buddha are washed with scented water. Stupas of sand are built on riverbanks or on temple grounds, and when New Year has dawned the sand is carried away by the river or leveled off to form a new floor, just as the bad deeds of the past year should be cleared away.

VESAKHA
(Full moon of Vesakha) Marks the Buddha's birth, enlightenment and his passing into nirvana at death. Celebrations range from walking around the temple or stupa three times (to honor the Three Jewels) to watering bodhi-trees with scented water, decorating houses, lighting lanterns and erecting street stalls or theaters.

ASALHA
(Full moon of Asalha) Commemorates the Buddha's first sermon. Ordination of Theravada monks generally takes place in the period leading up to this festival. This is also the beginning of the three-month rainy season known as *Vassa*, a time when monks stay in the monastery for study.

ASSAYUJA
(Third full moon of Vassa) According to tradition the Buddha ascended to Heaven during his lifetime, and passed on his teachings to his mother. This festival celebrates his return from Heaven and marks the end of Vassa.

KATTIKA
(Full moon of Kattika) Celebrates the first missionaries who went out to spread the teachings of the Buddha. If the rains continue longer than usual, Kattika is the latest date for the end of Vassa.

KATHINA
(End of Vassa) When the rainy season has ended, the Kathina celebrations take place as offerings—especially robes—are presented to the monasteries in elaborate ceremonies.

EASTERN BUDDHISM

THE BIRTH OF THE BUDDHA

(8th day of fourth lunar month; 8th April in Japan) Images of the Buddha as a child are bathed in scented water or tea. Also a time for compassion toward living creatures.

BIRTH, ENLIGHTENMENT AND DEATH OF KUAN YIN

(19th of the second, 19th of the sixth, and 19th of the ninth lunar months) The bodhisattva Kuan Yin is one of the most popular figures in Chinese Buddhism (in Japan and Korea she is known as Kwannon). Women hoping to have children seek her help. Offerings are made at the temple and divination poems are read.

1 **New Year Festival**
2 **Vesakha**
3 **Asalha**
4 **Assayuja**
5 **Kattika**
6 **Kathina** (depending on the end of Vassa)
7 **Birth of the Buddha**
8 **Birth of Kuan Yin**
9 **Enlightenment of Kuan Yin**
10 **Death of Kuan Yin**
11 **Hungry Ghost Festival**

HUNGRY GHOST FESTIVAL

(8th to 15th day of the seventh lunar month) The activities calm the unsettled spirits of the dead. The monks chant to ease their suffering, and the laity burn paper boats and make food offerings enabling them to pass peacefully out of this world.

O-BON

(In Japan: 13th to 15th of July) This festival remembers ancestors and is a time of family reunion. For two days the ancestors are celebrated; on the third day the family bids them farewell with fires. Offerings are made to the Buddha, and monks visit home shrines to read from the scriptures.

NORTHERN BUDDHISM

TIBETAN NEW YEAR

(The new moon of February) Before the New Year celebrations, houses are cleaned to sweep away any lurking negative aspects from the past year. Costumed monks perform special rituals and chants while the people light firecrackers or torches and go through the house shouting loudly.

Lama dance, Festival of the Buddha's Enlightenment, Labrang Monastery, Tibet.

MONLAM CHENMO

(The Great Prayer Festival; 8th-15th of the first lunar month) Ornate butter sculptures are displayed in the monasteries as the festival draws to its climax on the 15th day. There may also be puppet shows depicting traditional Tibetan Buddhist stories. The traditional decorations and ritual meals were banned for several years by the Chinese government. They now take place on a smaller scale.

THE BUDDHA'S ENLIGHTENMENT AND PASSING INTO NIRVANA

(15th day of the fourth lunar month) Buddhist pilgrims visit the monasteries to make offerings and to see the colorful paintings of demons, spirits, Buddhas and bodhisattvas. Lamas dress in traditional costumes to perform Chan dancing.

12 **O-Bon**
13 **Tibetan New Year**
14 **Monlam Chenmo**
15 **Buddha's Enlightenment and passing into nirvana**
16 **Guru Rinpoche's birthday**
17 **Chokhor Duchen**
18 **Lhabab Duchen**

GURU RINPOCHE'S BIRTHDAY

(10th day of the sixth lunar month) Guru Rinpoche is the title given to the Indian teacher Padmasambhava who helped to establish Buddhist teachings in Tibet toward the end of the 8th century CE.

CHOKHOR DUCHEN

(4th day of the sixth lunar month) Celebrates the Buddha's first sermon after his enlightenment.

LHABAB DUCHEN

(22nd day of the ninth lunar month) Commemorates the descent of the Buddha from Heaven after giving the teachings to his mother.

Practicing the Path: Mindfulness and Compassion

According to Buddhist teachings, all things in this world are in a state of constant change and are little more than illusions.

> Thus shall you think of all this fleeting world;
> A star at dawn, a bubble in a stream;
> A flash of lightning in a summer cloud,
> A flickering lamp, a phantom and a dream.
> Diamond Sutra, verse 32

Woman offering food to a Buddhist monk. The more individuals give to others the less they are attached to the material goals of this world and by doing so are refining their spiritual path

Novice monks in a Cambodian temple. During the rainy season in Southeast Asian countries the number of monks increases due to the many young men taking temporary ordination in preparation for adult life. Older people may also spend periods of time living and studying in a monastery as a way of gaining merit toward their next life.

For the practicing Buddhist, it is important not just to hear and know the teachings but also to understand them so that they can be applied in day-to-day life. According to the Buddha's teaching, all pain and suffering is caused by desire and self-centered actions. Buddhist practice aims to reduce self-centeredness and develop compassion in action and thought. But before self-centeredness can be overcome, a Buddhist must first of all be aware of it. According to the seventh step of the Eightfold Path (see page 109), all actions, even the most ordinary, should be performed with mindfulness. Mindfulness means attention to thought and action and their effect on other people.

Compassion is very important in Buddhist practice. For Buddhists, compassion means unselfish behavior—putting others before oneself. So the more one practices compassion, the more one is free from the mistake of selfish thinking.

The instructions that the Buddha passed on to his disciples are all, in one way or another, designed to help people become more mindful and more compassionate. The second of the Five Precepts (see box on opposite page) warns against stealing, because that is selfish behavior. The fifth precept warns against the use of alcohol or other drugs, because the

TIBETAN LAMA

In Tibetan Buddhism the role of the teacher or *lama* is particularly important. The lama is sometimes seen as the fourth Jewel, since without the lama the Three Jewels cannot be taught; in a certain sense, the lama embodies the Three Jewels. Some lamas—called *tulkus* —are said to be reincarnations of previous lamas. When such a lama dies, he is believed to be reincarnated almost immediately into the body of a young child. The lama's followers must then find the reincarnation of their teacher, who will be taken to a monastery to train for another lifetime of teaching. Some of these lines of succession can be traced back for hundreds of years, and are associated with particular bodhisattvas.

resulting intoxication would prevent mindfulness. The precept against harming living beings means that many Buddhists are vegetarians; some early monks would not grow their own grain in case they broke this instruction. Because the Buddha's instructions may be hard for lay people to follow, the lifestyle of the monk or nun is normally seen by Buddhists as the best example of an unselfish way of life, and the average layperson is not expected to follow it as fully.

Monasticism

The Sangha follow a code of training rules designed to help them avoid the distractions of everyday life that lead to greed, hatred or delusion. These are rules that guide spiritual practice, as well as a code of behavior that benefits community life.

Many members of the Sangha, monks and nuns, live a celibate lifestyle attached to a monastery, although in some traditions monks do marry and live with their families in or around monasteries.

At times individuals may choose to leave their shared monastic life for periods of meditation and study in secluded dwellings such as huts or caves; sometimes they may take any shelter that is available on a mountain or in a forest. However, the heart of the Sangha lies in the teaching, discipline, study and support of communal life.

DHARMA, DANA AND THE FIVE PRECEPTS

THE DHARMA

The *Dharma* can be understood in several ways in Buddhist teachings. It is the Buddhist teachings, the true path, and the true nature of all things. The enlightened Buddha not only understands Dharma but has also become Dharma. In the words of the Buddha, "whoever sees Dharma, sees me; whoever sees me, sees Dharma."

The Buddha's first sermon after his enlightenment has been described as "the setting in motion of the wheel of Dharma."

DANA

Dana (giving) is at the center of Buddhist practice. The act of giving produces merit that improves karma in this life and the next.

To the Sangha, alms-giving is an important aspect of Dana since the religious community largely depends upon laypeople for food, clothes, housing and other needs. In return the Sangha offer the more precious gift of the Dharma. But Buddhists also support hospitals, schools, festivals, funerals, ordinations, the printing of religious texts, and other organizations and events that affect the life and well-being of the community.

By practicing dana, Buddhists become more sensitive and compassionate to the needs of others. Through dana they have laid the foundations for cultivating virtue. This is developed by observing ethical rules, the most common of which are the Five Precepts or "rules of training." Each of these precepts is a promise or a vow—an acceptance of Buddhist teaching as a guide to life. To commit oneself to these precepts, it is traditional to have a monk chant them first and then repeat them. However, one can also decide to take these on by chanting them oneself. After this the precepts are chanted on many occasions, before undertaking day-to-day activities or at festivals and ceremonies.

THE FIVE PRECEPTS

I undertake the rule of training of refraining from:
harming living beings;
taking what is not given;
misuse of the senses;
false speech;
self-intoxication due to alcoholic drink or drugs.

Buddhist nuns in one of the gardens at Chithurst Monastery in the UK. As well as being a center of teaching and meditation, the community here has revived an ancient English woodland. Caring for the environment is one of the ways Buddhist teachings can be applied in everyday life.

The Spread of Buddhism and Modern Developments

D uring the twentieth century, Buddhism has been subjected to greater suppression than at any time during its history, but many of these controls on Buddhist practice are now being eased and Buddhism is reemerging.

Buddhism in Asia
While Buddhism is flourishing in parts of Asia, there are other areas where practice is restricted or state-controlled. After the Vietnam War (1964-75), many monasteries were closed and the Vietnamese Sangha was in decline but in recent years there has been a revitalization of Buddhist practice privately and publicly although tensions remain between the socialist regime and the Sangha. In Cambodia, the effects of the Vietnam War were compounded by the rule of the Khmer Rouge, during which almost the entire Sangha was forced into lay life or killed. After the fall of the Khmer Rouge the main task was to re-establish the Sangha. There is now a new confidence in the Cambodian Sangha who are becoming increasingly involved in social, development and environmental issues. Laos became a communist state

A Zen nun at a Buddhist community in Los Angeles. Zen is one of the longest-established Buddhist traditions in the United States: groups were formed in California in the early 1920s,

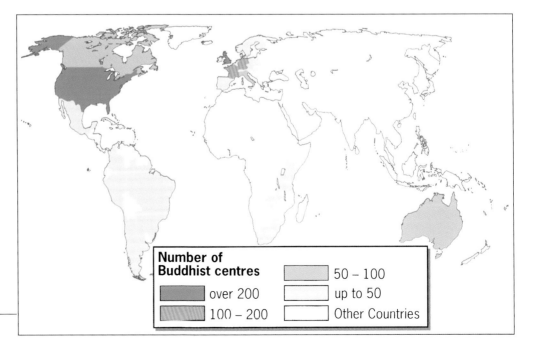

Number of Buddhist centres

over 200	50 – 100
100 – 200	up to 50
	Other Countries

in 1975, the Sangha no longer had an independent central role and many monks fled to Thailand although Buddhism privately remained the majority religion. It is now widely practiced and has regained much of its social position although the activities of the Sangha are still regulated by the Marxist government.

However, there are many other areas where the Sangha remains central or is gaining influence. In Thailand and Sri Lanka, Buddhism is the majority religion, and it is still the state religion of Thailand and of the Himalayan kingdom of Bhutan. Small groups of Buddhists still practice in Russia, in the republics of Buryat, Tuva and Kalmyk. The influence of Buddhist revivals and new movements is seen in Indonesia, Taiwan, Hong Kong, Singapore, South Korea and Nepal, as well as China and Japan. India's Buddhist population is also growing, due partly to the influx of refugees from Tibet and partly to the conversion to Buddhism of several million "untouchables" (now known as "scheduled castes").

Western interest in Buddhism continues to grow, but it is impossible to say how many Buddhists there are in the West as many do not join organized religious orders.

In 1959 many Tibetans followed their Buddhist leader, the Dalai Lama, when he fled to India and established a community at Dharamsala in northern India. The Dalai Lama has become well known worldwide for his campaigns on behalf of freedom for Tibet, resettling Tibetan exiles and for his work on peace issues.

BUDDHISM UNDER COMMUNIST RULE

Mongolian monks are now free to follow Buddhist traditions once again and monastic life has been re-established. Monasteries are being rebuilt; novice monks are joining communities; and religious texts are being reprinted.

In the twentieth century, several eastern Buddhist countries came under Communist control that has often been intolerant toward Buddhist traditions and in many cases destructive of Buddhist culture.

MONGOLIA
When Mongolia, a majority Buddhist country, came under Communist rule in 1924, religious practice was suppressed and by the early 1930s it was forbidden. Buddhist monks and nuns had to leave their religious communities, and monasteries were destroyed or abandoned. For sixty years no new monks could be trained or scriptures printed.

CHINA
As communism took hold in China after the Second World War, religious communities were broken up and religious practice was restricted. Followers of Buddhism and other religions received their most serious blow in the Cultural Revolution (1966-76), when nearly all monasteries and temples were closed, reused for other purposes or destroyed, and Buddhists could no longer teach or follow their traditions in public.

Since 1977 monasteries and temples have been allowed to open, and in 1980 ordination of monks (banned in 1951) was once again permitted. Buddhism is now beginning to grow in strength in China, especially in the north. It is popular with young people in China because of its philosophic and international dimensions.

TIBET
Chinese Communist forces invaded Tibet in 1950 and nine years later the Tibetans staged an uprising in protest against Chinese rule. This uprising was quelled and in the years that followed the Chinese forces tried to eradicate Tibetan Buddhist culture by destroying religious art and thousands of monasteries and libraries.

Since the 1980s monasteries have begun to open again and Tibetan Buddhist scriptures are being reprinted.

Origins and Development of Jainism

Worshipers washing the feet of a statue of one of the Tirthankaras at a Jain temple in southern India. Bathing or washing the statue is a way of showing reverence and gratitude to the Tirthankaras.

The word *Jain* refers to those who conquer their inner feelings of hate, greed and selfishness: Overcoming desires is the chief principle of Jainism. Jains believe that all individuals are bound to this world by deeds done in previous lives – *karma* – and it is only by renouncing materialistic desires that these bonds can be broken and the soul achieve the blissful state of *moksha*.

Lord Mahavira

Jains believe in twenty-four Tirthankaras in each cycle of history. Vardhamana Mahavira, the last of these teachers, is the most important. Born in Bharat, India, around 540 BCE, he took up a wandering ascetic life at the age of thirty. He wandered naked, lived only on what little food he received as alms, spent most of his time in silence and frequently stood totally still with his body like a statue.

After twelve years of suffering he achieved omniscience (*kevala*). His first message after this is found in a Buddhist text, the *Majjhima Nikaya*:

I am all-knowing and all-seeing,
and possessed of an infinite knowledge.
Whether I am walking or standing still,
whether I sleep or remain awake,
the supreme knowledge and intuition
are present with me – constantly and
*   continuously.*

Mahavira began to teach others, including eleven Hindu Brahmins, who one after the other heard of this new teacher and came to challenge him in debate. They were converted by Mahavira's wisdom and explanation of the Vedas, and became his main disciples.

The Jain movement

Mahavira organized his followers into four groups: monk (*sadhu*), nun, layman and laywoman. The group as a whole became known as the Jains.

At the age of seventy-two Mahavira broke the bonds of karma and achieved moksha. His senior disciples took over leadership of the movement, which then numbered several hundred thousand, and by the fifth century CE the Jains were an influential force within India. But by the twelfth century Jainism was beginning to decline. The rise of other religions, particularly increasing numbers of Hindus and Muslims, led to the Jains being mainly concentrated in northwestern India. There are more than 7.5 million Jains in India today, mainly in the provinces of Gujarat and Maharastra. There are also small Jain communities abroad, particularly in the United States.

Meditating in the Adinath temple in Ranandpur, India. Meditation is one way of working toward detachment from material things and eventual enlightenment.

Jain Life: Beliefs and Practices

The central doctrine of Jainism is that the world is a place of evil and suffering. There is an infinite number of individual souls trapped in the material world, bound to it in a cycle of reincarnations because of *karma*—spiritual residue accumulated from wrongdoing in previous lives. Good deeds abolish this karma and allow the soul eventually to transcend the world and reach a state of *moksha*, eternal spiritual bliss. Bad deeds and concentration on material pleasures tie the soul even closer to the world.

Daily life

Because of the principle of *ahimsa* (non-injury) all Jains follow a completely vegetarian lifestyle. They often pursue trade as a profession, for most other occupations involve doing harm to other beings, even unintentionally. For example, by plowing the earth a farmer may be destroying thousands of tiny creatures.

Jain monks and nuns are even more strict in their pursuit of ahimsa. They always carry a small brush with which they gently sweep the path when walking, so as to avoid treading on any insect. They strain their drinking water, and some wear a small mask over their face to stop any insects accidentally flying in and being harmed.

Temple worship

Jain temples are dedicated to the twenty-four Tirthankaras, each of which is represented by a statue. The statues are identical, to indicate spiritual perfection, but each Tirthankara has a particular symbol—the one for Mahavira, for example, is a lion.

The seated image of a particular Tirthankara almost always dominates a Jain temple. The worshipers perform *puja* (worship) to the image every day, preferably in the early morning, or do the same in a home shrine. Worship begins with the reciting of this mantra:

> I bow to the Jinas!
> I bow to the souls that have obtained release!
> I bow to the leaders of the Jain orders!
> I bow to the preceptors!
> I bow to all the Jain monks in the world!

Then the worshiper forms a design with grains of rice, and showers the statue with water or offers a symbolic bath. An offering of eight symbolic substances is made, each representing a particular virtue. More elaborate ceremonies are held on important occasions, when the statue may be decorated with flowers or other offerings.

Festivals and pilgrimages

Jain festivals are often celebrated through pilgrimage, and last for several days. There are many Jain holy sites, often vast complexes of temples and shrines, to which pilgrims travel regularly. The cycle of festivals and pilgrimages is linked to significant events in the lives of the Tirthankaras. Major sites include Sameta Sikhara, Pavapira, and Mount Girnar, at all of which a Tirthankara achieved enlightenment.

The birth and enlightenment dates of Mahavira are particularly celebrated. These

Pilgrims climbing the sacred hill of Palitana in the Shatrunjaya Hills, Gujarat, India. The whole area is sacred to Jains, and at the top of many of the hills there are large complexes of temples celebrating the Tirthankaras and other Jain saints.

take place in Caitra (March/April) and Kartik (October/November) respectively. The most significant holiday is Paryushana, an eight-day period of confession, forgiveness and often fasting, which takes place in Bhadra (August/September).

Jain groups

During the centuries after Mahavira's death, the Jain movement split into two main factions, the chief difference between them being in the degree of asceticism they thought necessary. The Digambara (sky-clad) faction believed that complete nudity was necessary to signify detachment from material things, whereas the Shvetambara (white-clad) faction held that simple white robes would be equally acceptable. The Digambaras will not admit women to full monastic vows, holding that they are incapable of achieving enlightenment and must wait to be reborn as men. The two factions developed separate bodies of religious literature and still exist today, with the Digambaras largely based in the north of India and the Shvetambaras in the south. The Digambaras now wear robes in public, however. The small Sthanakavasi group, which originated in the seventeenth century, is even more rigorous in its discipline and also opposes any form of image worship.

THE FIVE PRINCIPLES

Ahimsa: this is the complete avoidance of harm and is essential to the pursuit of moksha. All living beings are equal and none of them should be harmed, for in doing so one will only harm oneself.

Truthfulness (*Satya*): this does not mean tactlessness, but includes deliberation before any speech and avoidance of saying anything painful to others.

Non-stealing (*Asteya*): this also includes avoidance of greed and exploitation.

Chastity (*Brahmacharya*): monks and nuns are celibate, and for Jain laypeople monogamy and faithfulness are important.

Detachment from material things (*Aparigraha*): material pleasures are transitory illusions, and Jains try to limit their acquisition of wealth, contributing instead to humanitarian causes.

THE HUMAN CONDITION

The difficulty of freeing oneself from karma is one of the central Jain beliefs, which is explained in many different ways in Jain literature. The following story is one of the intricate analogies that are used to explain the suffering of the soul in the world.

In a dense forest, a man was pursued by an elephant. He turned to flee, but a demon with a sword barred his path. He tried to climb a great tree, but its trunk was too slippery and he fell into a deep well. At the edge of the well was a small clump of roots, which he just managed to grasp to prevent his fall, but looking down he saw snakes, including a great python, ready to devour him. When he raised his head again, to his horror he saw mice nibbling at the roots to which he was clinging. Meanwhile the enraged elephant had dislodged a wild bees' nest, disturbing the bees which began to sting the man. However, a single drop of honey fell upon his tongue and he immediately forgot his perils and thought only of getting another drop of honey.

The man is the soul and the forest represents *samsara*, the endless wheel of reincarnation. The elephant is death, while the demon is old age. The well represents human life; the serpents are passion; and the python is hell. The tree represents enlightenment, far too difficult for an ordinary soul to achieve. The bees are disease and pain, while the honey represents the trivial pleasures of life, distracting from the true suffering of existence.

Pilgrims singing and praying in the Adinath temple in Ranandpur, India.

CHAPTER SIX

OTHER MAJOR TRADITIONS

This section deals with religions of great antiquity and with two of the most recent. Between them they illustrate the tremendous range of faiths in the world that fall outside the two broad categories of Abrahamic and Vedic religions. Their significance lies in their diversity, history and originality.

The faiths assembled in this last section do not have such clear links and have developed in a variety of ways. Sikhism and the Baha'i faith owe much to earlier faiths. The Baha'is recognize teachers and writings from many of the major world faiths but believe that they have been superseded by the revelation to Baha'u'llah.

Sikhism arose in a context of debate and conflict between Hinduism and Islam, and quite specifically set out to take what it saw as the best of each.

Taoism in China and Shinto in Japan are indigenous religions, arising from the specific conditions, myths and legends of their own lands. However, they have developed texts, written liturgies and ritual traditions and they have developed complex cosmologies.

Most indigenous traditions remain within a definable group of people in a specific area. In contrast, Taoism especially has traveled far beyond China, with its classic texts being translated into a variety of languages, and its observance in many different countries by both Chinese emigrants and non-Chinese converts. This change in Taoism, from an indigenous religion with a literature to a religion with adherents worldwide, has happened in the last quarter of the twentieth century.

A footpath leading to one of the peaks of Song Shan, a Taoist sacred mountain in central China. Temples and shrines have been built here for more than two thousand years.

The Guru Granth Sahib being read in the worhip room of the House of God, also known as the Golden Temple, in Amritsar, India. This is a major center of pilgrimage for Sikhs worldwide.

Shinto: Beliefs, History and Development

A portable shrine is carried to a waterfall as part of a community festival. At these festivals the symbol of the local kami is removed from its usual place in the inner sanctuary of the shrine and taken on a tour in order to bestow new life on the area.

Shinto—meaning the way of the gods —is the collective term for the oldest religions of pre-Buddhist Japan. The heart of Shinto is worship of *kami*—spirits or deities whose presence is felt everywhere. The kami are of different kinds, ranging from spirits that reside in trees, rocks or even entire mountains through spirits that act as patron deities to particular trade groups such as fishermen or carvers, to the founder deities of families, villages or the nation itself. The rise of Buddhism from the sixth century onward profoundly affected Shinto and forced it to become more self-defining. At times Shinto and Buddhist practices have been almost complementary, while at other times Shinto has competed with Buddhism. Today most Japanese describe themselves as both Buddhist and Shinto, using aspects of each faith to deal with different needs throughout the year and through life.

In 1870, in an attempt to purify Japanese culture, the government banned all temples that adhered to a combination of Shinto and Buddhist deities and traditions. This was the emergence of the concept of State Shinto, with its strong nationalistic and racial overtones. Shinto priests became civil servants and the cult of the emperor was enhanced to form a new focus for national State Shinto. Many Shinto priests, temples and groups opposed this, but State Shinto was made mandatory. The height of State Shinto was the entry of Japan into the Second World War. When Japan was defeated, State Shinto was left officially discredited and was therefore banned by the new constitution.

Today Shinto is more local, nature-based and family or clan-orientated than it was in the days of State Shinto. But it has also responded to the modern world by producing new forms of Shinto, often based around a charismatic medium who channels teachings from the kami. These new forms are gaining in popularity, especially because of their emphasis on the natural world of Japan.

Shinto and the Imperial Family.

The most famous kami site is at Ise. Here, in a site probably two thousand years old, is the shrine of the Sun goddess Amaterasu, who is believed to be the founder of the Japanese imperial family and thus, in effect, the founder of the Japanese. Until the defeat of Japan in 1945, the emperor was held to be divine—a direct descendent of the goddess. Many Shinto followers still believe this to be the case.

Mount Fuji towers above a pilgrims' center in its foothills. Mount Fuji is known and venerated throughout Japan as a home of the gods and of the departed. Mountains are especially important because they are homes of the kami and also of the dead.

Worship, Rituals and Ceremonies

A t its heart Shinto is concerned with continuity and with balance and purity in this life, because of the interaction of the material world and the spiritual world. It is concerned with order and with passing the values and traditions of the past from generation to generation.

A couple are married according to Shinto rites. Many rites of passage and community celebrations in Japanese life are marked by Shinto ceremonies. However, Shinto practice is sometimes understood as a social rather than a personal commitment, a way of maintaining family traditions and affirming links to the community. It is perfectly possible to combine faithful practice of the Shinto traditions with a personal devotion to another religious tradition, such as Buddhism or Christianity.

Shrines

Shinto shrines can be vast complexes such as Ise or tiny shrines perched beside a rock or surrounding a venerable tree. The most common deity worshipped in these shrines is Inari, the kami associated with rice, the protection of the home and various trades. Fox statues and images are often found at Inari shrines because it is believed the fox is a messenger of Inari.

Many Shinto shrines are too small to have their own resident priest. Instead, local people look after them, making food offerings and opening and shutting the shrine doors at daybreak and dusk.

A Shinto priest banging a drum close to the shrine of the kami. The noise of the drum is a way of alerting the kami to the presence of the priest.

Worship at the shrine

Before entering a shrine area, the worshiper or visitor performs a ritual washing. This consists of rinsing the mouth and washing the hands—acts that symbolize both internal and external cleansing. Purity is very important in Shinto, so those who have recently been in contact with blood, such as a menstruating woman or anyone who has just touched a corpse, is forbidden to enter.

Once inside the shrine area, which combines simple temple buildings with landscaping to express the harmony between the human and natural worlds, the worshiper may purchase an amulet for protection, or a prayer board. Many major temples have wooden prayer boards with printed prayers for sale, which, once bought, can be hung near the main shrine. They often carry the animal sign for the year, as it is believed that the spirit of the kamis is recharged or enhanced by the spirit of the animal of the year. The prayer boards are very popular with students, who come to ask for help in the school or college exams that are so crucial to success in Japan.

Upon approaching the shrine itself, the worshiper rings a bell or claps the hands together to alert the kami to his or her presence. Then an offering of money is thrown into a large box in front of the shrine. In a few

shrines, statues of the kami are present, but images are not usually found. The most common representation of the kami in a shrine is a mirror. This relates to the legend that when Sun Goddess Amaterasu departed, she left a mirror behind to represent her presence. In the larger shrines, priests run the liturgical life of the temple and laypeople come primarily for festivals or to make offerings and prayers in times of need.

One ceremony that priests conduct is a further purification ritual, again believed to operate both internally and externally. The worshiper stands before the shrine while the priest, following the reciting of various prayers, passes a purification stick over the head of the penitent. The purpose of this is to draw out all pollution and thus to purify the worshiper. Following this, offerings of twigs from the sacred sakaki tree are made, along with food and drink offerings.

Home altars

Before 1945 many homes used to have a kami altar and a Buddha altar. Today these altars are less common, although some rural households still maintain them.

Offerings are made to domestic kami for the well-being of the family and the productivity of the land. The offerings made at the Buddha altar are for the ancestral spirits and for those who are about to become ancestors.

The torii

Every Shinto shrine has at least one *torii*—the special gateway. Many shrines have hundreds of them, often forming a corridor of scores or more in line.

The torii is believed to have originated in antiquity as a place where the sacred birds of the site sat. The word *torii* means bird. The birds heralded the start of day and thus the start of worship. Today the torii signifies entry into a sacred Shinto place and helps delineate the boundaries between the secular world and the sacred. Toriis are sometimes sited in lakes, and in these cases they are a sign of the sacred nature of the place itself.

FESTIVALS

The main form of Shinto festival is the *matsuri*, when the kami are summoned through dance, music, chants and prayers. Such festivals are often held at the request of a village or an association, and through it the intervention, guidance and blessing of the kami is sought.

The word *matsuri* also describes daily worship and openness to the kami. This covers the activities of the daily visit to the local shrine or the moment of prayer and reflection at the start of the day in the home where the worshiper seeks to be in touch with the forces of the universe as manifest in the kami.

NEW YEAR'S DAY.

One of the biggest matsuri is the festival of New Year's Day. On this day millions pack the great shrines to worship and to seek the blessing of the kami for the new year. It is believed that the coming of the new year revitalizes the kami themselves and thus this is a most auspicious time to seek their blessing. Seeking the kami blessing is a vital activity for millions of families since it is believed this ritual marks an auspicious start to the new year. Each shrine will also have its kami's day—a special day when the kami tours his or her area and is celebrated by a local matsuri.

CHERRY BLOSSOM FESTIVAL.

The most famous Japanese festival is probably the Cherry Blossom Festival of early spring. Celebration of the beauties of cherry blossom trees, especially wild ones, goes back to ancient Japan. There is no specific religious significance to the festival, though many of the best examples of cherry blossoms are found within the confines of Shinto shrines or on Shinto holy mountains. This illustrates the close ties between the beauties of nature and Shinto practice.

Families and friends sharing picnics beneath the cherry blossom trees in Tokyo, Japan

The Tao—the Way of Heaven

aoism emerged around the first century CE and takes its name from the Chinese character for *path* or *way*—*Tao*. The Tao is not a divine force, but simply the natural force that makes the universe act as it does.

Yin and yang

The Tao creates everything—the One—the unity of all existence at the beginning of time. The One creates two forces when it splits: the twin and opposed forces of *yin* and *yang*. Yin is heavy, dark, moist, earthy, lunar and feminine. Yang is airy, light, dry, hot, heavenly, solar and masculine. These two forces are in everything, locked into an eternal struggle in which neither can destroy the other.

Traditional Chinese philosophy holds that these two natural forces create the energy of life through their interaction, but they are not deities, nor do they have divine power. Their interaction is seen in the changing of the seasons or in the health of an individual.

The dynamic tension of the two creates the three: Heaven, Earth and Humanity. Heaven and Earth are the spiritual and the physical worlds, as in the earlier beliefs of shamanism (see page 134). Humanity's role is to help keep the balance between these two worlds, which are also reflections of yin and yang. However, it is believed that wicked human behavior can disturb this relationship. Therefore, part of Taoist ritual is to make offerings and prayers to ask for forgiveness for human wrongdoing that has disturbed the balance of life.

Finally, all life is made possible by *ch'i*, which is the life breath and energy of the universe. Taoists believe that this life breath is in everyone and everything. When people are born, they have within them all the breath that they will ever have. All things die when their original breath expires. Thus Taoism has developed breathing exercises and meditations, designed to help people preserve their ch'i. This is part of the quest for immortality (see page 136).

Gods and goddesses.

The world of nature and the universe is full of deities in Taoism. Until the Communists took power nationwide in 1949, every aspect of life from different illnesses to every individual household had its own deities. Most of this was swept away in Communist attacks on religion. Since increased religious freedom returned in the late 1970s, temples have been rebuilt and the statues of gods remade. In the process, many deities have disappeared from all but a few temples.

Today the most popular deities are those to do with childbirth, wealth and health. However, the Three Pure Ones of Taoism are also to be found again. These Three express the three ideas of the Tao in divine form. The Three Pure Ones represent Pure Tao as the origin of origins, the Tao of the Revealed Scriptures that links Heaven and Earth, and the final Pure One is the human manifestation of the Tao. This is often taken to be the legendary sage Lao Tzu, author of the *Tao Te Ching*, who is also seen as the founder spirit of Taoism as a specific religion.

Pictures of the God of Myriad Blessings are traditionally pasted on the front door of homes at Chinese New Year. He is believed to bring good fortune and prosperity to those who live in or enter the building. Paper posters such as this one are sold at the divination stalls that are often found in the grounds of Taoist temples.

A tripod for holding joss sticks in front of the main temple entrance. When the joss sticks are lit, the rising incense symbolizes prayers that are offered to Heaven. The dragons on either side of the tripod and on the temple roof symbolize strength, energy and the life force.

Taoist Traditions, Beliefs, and Practices

 aoism contains elements of shamanism, the oldest religious tradition in China, which involves belief in the existence of two worlds: this physical one and a spiritual one. Communication with the spiritual world is through shamans, who enter a trancelike state.

Shamanism spread to China from Siberia at some time in remote antiquity—probably over 10,000 years ago. Its concern with communication between the physical and spiritual worlds and its shamans, who could take animal forms, pervade Chinese religion from the earliest written sources to the present day. The oldest surviving Chinese religious text, the *I Ching*, a divination text, was first created by shamans receiving messages from the spirit world that gave answers to questions put by tribal leaders.

The *I Ching* dates from around 1000 BCE. In early Chinese myths, the founder figures of Chinese culture and life are often half human, half animal. The greatest two, Fu Tzu and Nu Kua, had snake forms. Others could transform into bears—the traditional shamanic animal. This is the case with hero deities such as Yu the Great, who for ten years fought to control the Yellow River. Shamans were the ruler-priests of much of China until around 1500 BCE. After that they became the priests of the local kings until the rise of the Confucians in the fourth to the first centuries BCE. The Confucians hated the spontaneous, ecstatic ways of the shamans and forced them out of power.

Much of the spirituality of shamanism lived on at sites such as the great sacred mountains.

The Suspended Temple on Heng Shan, a Taoist sacred mountain in the north of China. There are five major sacred mountains that are still centers of Taoism, and countless smaller ones scattered across China. The sacred mountains are especially associated with sages and those who are believed to have achieved immortality.

Taoism emerged as a distinct religion in the first century CE, offering healing, well-being and ability to communicate with the deities. In many ways it was shamanism reinvented and with a more developed cosmology.

Feng Shui

Feng shui is used to establish or restore the balance of yin and yang in the landscape. This ancient art is also a way of determining the flow of ch'i in and around buildings or over natural features. Feng shui works on the basis that the world is alive with forces that shape the land and all life on it. When people build a house, dig a tomb or make a road, they should be in harmony with the flow of energy around them so that buildings will enhance, rather than dominate, their surroundings.

Ghosts and spirits

The fighting of ghosts and evil spirits is a substantial aspect of Taoism, and its great leaders were all exorcists. The ghost-catching sword of Chang Tao Ling (around the second century CE) was revered for nearly two thousand years until removed by the Communists. His charms are still sold from Taoist temples today.

Divination

Fortune-telling can now be seen again around the temples of China. While fortune-tellers can be found at both Buddhist and Taoist temples, Taoist priests are believed to be the more skilled. The usual method is to use a hundred fortune sticks that the person seeking guidance holds and shakes until one falls out. Each stick is numbered and the number relates to a divination message from a Taoist deity such as the Jade Emperor, ruler of Heaven, or Lao Tzu, the deity who is seen as the founder of Taoism. Fortune-tellers stress that fortune is in the hands of the individual and that actions can change fortune. A fortune-teller gives guidance but does not fix fortunes. Taoists believe that certain things in life, such as family and inherited wealth, are fixed. The rest of life is in the hands of the individual and depends on living in harmony with the flow of the Tao.

THE TAO AND THE TEACHERS

Between the fifth and the third centuries BCE, many schools of philosophy arose in China, and this time is known as the period of the Hundred Schools. Most of the schools were concerned with the meaning and significance of the Tao. The most significant books written during this period were the *Tao Te Ching* of Lao Tzu, the Book of the sage Chuang Tzu and the writings of Kung Fu Tzu (Confucius).

LAO TZU AND CHUANG TZU

The name Lao Tzu means "Old Master," but although he is the most famous Taoist sage, very little is known about him. He probably did not write the *Tao Te Ching*, but various sayings became associated with him. We do know about Chuang Tzu because he recounts many stories about himself in his book.

CONFUCIUS

Kung Fu Tzu is well recorded in history, not least because his followers often opposed Taoism. Confucius lived between 551 and 479 BCE, but was considered a failure during his lifetime. It was only after his death that his disciples slowly gained power as the philosophers and bureaucrats of emerging imperial China. Confucius taught that the Tao was reflected in order and hierachy. If everyone obeyed those in authority above them and ruled justly over those below them, then Heaven and Earth would be in harmony. Confucius stressed that sons should obey fathers, wives obey husbands, the people obey the emperor, the emperor obey Heaven.

Confucianists regarded Taoism as emotional, irrational and magical, while the Taoists regarded Confucian teachings as bureaucratic and imperialistic. It was, however, the rigid hierachical system created by Confucianism that shaped China for over two thousand years.

This statue of Lao Tzu is carved from the stone of the mountain and reflects the harmony of the Tao.

Taoist Rituals—Honoring the Ancestors

The key concerns of Taoism and its associated festivals are reconciling Heaven and Earth, care for the dead, pursuit of immortality and perpetuation of the ancient deities inherited from shamanism. The main Chinese festivals are celebrated by both Taoists and Buddhists.

Immortality

Taoism is unique in world religions in teaching that immortality is achieved through preservation of the human, mortal body. Becoming immortal involves changing the body into an imperishable form. This is believed to be a path that requires years of rigorous training and skilled practice. Some try to accomplish it by eating imperishable items such as gold or jade, others through exercises designed to promote the constant flow of ch'i energy. Still others see meditation as the way to become one with the Tao, the flow of Nature, and thus to ensure that the body never dies. In Taoist belief those honored as immortals may appear to die, but their body then disappears because the immortal has left the place of burial. The most popular figures in Chinese folklore are the Eight Immortals, a company of comic and tragic figures who help the poor and punish the wicked. Their stories are often told at the Festival of Ching Ming, a day when families gather to honor their dead ancestors.

Hungry Ghosts

The Hungry Ghosts are the spirits of the dead who have been buried without proper funeral rites and have no family to honor them. Each year, on the fifteenth day of the seventh month, offerings, prayers and liturgies are given to calm the ghosts and prevent them from causing disasters. Whole communities fund this festival to placate the hungry ghosts and ensure that they are benevolent toward the people.

A Taoist funeral procession passing through the streets on its way to the cemetery. The family and friends of the deceased man are wearing white, which is the traditional color of mourning in China.

CHINESE NEW YEAR.

This is the major festival. It is a time when families reunite and lavish gifts are given to children and young people. Traditionally it is the time when the new paper statues of the kitchen god and protecting charms are put up in the house. It is believed that just before New Year the kitchen god visits Heaven to report on the behavior of the family. Just before his paper statue is burnt to allow him to fly to Heaven, it is customary to smear his lips with honey so he will make a good report to the Jade Emperor, ruler of Heaven. The door gods, two painted warriors who defend the house against evil spirits, are also replaced with new ones and good luck sayings hung over the doorways.

DRAGON BOAT FESTIVAL

This June festival, held on the fifth day of the fifth lunar month, commemorates the watery suicide of an honest official who tried to shock the emperor into being kinder to the poor. The dragon boat races commemorate the people's attempts to rescue his body in the lake from the dragons who rose to eat it. It has grown in popularity in recent years as a celebration of honest government and physical prowess.

HUNGRY GHOSTS FESTIVAL

This is held in the seventh month. According to tradition, it is the time when the gates of the underworld are opened, leaving the Hungry Ghosts free to wander. In addition to offerings and devotions made to pacify these unsettled ghosts, operas and other musical events are sometimes staged to entertain them.

MID-AUTUMN FESTIVAL

The bright harvest moon, which appears on the fifteenth day of the eighth lunar month, is celebrated in the thousands of festival lanterns.

The story behind the festival is of the goddess Sheng O, whose husband, having discovered the pill of immortality, was about to eat it and become a cruel ruler for eternity. But Sheng O swallowed it instead. He sought to kill her, but the gods saved her, transporting her to the Moon, where she lives to this day. Her husband repented of his ways and was taken to be the god of the Sun.

1 **Chinese New Year**
2 **Ching Ming**
3 **Dragon Boat Festival**
4 **Hungry Ghosts Festival**
5 **Mid-autumn Festival**

Ching Ming is the only Chinese festival fixed by a solar date. It falls on either April 4 or April 5 and marks the start of spring. Tombs are cleared, fresh offerings are made and the ancestors are venerated. Many families will try to return to ancestral villages from which their families might have migrated hundreds of years ago, but with which they are still linked through the family dead.

SIKHISM

The Sikh faith began in the Punjab in India in the early sixteenth century. Northern India at that time was ruled by the Muslim Mughal Empire, but the majority of the population was Hindu. It was a time of tension between the two faiths, but also of cross-fertilization.

Guru Nanak, the founder of Sikhism, taught a new faith that was different from both, and which rejected certain religious and social practices of the time. The Punjabi word *Sikh* means "follower" or "disciple." Guru Nanak was succeeded by nine further Gurus, or teachers, before the collection of Sikh writings was instituted in 1708 as the Guru for all time to come. Sikhs revere their scripture, the Guru Granth Sahib, as they would a living teacher.

Sikhs believe in one God, whom they call *Waheguru*, meaning "Great Teacher." They believe that God reveals himself to those who are ready when he chooses, and that he has done so throughout history. As a result the Sikh scriptures contain hymns and prayers from both Hindu and Muslim writers.

Sikhs also lay great emphasis on equality and service to others regardless of status. In many parts of India Sikh temples give food to hundreds of thousands of the poor every day through the free kitchen (*langar*), which is attached to each temple. A Sikh temple is known as a *gurdwara*.

Sikhs are among the most visually distinctive of religious communities for they wear five marks of their faith, as well as a turban, which is the most visible sign of a Sikh man.

Sikh tradition lays great emphasis on the defense of religious freedom and protection of the weak. The swords and turbans are a symbolic reminder of the need to be vigilant in defense of justice.

The Harimandir or "House of God" in Amritsar is more widely known as the Golden Temple. It houses the original copy of the Guru Granth Sahib, the Sikh scripture. A causeway crosses the pool to the temple itself, and pilgrims often bathe in the waters.

Origins, Spread and Development

G uru Nanak, who first taught the Sikh faith, was born to a Hindu family in 1469 at Talwandi in the Punjab area of what is now Pakistan. At his birth it was predicted that he would praise God and would teach many others to praise God.

The disappearance from the riverbank

As a young man working for a local Muslim governor he impressed all who knew him with his wisdom and ability. Throughout this time, Nanak continued to pray and meditate, and he discussed religion with both Hindus and Muslims. He formed a group of friends who met by the side of a river to pray and worship God together. One day Nanak's clothes were found on the riverbank but he could not be found, and it was feared that he had been drowned. After three days Nanak returned, but did not speak for a day. His first words were, "There is neither Hindu nor Muslim, so whose

Sikhs in Delhi with a picture of Guru Nanak fastened to their truck to commemorate his birth.

path shall I follow? I shall follow God's path. God is neither Hindu nor Muslim and the path I follow is God's."

Traveling and teaching

Nanak left his job with the governor and began a life of traveling and teaching. He became known as Guru ("Teacher") Nanak, and taught that external rituals are irrelevant and that God cannot be defined by any religion.

Attracted by his songs and his simple lifestyle, people began to follow Guru Nanak. He spoke out against the Hindu caste system of the time, insisting that all his followers were equal and that all should share whatever work had to be done. He established communities of Sikhs in many parts of India, traveling as far as Sri Lanka in the south, Makkah in Arabia, and Afghanistan to the north.

After Guru Nanak

Toward the end of his life, Guru Nanak established a community of Sikhs at Kartarpur in the Punjab. It was expected that he would appoint a successor from among his sons as future leader of this community. But Guru Nanak underlined again the principles of equality that he had been teaching by choosing as the next

Northern India, showing the extent of the Muslim Mughal Empire in the early years of Sikhism. Muslim forces from Persia had conquered most of northern India by the time of Guru Nanak. His birthplace, Talwandi, is now called Nankana Sahib.

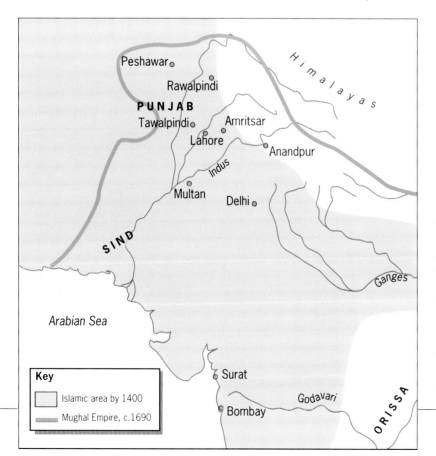

Peshawar
Rawalpindi
PUNJAB
Tawalpindi
Amritsar
Lahore
Anandpur
Himalayas
Indus
Multan
Delhi
SIND
Arabian Sea
Ganges
Surat
Godavari
Bombay
ORISSA

Key
Islamic area by 1400
Mughal Empire, c.1690

leader a man called Lehna who had been particularly devoted to him and willing to perform any task, however humble or unpleasant. Guru Nanak renamed him Angad, meaning "part of me." In all there were nine successors to Guru Nanak, each one indicating his successor (see pages 142-143). Before Guru Gobind Singh, the final human Guru, died in 1708, he declared that the collection of hymns and poems now known as the Guru Granth Sahib should be from that time on the Guru for the Sikhs. Leadership also passed to the Khalsa, the brotherhood of committed Sikhs founded by Guru Gobind Singh (see page 146).

Later development

Throughout the eighteenth century there was continued armed struggle between the Sikhs and the Mughal emperors, until Maharajah Ranjit Singh succeeded in forming an independent Sikh kingdom in the Punjab. This was short-lived, and in 1849 the British annexed the Punjab.

In the face of increased missionary activity from both Christians and Hindus, in 1873 the Singh Saba movement was formed, which campaigned for the revival of Sikhism and its recognition by the British rulers. In 1925 the Sikhs regained control of their gurdwaras and

holy places, which had often passed into Hindu control. When the Indian subcontinent was partitioned in 1947, the western Punjab became Pakistani territory and the eastern Punjab part of India. In the unrest and violence that followed, about 2 million Sikhs left the eastern part, and a similar number of Muslims migrated from the west. Many people were killed or injured, and enmity between Sikhs and Muslims has left a painful legacy.

Musicians (ragis) *playing at a Sikh service. When Guru Nanak was asked a question, he often replied with a poem or a song, which he sang with his friend Mardana. One of the songs describes the change in Nanak's life:*

> *I was like a singer with*
> *no one to sing for,*
> *The Lord gave me a*
> *song to sing.*
> *He said, "Night and*
> *day, sing my praise."*
> *I will sing your song,*
> *O Lord.*
> *I will spread your word.*

Music still plays a major part in Sikh worship.

Dera Sahib Gurdwara, Lahore, Pakistan. A Sikh temple is known as a gurdwara—"the door of the Guru." This style of architecture, with its distinctively shaped domes, is characteristic of gurdwaras in the Punjab area.

Basic Beliefs and the Eleven Gurus

ikhs sum up their basic beliefs in the words of the *Mool Mantra*, the first hymn to be written by Guru Nanak. These words appear at the beginning of every chapter of the Guru Granth Sahib:

> *There is only one God. Truth is his name.*
> *He is the Creator. He is without fear. He is*
> *without hate. He is timeless and without*
> *form. He is beyond death, the enlightened*
> *one. He can be known by the Guru's grace.*

The Guru Granth Sahib enthroned in the House of God (Harimandir Sahib) in Amritsar. Sikhs look to the Guru Ganth Sahib for guidance and inspiration in their lives, just as earlier Sikhs looked to their human Gurus.

God the Guru

When Sikhs speak of "the Guru" they are referring to God, the Great Teacher, whose spirit lived in all the human Gurus. God, the unknowable, becomes the teacher who reveals God to those who are ready. God created everything, so all life is good, but attachment to the material things of life leads to reincarnation and rebirth. After death God judges each soul, and if it is pure enough, it will rest with him instead of being reborn.

THE GURUS

Each of the ten human Gurus contributed in different ways to the development of the Sikh faith and the Sikh community.

1 GURU NANAK
(1469–1539)
First taught the Sikh faith, and wrote many hymns, now collected in the Guru Granth Sahib. Founded the Sikh town of Kartarpur.

2 GURU ANGAD
(1504–1552, became Guru 1539)
The beloved friend of Guru Nanak, known for his devotion and humility. He was originally called Lehna, but renamed by Guru Nanak. He developed the Gurmukhi script in which the Sikh hymns were written down. His hymns are also included in the Guru Granth Sahib.

3 GURU AMAR DAS
(1479–1574, became Guru 1552)
He organized the Sikh community into geographical divisions and introduced the custom of calling Sikhs together at the festivals of Baisakhi and Divali. He developed the custom of the *langar*, or communal meal.

4 GURU RAM DAS
(1534–1581, became Guru 1574)
The son-in-law of Guru Amar Das. He founded the city of Amritsar and had the great religious bathing pool dug there, making Amritsar the focal point of Sikh gatherings. Hundreds of his compositions are included in the Guru Granth Sahib, including the Sikh wedding hymn known as *Lavan*.

5 GURU ARJAN
(1563–1606, became Guru 1581)
Son of Guru Ram Das. Completed the building of the Harimandir Sahib at Amritsar. He collected the hymns of his predecessors into the collection known as the Adi Granth ("first book"), and installed this in the Harimandir Sahib. His relations with the Mughal Empire were cordial during Emperor Akbar's time, but when Akbar died in 1605, his successor Jehangir suspected Guru Arjan of supporting his rival. Guru Arjan was tortured and killed. He is honored as the first Sikh martyr.

The Three Golden Rules

Sikhs emphasize three aspects of daily life: Nam Jap – remembrance of and devotion to God, Vandh Cahak – earning an honest living, and Kirt Karan – charity and service to others. The concepts of service and equality go hand in hand. All men and women are equal and none should consider any jobs beneath them.

6 GURU HARGOBIND
(1595-1644, became Guru 1606)
Son of Guru Arjan. Although he was imprisoned for a short while, he had generally good relations with Emperor Jehangir, for which some people criticized him. He built gurdwaras and repaired others at places associated with earlier Gurus, and developed government based on Sikh teachings.

7 GURU HAR RAI
(1630-1661, became Guru 1644)
Grandson of Guru Hargobind. He had a reputation for his knowledge of medicines, and supplied a remedy for an illness of the son of Emperor Shah Jehan. He opened hospitals where treatment was given free.

8 GURU HAR KRISHAN
(1656-1664, became Guru 1661)
Younger son of Guru Har Rai, he is known as "the boy Guru," as he was only five when he became Guru. He was viewed with suspicion by Emperor Aurangzab, who kept his younger brother at the court in an effort to sow dissension among Sikhs. He was summoned to Delhi and kept under house arrest, during which he contracted smallpox after caring for its victims and died aged only eight.

9 GURU TEGH BAHADUR
(1621-1675, became Guru 1664)
Second son of Guru Hargobind, he became Guru only after the deaths of his nephew and great-nephew. His given name was Tyag Mal, but before he became Guru he was given the name Degh Bahadur ("brave cooking pot") because of his devotion to feeding the hungry. After he became Guru, his resistance to Emperor Aurangzeb's attempt to impose Islam on all his subjects earned him the name Tegh Bahadur ("brave sword"). He wrote many hymns now in the Guru Granth Sahib. He was executed after refusing to accept Islam.

10 GURU GOBIND SINGH
(1666-1708, became Guru 1675)
Son of Guru Tegh Bahadur, he was originally named Gobind Rai, but took the name Singh, along with all other Sikhs, when he founded the Khalsa. He was a soldier who sanctioned the use of military force in defense of justice. He wrote many hymns that were collected after his death into the Dasam Granth. His children were martyred by the emperor. He was killed by an assassin.

11 THE GURU GRANTH SAHIB
Guru Nanak's followers wrote down his hymns, and several later Gurus also wrote hymns of great beauty. These were collected by Guru Arjan, who added hymns and poems written by devout Muslims and Hindus. This collection was known as the Adi Granth, or "first book." Guru Gobind Singh declared that this collection should be the Guru for all time. The Guru Granth Sahib is written in Gurmukhi (the written form of Punjabi). In the nineteenth century the writing was standardized, so now every copy has exactly the same number of pages. The book is treated as one would treat a highly honored human Guru. It always has its own room, and whenever it is moved it is attended by five Sikhs, who represent the Panj Pyares ("five beloved"), the five men who came forward to start the Khalsa.

Guru Nanak is shown in the center, with his friends Bhai Bala and Mardana the musician. Sikhs regard the other nine Gurus as embodying the same spirit and teaching the same message.

143

Worship and Life around the Gurdwara

The word *gurdwara* means "the door of the Guru," and it is the center of Sikh worship because it is the home of the Guru Granth Sahib. Services may take place at any time, the gurdwara is open to all and there is no special day of worship.

Sikh services

The Guru Granth Sahib is at the center of all services. Many of its hymns are set to music and sung by the congregation or by a group of musicians, since music forms an important part of Sikh worship. The Guru Granth Sahib is read by the *Granthi* (who is a reader, not a priest) and interpretations are often given by the Granthi, but any member of the congregation, male or female, may speak..

At the end of a service, everyone stands for the final prayer (*ardas*) and a sweet food, *Karah Parshad*, is served. In India, those visiting a gurdwara purchase Karah Parshad that is donated to the gurdwara. Everyone then receives the food, whether they have donated or not. During the service, people come and go informally, and children are allowed to move about, but the atmosphere in the prayer room remains reverent and peaceful.

After every major Sikh service, a meal, called the *langar*, is served to anyone who wishes to take part. In Delhi, for example, 30,000 people eat in just one of the major langars every day, and 100,000 on Sunday, the most popular day for worship. The food is vegetarian in order not to conflict with any religious food rules.

In accordance with the Sikh principles of equality and service, men and women share the task of preparing and serving the meal.

In the worship room of the gurdwara the Guru Granth Sahib is enthroned on a quilt and three cushions known as the *Manji Sahib*, and covered with an embroidered cloth called a *rumala*. In a hot region like the Punjab, a disciple will stand near a Guru, waving insects away. Whenever the Guru Granth Sahib is open, Sikhs take it in turns to wave the special implement called the *chauri* over it. This is made of long hairs embedded in a handle, and recalls the personal care of a living Guru in a hot climate. As worshipers enter, they kneel or bow before the Guru Granth Sahib and bring offerings of food or money, which contribute toward the langar or to welfare work.

All members of the Sikh community take a turn at preparing food for the langar, the free meal served after every service.

SIKH HOLY PLACES AND PILGRIMAGE

Sikh places of pilgrimage tend to be associated with bathing places; Guru Amar Das instituted a bathing well at Goindwal and Guru Ram Das a bathing pool at Amritsar. The Sikh scriptures are nevertheless quite clear that bathing in such places does not purify or lead to salvation: "True pilgrimage is contemplation on God" (Guru Granth Sahib 687). Bathing and pilgrimage are therefore seen as a discipline that enables the mind to concentrate on God.

Guru Ram Das also began building the holy city of Amritsar, in the Punjab. Here the House of God (Harimandir Sahib) houses the first copy of the Guru Granth Sahib. The city is the spiritual center of Sikhism.

Anandpur is a popular destination, and in the gurdwara there, the sword that Guru Gobind Singh used when he founded the Khalsa can be seen, along with other great weapons of the Gurus and of Sikh history.

Other major pilgrim sites include places of martyrdom, such as the remains of the brick wall at Sarhind in which the two youngest sons of Guru Gobind Singh were immured and killed.

PRAYER

Because of the need for the Guru Granth Sahib to have its own room, just as a living Guru would, few Sikhs have their own copies of the Guru Granth Sahib. However, many Sikhs have a copy of certain excerpts, known as the *Gutkha*, and set prayers from it are said every morning and evening. There are 39 'steps' in the morning prayer which are obligatory to members of the Khalsa, but many families recite just the first five.

THE GURDWARA

The gurdwara is the center of activity for the Sikh community, and there may be classes held in reading Gurmukhi, in Sikh music, and in various physical activities, since Sikhs are expected to be strong and active enough to defend their faith and protect the weak. Bookshops and facilities for travelers are also provided at major sites

MUSICIANS
Music is an important part of Sikh worship. Each hymn in the Guru Granth Sahib has its own traditional tune.

KARAH PARSHAD
The last ceremony in a Sikh service is the distribution of Karah Parshad, a sweet paste that has been mixed using a kirpan while the prayer Ardas is said. Everyone receives a small portion as a symbol of their equality.

At night five Sikhs carry the Guru Granth Sahib to a separate room.

GURU GRANTH SAHIB
Everyone removes their shoes, covers their head and washes their hands before coming into the presence of the Guru Granth Sahib.

FLAG
The Sikh flag always flies outside the gurdwara. Once a year, at the festival of Baisakhi (see page 147), the flag is lowered and a new one raised. The symbol consists of two swords, symbolizing a Sikh's duty to teach truth and defend right, a circle, symbolizing that God is one, and a *khanda*, the double-edged sword used to prepare amrit.

Sikhs at prayer in the gurdwara. Although people come and go during the service, the atmosphere is peaceful and meditative. The music of the hymns calms the mind and aids prayer.

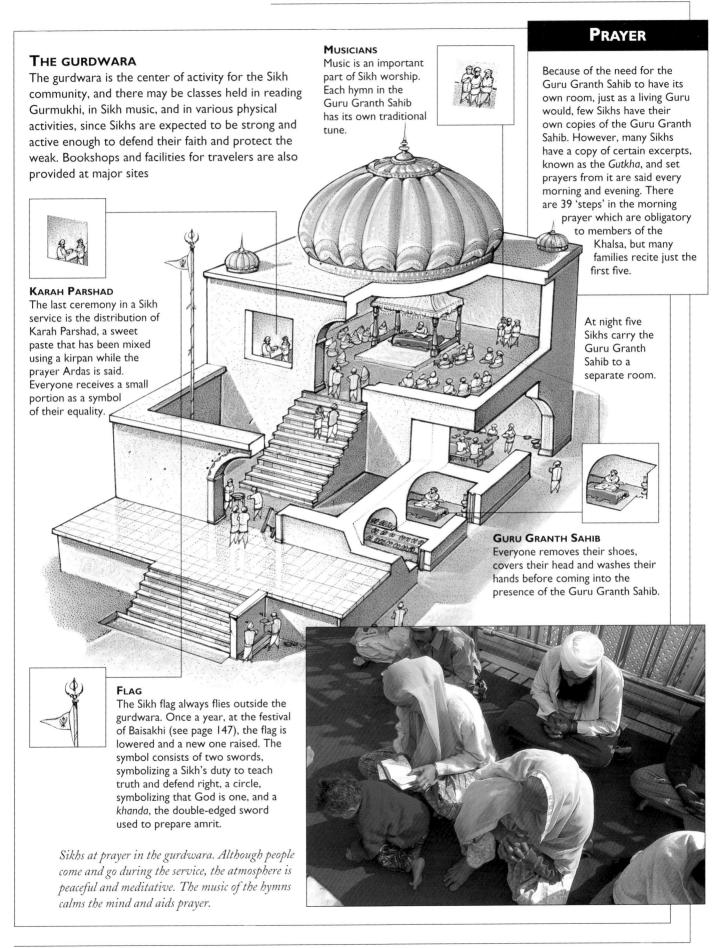

The Khalsa and the Five K's

THE FIVE K'S
Sikh men all wear five signs of
their faith. Each of these begins
with the letter K in Punjabi, so
they are known as "the five K's":

Kesh: uncut hair. Devout Sikhs
do not cut their hair or beard at
any time.

Kanga: a comb to keep the hair
in place.

Kara: a steel bangle, a complete
circle symbolizing one God and
one truth without beginning or
end. The steel symbolizes
strength.

Kirpan: a small sword or dagger
reminding the Sikh of the need
to fight against oppression in
any form.

Kacchera: short trousers or
breeches, dating from a time
when men usually wore robes.
The breeches signify readiness
to ride into battle.

The Khalsa was founded by Guru Gobind Singh to be a community of those who undertake to uphold the Sikh religion and values and to defend all those in need, regardless of religion or caste.

In 1699 the persecution that Sikhs had suffered for many years in the Punjab reached new levels. Guru Gobind Singh, the last human Guru, gathered the Sikhs at Anandpur to celebrate their harvest festival. At this gathering he called for a man who was willing to die for his faith. One man stepped forward and went into a tent with the Guru. Then the Guru reappeared with his sword covered in blood and asked for another volunteer. Another man came forward and, again, the Guru came out of the tent with a bloody sword, and asked for another volunteer. In all, five men came forward, and as far as the crowd could tell, met their deaths in the tent. Then the Guru opened the tent and revealed the five men alive.

This was the beginning of the Khalsa, the community of committed Sikhs who are willing to give their lives to uphold their faith and defend the weak.

At the same time, Guru Gobind Singh gave all Sikhs the name *Singh* ("lion") for men and *Kaur* ("princess") for women, to abolish all traces of the caste system.

Initiation into the Khalsa

Joining the Khalsa is a major step, and many Sikhs wait until quite late in life, when they feel they are ready. However, it is quite common for boys between the ages of fourteen and sixteen to enter formally into the Khalsa. Women may also join the Khalsa, but this is less common. Any candidate has to be accepted first by the other members of the Khalsa in the area.

The entry ritual is a private one, undertaken in the gurdwara with perhaps the close family attending. The initiation ceremony is called *amrit sanskar* or *pahul* and is often performed at the festival of Baisakhi because this is when the Khalsa was formed. Five members of the Khalsa must be present and they each hand the new member one of the five K's. The candidate vows to defend the faith, to serve others, to refrain from alcohol, tobacco and other drugs and to pray regularly, morning and evening. He is given *amrit* (sugar crystals and water) to drink and then says: "The Khalsa is of God and the victory is to God." The amrit is then sprinkled on his hair and eyes and this process is repeated five times. The Mool Mantra is recited and the Ardas prayer chanted. As usual the ceremony ends with the sharing of Karah Parshad. The five K's signify that the wearer is a full member of the Khalsa.

Nearly all Sikhs also wear a turban. This is not one of the five K's, but is worn to keep the hair tidy, and to resemble Guru Gobind Singh as closely as possible, and as a visible sign of commitment to their faith.

Sikhs wearing the 5 K's preparing for the initiation ceremony. For this ceremony, and whenever the Guru Granth Sahib is moved, there must be five Khalsa Sikhs present, representing the Panj Pyares—the "five beloved," the first five volunteers to the Khalsa.

FESTIVALS

Sikh festivals are often celebrated at the same time as Hindu festivals but reflect a very different attitude. They are times for quiet meditation on the Guru Granth Sahib but also times of great activity. Athletic activities, horseriding displays, mock battles, fireworks and vast langars are aspects of Sikh festivals. The major gurdwaras are lit with thousands of electric bulbs, and huge processions wind through the streets of the major cities in India. In Delhi, on Guru Nanak's birthday, Sikhs decorate up to ten miles of roadways and the procession may be two or even three miles long.

All Sikh festivals are preceded by a full reading of the Guru Granth Sahib, taking about 48 hours. Others come to hear part of the reading, called the *Akand Path*.

BAISAKHI

(13th April) The festival of Baisakhi, originally a harvest festival, is fixed by a solar calendar and very occasionally it is on 14th April. It commemorates the founding of the Khalsa, and is the usual time when Sikhs join the Khalsa. The flag that flies outside every gurdwara is taken down at this time, the flagpole washed and new coverings put on with prayers.

MARTYRDOM OF GURU ARJAN DEV

(4th Jaistha) A time of both sorrow and celebration. The usual events of reading the Guru Granth Sahib and of processions take place, but with a special emphasis on remembering those who suffered for the faith.

Sikhs in the Punjab celebrate Hola Mohalla.

DIVALI

(Four-day festival, ends on 2nd day of Kartik) Again, this falls at the same time as the Hindu festival (see page 101). Sikhs light lamps in their homes to celebrate the release from prison of Guru Hargobind, who had been imprisoned by the Emperor Jehangir, along with fifty-two Hindu princes. The emperor offered to release Guru Hargobind, but he refused to leave prison until the princes were also released. At Divali the Harimandir Sahib in Amritsar is illuminated, and there are firework displays and grand processions.

GURU NANAK'S BIRTHDAY

(Full moon day of Kartik) Stories of Guru Nanak are told and his hymns are sung in the gurdwara. In many parts of India processions are held through the streets, which are decorated for this occasion.

HOLA MOHALLA

(Full moon day of Phalgun) This falls at the same time as the Hindu festival of Holi (see page 100), but whereas Hindus celebrate with games and pranks, Sikhs have contests of athletics, horsemanship and martial arts. The greatest of these are held at Anandpur, site of the foundation of the Khalsa.

1 **Baisakhi**
2 **Martyrdom of Guru Arjan Dev**
3 **Divali**
4 **Guru Nanak's Birthday**
5 **Hola Mohalla**

Being a Sikh: Sikhism Today

Sikhs today continue to live the values espoused by the Gurus and set forth as the guiding principles of the Khalsa. In particular the notion of service is held in high esteem. Throughout India and worldwide, Sikh langars feed many of the poor and defenseless. Through hospitals and other such institutions, Sikhs help those in need. Sikhs also value education very highly and Sikh educational institutions offer both practical and theoretical training in many subjects. All this is underpinned by devotional life both at home and at the gurdwara.

Women at the House of God in Amritsar, which continues to be an important center of Sikhism today. One of the five Jathedars or spiritual leaders of Sikhism is based here and is the first among equals in power and authority. Amritsar is also the headquarters of the new Sikh World Council that works to unite Sikhs worldwide in service, study and understanding of Sikhism.

A class of Sikh children learns about Guru Nanak. Education is an important part of Sikh life, and as well as learning to read the Guru Granth Sahib, children learn to accompany the hymns with traditional music.

Service

Service to the community and menial work undertaken for the sake of others is an important part of Sikh teaching. Sikhs take it in turns to do practical work in the gurdwara and also run welfare clubs for the benefit of the whole community, not just Sikhs.

Diet

Many Sikhs are vegetarian, and while Sikhs may eat meat, they will not eat any slaughtered according to the rules of Islam or Judaism. They see those methods of killing as unnecessarily cruel. Furthermore, animals should not be killed wantonly, but only out of need. To respect Hindu views, beef is rarely if at all eaten. The Sikh faith discourages the use of any drugs (except medicinally), including tobacco and alcohol. Members of the Khalsa are expected to refrain from these altogether.

Sikhism today

In 1993 India had approximately 13 million Sikhs—1.9 percent of the population. Small communities of Sikhs also exist in the United Kingdom, Canada, the United States, Malaysia and East Africa.

Since the Partition of India in 1947, Sikh leaders have been conducting a campaign to obtain equal recognition and rights promised in pre-Independence negotiations. In the early 1980's what many regarded as a suppression of Sikh culture, identity and economic opportu-

RITES OF PASSAGE

A couple kneel in front of the Guru Granth Sahib at a Sikh wedding.

nity led to some Sikhs, including members of the leading Sikh party, the Akali Dal, to call for the establishment of an independent nation (Khalistan). Political tensions rose resulting in widespread clashes in the Punjab between Hindus and Sikhs. In 1983 the central government of India took control of the Punjab and by April 1984, 50,000 troops occupied the Punjab and the neighbouring state of Haryana. In June 1984, Indian troops attacked the House of God at Amritsar. The shrine was damaged and the Sikh militants quashed but many pilgrims were caught up in the three day cross-fire. The attack angered many Sikhs and was believed to have led to the assassination of Indian Prime Minister Indira Gandhi by Sikh members of her bodyguard later that year.

This in turn led to terrible riots throughout India, directed against Sikhs. Many were killed and their homes and businesses burnt. Since that time the situation has calmed but the undercurrent of resentment is still an issue within the global Sikh community that continues to feel under-represented as a minority community within India.

Another focus of concern for today's Sikhs, especially for the diaspora Sikh community, is the question of how to maintain and redefine their identity and values in an increasingly westernized global community.

To celebrate rites of passage, the entire Guru Granth Sahib is often read aloud, taking two or three days, and families give food for the langar or gifts of money to charity.

BIRTH AND NAMING

When a baby is born, the words of the Mool Mantra may be whispered in its ear, and a drop of honey placed on its tongue to symbolize good and pure words. Later on the baby is taken to the gurdwara for the first time, when the name is given. Hymns are sung expressing gratitude for the birth of a baby. When the random reading is taken for the day, the family chooses a name for their child that begins with the first letter of the reading.

MARRIAGE

The family assists in choosing a partner. Great care is taken and no one is made to marry against his or her will. During the ceremony, which follows the usual form of service, the couple are given advice on marriage and a hymn, the *Lavan*, is sung. After each verse the couple walk around the Guru Granth Sahib, with their families in attendance to show support for the couple.

INITIATION

See page 146 for a description of the initiation into the Khalsa.

DEATH

Sikhs believe in a cycle of reincarnation so they teach that it is wrong to mourn excessively for someone who has died, since they live on in another body. Family and friends may read hymns from the Guru Granth Sahib. After death, the body is washed and dressed in the five K's if the person was a member of the Khalsa. Then the body is cremated—in India on a funeral pyre, elsewhere usually at a crematorium. A prayer for the peace of the soul is said, followed by the evening or bedtime prayer. The ashes, and the Kirpan and Kara, which are made of metal and will not burn, are scattered on running water—a stream or a river. There is a service at the gurdwara and a meal is served in the langar. It is customary for the family to give gifts to charity.

Development of the Baha'i Faith

The Baha'i faith originated in the mid-nineteenth century in the region of present-day Iran. It is based on the belief that the man born as Mirza Husayn Ali in 1817 was the prophet sent by God to the present age. He is now known as Baha'u'llah—"the Glory of God."

In 1844 a young Shi'a Muslim, Siyyid Ali-Muhammad, announced that he was a Bab—according to Shi'a tradition a "gate" through whom God communicates with humanity. This brought fierce opposition, though he gained many followers, known as Babis, who believed a new era of revelation was occurring.

The shrine of Baha'u'llah in Haifa. In 1877 Baha'u'llah selected sites for the shrine of the Bab and for the Baha'i center, both on the side of Mount Carmel. The Baha'is' international headquarters are now in Haifa, Israel, on the side of Mount Carmel.

The Bab was executed in 1850 and terrible persecution of his disciples followed. Before he died, the Bab predicted that a new prophet would arise: "He Whom God Will Make Manifest." Baha'is believe that this new prophet is Baha'u'llah.

Baha'u'llah was born into a wealthy Persian Muslim family. A prominent follower of the Bab, he was arrested after the Bab's execution and thrown into jail. Here he had a mystical experience revealing him as He Whom God Will Make Manifest. On his release from prison in 1853 he was exiled to the neighboring Ottoman Empire, and here a group of Babis gathered around him. He had told no one of his belief that he was the new prophet, and not all Babis accepted his claims to be the successor to the Bab, so he withdrew for two years into solitary retreat.

In 1863 Baha'u'llah eventually declared to his closest followers that he was the new prophet. The Ottoman rulers, unsure of how to treat him, kept him under house arrest until 1868, when he and his family were exiled to the remote and bleak city of Acre, in present-day Israel. From here the Baha'i faith began to spread. Baha'u'llah was a prolific writer and his writings are regarded as revelation from God.

Baha'u'llah died in 1892, having appointed his son, Abdul Baha, as the only authority capable of interpreting his revelations. During Abdul Baha's time the Baha'is became an international faith.

LITERATURE AND LEADERSHIP
The writings of Abdul Baha, who died in 1921, are also considered revelation, and together with those of Baha'u'llah, form the main body of Baha'i sacred literature. At the time of Abdul Baha's death there were perhaps 100,000 Baha'is in Persia, with small groups scattered around the world. Today there are about 5 million. Leadership of the faith passed to Abdul Baha's grandson, Shoghi Effendi, who established a democratic structure that took over when he died in 1957. His interpretation and translation into English of the Baha'i sacred texts is considered definitive.

The shrine of the Bab on Mount Carmel, Israel.

Basic Beliefs, Calendar and Festivals

The Baha'is believe that God has, at different times, revealed himself through different prophets. Thus they see the texts revealed through Krishna, Moses, Buddha, Christ or Muhammad as being revelations that were all appropriate for their time but superseded by the next revelation.

Sacred texts

Baha'is believe that the written revelations of Baha'u'llah and Abdul Baha are the sacred texts for this era and supersede but do not contradict the earlier revelations of the Torah, the New Testament or the Qur'an. New revelations are necessary because humanity is becoming more mature and responsible. What was appropriate

A banner made by the Baha'i community in Benin, Africa. The words of the banner are taken from a saying of Baha'u'llah: "You are the fruits of the same tree."

for the people to whom Krishna, Buddha or Moses spoke was no longer appropriate to the more advanced people taught by Jesus and Muhammad. Baha'is believe that we now stand on the threshold of becoming adult in our behavior, and thus capable of forming one world rather than diverse nations, races and religions. The belief in the progressive development of humanity is central to Baha'i social and religious vision.

> *The Baha'i faith upholds the unity of God, recognises the unity of His prophets, and inculcates the principle of the oneness and wholeness of the entire human race.*
> Shoghi Effendi, *Guidance for Today and Tomorrow*, 3-4

This view is rooted in Islam, but the claim that the Baha'i sacred texts are the successor to the Qur'an has led to terrible persecutions of Baha'is in many Muslim lands. In Iran, the homeland of the Baha'i faith, Baha'is have been heavily persecuted and restricted, and while a considerable proportion of Baha'is is Persian, the majority today are not from Persia.

Baha'is believe in One God, creator of all, and thus follow the Abrahamic faiths. They also share the Abrahamic view that humanity is a distinct and special creation of God. They

believe that humanity is essentially good and that if we follow the true teachings of the prophets down through history we will be able to live good lives. As Baha'u'llah put it in his work *Gleanings*:

> Having created the world and all that liveth and moveth therein, He [God] through the direct operation of His unconstrained and sovereign Will, chose to confer upon man the unique distinction and capacity to know Him and to love Him – a capacity that must needs be regarded as the generating impulse and the primary purpose underlying the whole of creation.

Baha'is also stress the oneness of humanity, seeing the divisions between nations, races and religions as flaws that will disappear under the new dispensation of the Baha'i faith.

Baha'is place a strong emphasis on social concern and the need to create one world, under one government and one religion—the Baha'i faith. They are thus enthusiastic supporters of bodies such as the United Nations. Shoghi Effendi summed up the Baha'i outlook:

> ...the object of life to a Baha'i is to promote the oneness of mankind. The whole object of our lives is bound up with the lives of all human beings; not a personal salvation we are seeking but a universal one....Our aim is to produce a world civilization which will in turn react on the character of the individual.

Baha'i institutions

The Baha'i faith has established a world center at its international headquarters in Haifa, Israel, including an International House of Justice. This is in preparation for the time that they believe will come, when there will be one world government, guided by the Baha'i faith. The structure of Baha'i assemblies worldwide is democratic and participatory, reflecting the principles they wish to see universally adopted. Baha'is take great pride in the consultative style of their operations and in the equality given to all, regardless of class, race, gender or age, a tradition that goes back to the earliest days of the Babi movement.

PRAYER AND WORSHIP

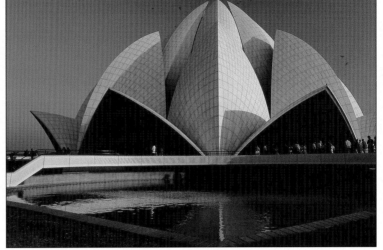

The Baha'i House of Worship, Delhi.

I bear witness, O my God, that Thou hast created me to know Thee and to worship Thee. I testify, at this moment, to my powerlessness and to Thy might, to my poverty and to Thy wealth. There is none other God but Thee, the Help in Peril, the Self-Subsisting. (A Baha'i daily prayer)

HOUSES OF WORSHIP

Baha'is worship daily, following a set series of prayers, and pray in the direction of Acre and Haifa. Private prayer is also very much encouraged and there are many collections of prayers given by Baha'u'llah and Abdul Baha. Three prayers were chosen as obligatory, and Baha'is always say at least one of these each day. The Baha'is have started to build great centers for collective prayer by people of all faiths. These houses of worship (*Mashriqul Adhkar*) have been placed in all the main continents as symbols of the spread of the faith. They have nine entrances, symbolizing the nine major faiths that Baha'is believe have been revealed through humanity's history. Baha'is see these houses of worship as precursors of such houses throughout the world, where the faithful will gather when the Baha'i faith has become the majority faith worldwide.

RULES OF LIFE

Baha'is have a strict code of conduct based upon the Kitab I Aqdas, or "Book of Laws," given by Baha'u'llah. Daily prayer is mandatory as is the fasting month of Ala (March 2-21st). This precedes New Year (*Naw Ruz*), which is a major festival. Narcotic or hallucinogenic drugs and drinking alcohol are strictly forbidden as is pre-marital sex and adultery. The smoking of tobacco is not forbidden but is strongly discouraged. Baha'u'llah also forbade gossip and backbiting among other patterns for good behavior. Marriage is very highly valued. Partners are free to choose each other but must then receive the permission of both sets of parents. Baha'is may vote but not take any active part in party politics. The vision of one world is seen to be of greater importance than the temporary state of national and even regional politics.

Faith in the Future

In each chapter of the book we have mentioned significant developments in recent years within each faith. Here we look at the wider trends that can be seen affecting the faiths across the world.

The last hundred years has perhaps witnessed the most concentrated assault ever on religious faith and practice. Persecution by ideologies such as Communism and Fascism, opposition from nationalism and imperialism and then the deliberate attempts to destroy certain faiths, for example Judaism under the Nazis, made it hard to hear the voice of faith in the late 20th century. But the years around the turn of the millennium have seen dramatic changes. From the Buddhists of Asia, through the Muslims of Central Asia to the Christians and Jews of Russia and Europe and on to indigenous faiths in South Africa and Mozambique, followers who had been oppressed have now found themselves free once again. With freedom comes responsibility and this shapes much of the development of religion around the world today.

The reconstruction of faith following traumas such as mass persecution, or sometimes as a response to changing cultural and political patterns, means that faiths do rethink their priorities. For example, the Heavenly Courts and Rulers that were a feature of Daoism are no longer prominent in the Taoist tradition just as the Earthly Imperial Court of China no longer exists. Or in countries that are becoming increasingly pluralist, such as the United Kingdom, Christianity does not see itself as the defining faith, but one of many that create a society of diversity. Now the faiths are being welcomed by seemingly unlikely partners such as the World Bank and the business community. The culture of pluralism is generally seen as the way forward, with an acceptance now by secular powers that religions have a right to be part of the pluralism of civil society and to have a voice on issues of the day. These issues range from HIV/AIDS to homosexuality, to development issues and economic models. And worldwide the faiths are recognized as playing a unique role in tackling the pressing issues which cause poverty and alienation in the world.

The principle of a secular state as the highest good is also being challenged in countries as diverse as India and France by increasing self-confidence amongst faith communities in the political arena. In many of the areas previously dominated by political ideologies, the traditional faith of the area is reasserting itself, often in conflict with secular powers, as is happening in much of Central Asia, or in competition with other faiths, as is the case in Russia. As the remaining Communist countries change, this struggle will become more important and already in China there are signs of a religiously based split emerging between the Muslim West and the Daoist/Buddhist East.

The greatest change since our first edition is the rise of a serious confrontation between, in particular, the United States and the militant face of Islam. Because Islam sees religion and daily life as one and the same thing, to many in the Islamic world, the West is Christianity and thus any action by 'The West' – be that the United States or Europe or both – can be interpreted as a Christian action against Islam. These tensions, fueled by terrorist attacks such as the attack on the World Trade Center in 2001 by extremists in the name of Islam and, to many in the Islamic world, similar aggressive acts of armies from the West in invading Afghanistan and Iraq, will shape the religious and secular world in years to come.

Representatives of nine major faiths at the International Summit on Religions and Conservation held at Windsor Castle in England in 1995.

Glossary of Religious Terms

Since many terms are specific to one particular religion, those in this glossary are identified according to the following key: [B] = Buddhist; [C] = Christian; [H] = Hindu; [I] = Islamic; [Ja] = Jain; [Ju] = Judaic; [S] = Sikh; [gen] = general religious vocabulary

absolution [C] a declaration of God's forgiveness given after confession.

ahimsa [H, Ja] the principle of non-violence.

Allah [I] the Arabic word for God.

amulet [gen.] a physical sign of spiritual protection, such as a symbol or passage of scripture enclosed in a pouch and worn around the neck or wrist.

Apocalypse [C] the end of time; more specifically, the account of the end of time given in the Revelation of St. John in the New Testament.

ark [Ju] in a synagogue, the cupboard or curtained alcove where the Torah scrolls are kept. In biblical times, the stone tablets of the Law were carried in a special ark or chest with carrying poles.

ascension [C] Jesus' return to heaven forty days after his resurrection.

atman [H] the personal, individual spirit or soul.

avatar [H] one of the incarnations of a god, especially Vishnu.

bar mitzvah [Ju] "Son of the Commandment"; a boy becomes an adult in religious terms on his thirteenth birthday, and this is celebrated by family and friends.

Beatitude [C] "Blessing"; Jesus' account of the people who can be considered blessed or happy.

bhakti [H] loving devotion to a particular deity.

bimah [Ju] a raised platform in the synagogue where the Torah is read.

bodhisattva [B] one who has achieved enlightenment but delays his or her final rebirth in order to help others to enlightenment.

Brahmin [H] a member of the highest caste, often a priest or teacher.

brahman [H] the energy that sustains the universe, the world soul.

caliph [I] "deputy"; one of the leaders of Islam who succeeded Muhammad.

canon [gen.] a collection of texts that has been agreed upon as forming the authentic scriptures.

caste [H] the ancient system of groups with a specific role and position in society.

demon [gen.] slightly different meanings in different cultures; generally, a spiritual being with evil or mischievous intentions.

denomination [C] a division of Christianity.

dhamma *see* dharma.

dharma [B, H] the natural, unchanging laws that sustain the universe; in Hinduism, law or social duty; in Buddhism, the teaching and the true path.

divination [gen.] the art of finding out what is hidden, such as the future or someone's character.

ecumenical [C] a modern movement that promotes collaboration between churches and denominations or tries to reunite them.

enlightenment [B] the state of being aware of, or awakened to, the true nature of existence and the realization of the way to end suffering.

Epiphany [C] "Manifestation"; refers particularly to the visit of the wise men to the baby Jesus, and also to his baptism as an adult.

Exodus [Ju, C] the release of the Hebrew people from captivity in Egypt and their journey to the Promised Land, as described in the Bible, the book of Exodus.

exorcism [gen.] the casting out or laying to rest of ghosts or evil spirits.

Gospel [C] one of the four accounts of the life of Jesus in the New Testament.

Guru [B, H, S] a religious teacher.

Hadith [I] the words of the Prophet Muhammad, carefully recorded and used as a guide to Muslim life.

hajj [I] pilgrimage to Makkah.

Harimandir [S] Also known as the Golden Temple at Amritsar.

Hijrah [I] the migration of Muslims from Makkah to found the first Islamic state in Medina in CE 622.

Holy Week [C] the week leading up to Easter Sunday.

imam [I] the leader and teacher of a Muslim community.

incarnation [C, H, B, Ja, S] taking on a body of flesh; used in Christianity to refer to the earthly life of God as Jesus, in Hinduism to refer either to the earthly lives of Vishnu; or, in several faiths, one of the many lives of an individual.

jihad [I] "struggle"—the struggle to live in submission to God's laws, and to defend the faith in the world.

Ka'ba [I] the House of God in Makkah, a cube-shaped structure, the center of Muslim prayer.

kamma *see* karma.

karma [B, H, Ja] the accumulated effects of actions in this and previous lives; the law of cause and effect.

kashrut [Ju] Jewish food laws.

kosher [Ju] food sanctioned by Jewish law.

lama [B] in Tibetan Buddhism, a religious teacher.

layman/laywoman [gen.] a believer who has not been ordained as a monk, nun or priest, an ordinary member of a religious community.

Lent [C] forty days (not counting Sundays) of fasting and repentance before Easter.

Mahayana [B] "Great Vehicle," the northern and eastern form of Buddhism.

mantra [B, H, Ja] words that are repeated as worship or meditation.

menorah [Ju] a lampstand or candelabrum. The traditional symbol of Judaism is a seven-branched menorah recalling the one in the Temple. At the festival of Hanukah a nine-branched menorah is lit.

Messiah [Ju, C] a Hebrew word meaning "anointed." God's chosen one, predicted by the prophets in the Hebrew Bible. Christians believe that Jesus was the promised Messiah; Jews still look forward to the Messiah's coming.

mezuzah [Ju] a box containing the Shema, fastened on the doorpost as a reminder of God's presence and laws.

mihrab [I] a niche in the wall of a mosque or other building, indicating the direction of Makkah.

minbar [I] a small set of steps in a mosque, from which a sermon is preached.

ministry [gen.] a religious task or calling.

minyan [Ju] the minimum number necessary for congregational prayer: ten adult Jewish men.

Mishnah [Ju] a second-century CE compilation of judgments and discussions by rabbis to help interpret the Torah.

moksha [H, Ja] release from the cycle of rebirth.

muezzin [I] one who makes the call to prayer five times a day from the mosque.

nibbana *see* nirvana.

nirvana [B] the final release from rebirth, disease, desires, suffering, and death; a state of supreme happiness.

pantheon [gen.] several gods within one faith or belief system.

prophet [Ju, C, I] a man or woman who acts as a messenger from God, either in words or actions.

Protestant [C] the Christian denominations that split from the Roman Catholic church during the Reformation in the sixteenth century.

puja [B, H, Ja] the act of worship or devotion.

Qur'an [I] the Muslim holy book, containing the revelations given to the Prophet Muhammad.

rabbi [Ju] Hebrew for "teacher." A rabbi leads the worship and study in a synagogue.

rakhi [H] a ribbon or thread tied round the wrist as a token of protection.

Ramadan [I] the month of fasting.

reincarnation [H, B, Ja, S] being reborn in a different body.

relic [gen.] part of the body or belongings of a holy person, revered by the faithful.

resurrection [C] rising from death; refers both to the belief that Jesus rose from death and to life after death for all Christians.

revelation [gen.] knowledge that is revealed by God, not found by human study. Many faiths teach that God can only be known by revelation.

sabbath [Ju] English version of the Hebrew word Shabbat—*see* shabbat.

sacrament [C] a ceremony or sign that conveys a blessing from God.

Saivite [H] a devotee of Shiva.

samsara [H, Ja] the endless cycle of reincarnation.

samskara [H] a ritual associated with a rite of passage.

Sangha [B] the community of Buddhist monks and nuns.

shabbat [Ju] the seventh day of the week, set aside for celebration and relaxation, when no work is done.

shari'ah [I] the system of Muslim civil and criminal law.

Shema [Ju] the first and most important words of the Ten Commandments, enjoining wholehearted worship of the one God. Named after the first word, *shema*—"hear" in Hebrew.

Shi'a [I] the smaller of the two main divisions of Islam, named after the "partisans" of Muhammad's son-in-law Ali.

stupa [B] a bell-shaped structure usually associated with a temple, which contains relics.

sukkah [Ju] a temporary shelter made for the festival of Sukkot.

sunnah [I] the actions of the Prophet Muhammad, carefully recorded and used as a guide to Muslim life.

Sunni [I] the largest division of Islam.

tallit [Ju] a fringed prayer shawl, a reminder of the Law.

Talmud [Ju] a sixth-century AD compilation of judgments and discussions by rabbis to help interpret the Torah.

terefah [Ju] a forbidden food, i.e., non-kosher.

Testament [C] "witness"; Christians divide the Bible into two parts, the Old Testament (the witness of the Jewish prophets) and the New Testament (the witnesses to the life of Jesus).

Theravada [B] "Teachings of the Elders," the southern form of Buddhism, found in Sri Lanka and Southeast Asia.

Torah [Ju] the Law: the word is used for God's everlasting law, for the particular laws as given to Moses on Mount Sinai, and for the first five books of the Hebrew Bible that contain these laws.

Tripitaka [B] "Three Baskets"; the three groups of Theravada Buddhist texts.

ummah [I] the worldwide community of all Muslims.

Vaisnavite [H] a devotee of Vishnu in one of his forms, often that of Krishna.

Veda [H, Ja] the most ancient Sanskrit scriptures.

wudu [I] ritual washing before prayer.

yoga [H] a discipline, whether of the mind or the body.

zakat [I] welfare tax paid as a proportion of wealth by all Muslims.

Select bibliography
Bowker, J. *World Religions*, Dorling Kindersley, London, 1997.

Breuilly, E. O'Brien, J. and Palmer, M. *Festivals of the World*, Checkmark Books/Facts On File, New York, 2002.

Cole, W. Owen (ed.). *World Religions* Series, Stanley Thornes and Hulton, Cheltenham, 1989-1992.

de Lange, N. *Atlas of the Jewish World*, Equinox, Oxford, 1984.

Harvey, P. *An Introduction to Buddhism*, Cambridge University Press, Cambridge, 1990.

Hinnells, John R. (ed.). *The New Penguin Handbook of Living Religions*, Penguin, London, 2000.

Hinnells, John R. (ed.). *The Penguin Dictionary of Religions*, Penguin, London, 2000.

Hinnells, John R. (ed.). *Who's Who of Religions*, Penguin, London, 1991.

Palmer, M. (ed.) *The Times World Religions*, Harper Collins, London, 2005.

Smart, N. *The World's Religions*, Cambridge University Press, Cambridge, 1989.

Smart, N. *Atlas of World Religions*, Oxford University Press, Oxford, 1999.

Zaehner, R. C. *Hinduism*, Oxford University Press, Oxford, 1962.

Zaehner, R. C. (ed.). *Hutchinson Encyclopedia of Living Faiths* (fourth edition), Hutchinson, London, 1988.

Index